Law on the battlefield

This new book concentrates on key areas of the law of wars as it applies to decisions made on the battlefield in conventional, international armed conflicts. It deals with the rules on targeting, precautions in attack, precautions against attacks, protection of cultural property and the environment and the responsibility of commanders.

The book discusses practical problems of international law arising in armed conflicts, illustrated by references to recent conflicts such as the Gulf war of 1990–91. It takes articles of Geneva Protocol I of 1977, examines them in their historical context, and provides guidance on their interpretation.

Major General Rogers is a practising military lawyer and a serving officer in the British Army.

D0892520

Melland Schill Studies in International Law

The Melland Schill name has a long established reputation for high standards of scholarship. Each volume in the series addresses major international law issues and current developments. Many of the previous volumes, published under the name 'Melland Schill Monographs', have become standard works of reference in the field. Interdisciplinary and accessible, the series is vital reading for students, scholars and practitioners of international law, international relations, politics, economics and development.
Series editor: Dr Dominic McGoldrick, University of Liverpool

Titles published in the *Melland Schill Monographs* and *Studies in International Law* series:

Melland Schill Monographs in International Law

I. M. Sinclair
The Vienna Convention on the Law of Treaties
R. B. Lillich
The human rights of aliens in contemporary international law
E. R. Cohen
Human rights in the Israeli-occupied territories
A. Carty
The decay of international law?
N. D. White
The United Nations and the maintenance of international peace and security
J. G. Merrills
The development of international law by the European Court of Human Rights
J. G. Merrills
Human rights in Europe
Wayne Mapp
The Iran-United States Claims Tribunal: the first ten years
N. D. White
Keeping the peace: the United Nations and the maintenance of international peace and security

Studies in International Law

Gamani Corea
Taming commodity markets: The Integrated Programme and the Common Fund in UNCTAD
Philippe Sands
Principles of international environmental law I: frameworks, standards and implementation
Philippe Sands, Richard Tarasofsky and Mary Weiss (eds)
Principles of international environmental law II: documents in international environmental law
Philippe Sands and Richard Tarasofsky (eds)
Principles of international environmental law III: documents in European Community environmental law

Law on
the battlefield

A. P. V. ROGERS

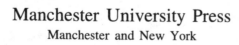

Manchester University Press
Manchester and New York

distributed exclusively in the USA and Canada by St Martin's Press

Published by Manchester University Press
Oxford Road, Manchester M13 9NR, UK
and Room 400, 175 Fifth Avenue, New York, NY 10010, USA

Distributed exclusively in the USA and Canada
by St Martin's Press, Inc., 175 Fifth Avenue, New York,
NY 10010, USA

British Library Cataloguing-in-Publication Data
A catalogue record for this book is available from the British Library

Library of Congress Cataloging-in-Publication Data
Rogers, A. P. V.
      Law on the battlefield / A. P. V. Rogers.
          p.   cm.
      Includes bibliographical references and index.
      ISBN 0–7190–4784–6 (hardback: alk. paper). — ISBN 0–7190–4785–4
(pbk.: alk. paper)
      1. War (International law)   I. Title.
   JX4511.R64   1996
   341.6'3—dc20   95–16860
                                                                                                          CIP

ISBN 0 7190 4784 6 *hardback*
      0 7190 4785 4 *paperback*

First published 1996

99 98 97 96 95   10 9 8 7 6 5 4 3 2 1

Typeset in Hong Kong
by Graphicraft Typesetters Ltd, Hong Kong
Printed in Great Britain
by Redwood Books, Trowbridge

Contents

Series editor's preface

The very title of this book is a challenging one. Many observers of world events will take much convincing that 'the law on the battlefield' is not a contradiction in terms. Yet General Rogers presents a powerful and informed case. On the basis of his extensive practical experience he offers expert guidance on how international humanitarian law can, and should, be integrated into military planning and doctrine. The civilising influence of that law needs to be firmly embedded in legal analysis and military planning. Political and military leaders need to be ever conscious of the restraints it imposes on them.

It is one of the tragic ironies of our time that continuing conflicts have heightened interest in the interpretation, application and function of international humanitarian law. The clarity and wisdom of this work will ensure that it attracts wide interest across a range of disciplines concerned with international conflicts.

Dominic McGoldrick,
International and European Law Unit,
University of Liverpool

Foreword

by

General Sir Michael Rose, KCB, CBE, DSO, QGM, MA

Although the idea that there can be any law governing something as conjectural and murderous as war may be regarded as surprising, the concept that behaviour under conditions of war should be subject to some sort of *jus in bello* can be traced back at least to the Age of Chivalry, when clear rules were developed for the treatment of prisoners and civilian populations following sieges. These rules were based not so much on natural law as on a perception among the combatants that there was some mutual benefit to be gained by recognizing some element of restraint. Over the centuries these restraints have become encapsulated in a law of war. The advent of weapons of mass destruction clearly challenged many of the legal assumptions contained in the various treaties, but the idea that there should be a law of war none the less survived, and continues to this day to be enshrined in a number of treaties and protocols.

However, it is clear that nowadays the majority of conflicts are increasingly taking the form of civil war, and this has made the laws of war more difficult to uphold. This is because these new forms of warfare not only have the savage character of the Hundred Years War in Europe but are marked by a total absence of any respect for human values or, indeed, the law of war. Such conflicts have combined to create chaotic situations of anarchy in which hatred and a spirit of revenge run unbridled. The extreme horrors caused by these changed circumstances need no further description, for they are daily illustrated on our TV screens. Within days modern cities are reduced to rubble by bombardment and entire populations are compelled to exist in conditions of total misery.

Inevitably there is an increasing tendency for the United Nations to become involved in these conflicts—often for humanitarian reasons. The Security Council resolutions on which all United Nations humanitarian and peacekeeping operations are founded *de facto* have the force of international law and provide the legal framework for all mission activities. In Bosnia the United Nations Protection Force is able to establish safe areas and exclusion zones and oblige the combatants to allow free passage for aid convoys through the practical application of the law of war. Any military force used by the United Nations in support of its mandate is required to comply with the guidelines which underpin all peacekeeping operations. Only a minimum level of force can be used to achieve a specific objective. Warning must be given where possible, all collateral damage must be avoided, and all use of force must be proportional, relevant and timely. Only by strict adherence to these rules can a mission avoid becoming party to the conflict itself—as happened with such disastrous results in Somalia in 1993. On a more general note, the civilian and military personnel who were taken hostage by the Iraqis in Kuwait in 1990 probably owe their release to the diplomatic pressure brought to bear through the Geneva Convention of 1949, under whose protective status they found themselves. In sum, the aim of the law of war is to save life and limb by encouraging humane treatment and by preventing unnecessary suffering and destruction.

As war has become more complicated, so, sadly, has the language of the treaties and protocols. If the law of war is to be successfully applied, it must clearly be understood by those to whom it is addressed. It is important that the language used should not be obscure. This book makes a most useful contribution to the understanding of the law of war. It takes key provisions of the 1977 Geneva Protocol I and explains their context, their negotiating history as well as their meaning and relevance today. I commend it not only to military lawyers but also to those who plan and conduct operations of peacekeeping and war. The book will also appeal to those who would like to resolve in their own minds the apparent incompatibility between law and war.

M. R.
April 1995

Preface

As a military lawyer I first became interested in the law of war when I attended the congress of the International Society for Military Law and the Law of War in The Hague in 1973. Preparation the following year of a paper on Penal and Disciplinary Sanctions against Prisoners of War was my first academic foray in this field. A posting to the international legal staff of Supreme Headquarters Allied Powers Europe prompted me to read the *Manual of Military Law* Part III (*The Law of War on Land*) from cover to cover, which stood me in good stead. There followed a specialist appointment in the United Kingdom where I was responsible for law of war training and advice within the army. This included being a delegate at the UN Weapons Conference in 1979 and 1980. My interest in the law of war in the following years was kept alive by my involvement in the International Society, as an occasional lecturer at the International Institute of Humanitarian Law or at seminars arranged by the International Committee of the Red Cross and the British Red Cross Society and as a regular attender at the Law of Armed Conflict discussion group of the British Institute of International and Comparative Law. From 1987, further appointments at the Ministry of Defence, where I was responsible for law of war advice, especially during the Gulf War of 1990–91, gave me an opportunity to practise the theory that I had absorbed over the years. I also attended meetings of experts arranged by the International Committee of the Red Cross to discuss laser weapons and anti-personnel mines.

However, my education in the law of war had been entirely 'on the job'. I had developed a special interest in the decisions that have to be made by commanders, staff officers and military lawyers in the context of land warfare, often under severe time pressure, which require a careful balancing of military and humanitarian requirements and was looking for an opportunity to study these problems in greater depth, so was glad to embark, on a part-time basis, upon a thesis of the same title as this book which eventually led to the award of the degree of Master of Laws by Liverpool University in July 1994.

I am grateful to Major General M. T. Fugard, then Director of Army Legal

Services, for launching me on this project and to him and his successors for providing financial support for my studies; to my supervisor, Professor Peter Rowe of Liverpool University, for his many suggestions, guidance and wise counsel; to Dr Dominic McGoldrick of Liverpool University for his energy in persuading the publishers to accept this work; to Richard Purslow, the editorial director, for his patience; to Miss Kim Spreadbury for her dedicated work on the word processor; especially to the many authorities I have quoted for enlightening me; and, not least, to my wife, Annekatrin, for her patient support and encouragement of work done almost entirely in my spare time, often in the early hours of the morning!

I take full responsibility for the final result, which is not a statement of British government policy nor to be seen as official endorsement of any facts stated or conclusions reached but is solely a reflection of my personal views.

The scope of the book is limited. It does not deal with the law relating to the protection of the victims of war, to civil wars, naval warfare or the use of weapons. It is a critical study of the key provisions of the law relating to the conduct of combat in international armed conflicts on land, illustrated by reference to problems that have arisen in recent armed conflicts. The study that led to the book has helped to clear my mind on a number of issues and enabled me to see things more clearly. My only hope is that the book will assist readers in the same way to a better understanding and so facilitate, in a very modest way, the ultimate aim of the laws of armed conflict, which is to reduce the sufferings of war.

A.P.V.R.
Tidworth, January 1995

Abbreviations

AFP 110–31 International Law—The Conduct of Armed Conflict and Air Operations, US Department of the Air Force, 1976

AFP 110–34 Commander's Handbook on the Law of Armed Conflict, US Department of the Air Force, 1980

Air Warfare Rules Hague Rules of Aerial Warfare, 1923 (UK Misc. 14 of 1924 (Cm. 2201))

Annual Digest H. Lauterpacht (ed.), *Annual Digest and Reports of Public International Law Cases*, Butterworth

[ ] All ER All England Law Reports 1936 onwards

art(s). article(s)

Brussels Code Project of an International Declaration Concerning the Laws and Customs of War attached to the Final Protocol of the Brussels Conference of 1874 (65 *British and Foreign State Papers* 1005)

CDDH Diplomatic Conference on the Reaffirmation and Development of International Humanitarian Law applicable in Armed Conflicts, Geneva, 1974–77

Civilian Convention Geneva Convention relative to the Protection of Civilian Persons in time of War, 1949 (75 UNTS (1950) 287 (No. 973))

CO commanding officer

col. column

ICRC *Commentary* ICRC *Commentary on the Additional Protocols of 1977 to the Geneva Conventions of 1949*, Nijhoff, 1987

Cultural Convention Convention for the Protection of Cultural Property in the Event of Armed Conflict, The Hague, 1954 (249 UNTS 214 at p. 240 (No. 3511))

Cultural Protocol Protocol to the Cultural Convention (249 UNTS 358–364)

Cultural Regulations Regulations for the Execution of the Cultural Convention (249 UNTS 270)

DA PAM 27–161–2 International Law vol. II, US Department of the Army, October, 1962

Despatch P. Hine, Despatch by Joint Commander of Operation Granby, 2nd Supplement to the *London Gazette*, 28 June 1991

DOD Interim Report Conduct of the Persian Gulf Campaign, US Department of Defense Interim Report to Congress, July 1991

DOD Report Conduct of the Persian Gulf War, US Department of Defense Final Report to Congress, April 1992

ENMOD Convention Convention on the Prohibition of Military or any other Hostile Use of Environmental Modification Techniques, 1977 (1108 UNTS 151–178 (No. 17119))

et seq. *et sequentia*, and the sections that follow

FM 27–10 The Law of Land Warfare, US Department of the Army, 1956

GYIL *German Yearbook of International Law*

Hague Regulations Regulations annexed to Hague Convention IV of 1907 (100 *British and Foreign State Papers* 338)

HMSO Her Majesty's Stationery Office

ibid. *ibidem,* in the same book, chapter as the case may be

ICRC International Committee of the Red Cross

ICRC Draft Rules ICRC Draft Rules, ICRC, 1956

JSM Joint Service Manual on the Law of Armed Conflict (JSP 383), HMSO, [to be published]

Lieber Code Instructions for the Government of Armies of the United States in the Field, prepared by Francis Lieber and promulgated by President Lincoln as General Orders No. 100 on 24 April 1863

NATO North Atlantic Treaty Organization

Naval Bombardment Convention Hague Convention IX of 1907 Concerning Bombardment by Naval Forces in Time of War (100 *British and Foreign State Papers* 401)

op. cit. *opere citato*, in the work just referred to

p. (pp). page (pages)

para(s). paragraph(s)

Protocol I First additional Protocol of 1977 to the Geneva Conventions of 1949, (UK Misc. No. 19 (1977), Cmnd. 6927; 1125 UNTS 3–608 (No. 17119))

reg(s). regulation(s)

resn(s). resolution(s)

Roerich Pact Treaty on the Protection of Artistic and Scientific Institutions and Historic Monuments, Washington, 1935 (reproduced in C. I. Bevans, Treaties & Other International Agreements of the United States of America, 1776–1949, Department of State, vol. 3, p. 254)

St Petersburg Declaration St Petersburg Declaration of 1868 renouncing the Use, in Time of War, of Explosive Projectiles under 400 Grammes Weight (58 *British and Foreign State Papers* 16)

UN United Nations

UNESCO UN Educational, Scientific and Cultural Organization

WCR Law Reports of Trials of War Criminals, selected and prepared by the UN War Crimes Commission, 15 vols, HMSO, 1946–49

Weapons Convention Convention on Prohibitions or Restrictions on the Use of certain Conventional Weapons which may be deemed to be excessively injurious or to have indiscriminate effects, 1981 (UK Misc. No. 23 (1981), Cmnd. 8370)

Wounded Convention Geneva Convention for the Amelioration of the Condition of Wounded and Sick in Armed Forces in the Field, 1949 (75 UNTS 31–83 (No. 970))

ZDv 15/2 *Humanitäres Völkerrecht in bewaffneten Konflikten* (also available in English as Humanitarian Law in Armed Conflicts), German Ministry of Defence, August 1992

ZDv 15/9 The Protection of Cultural Property in Armed Conflicts, German Ministry of Defence, July 1964

To Annekatrin

1

General principles

Introduction

Writers delve back through the history of centuries to the ancient civilizations of India and Egypt to find in their writings evidence of practices intended to alleviate the sufferings of war. This evidence is to be found in agreements and treaties, in the works of religious leaders and philosophers, in regulations and articles of war issued by military leaders, and in the rules of chivalry.[1] It is said that the first systematic code of war was that of the Saracens and was based on the Koran.[2] The writers of the Age of Enlightenment, notably Grotius[3] and Vattel,[4] were especially influential. It has been suggested that more humane rules were able to flourish in the period of limited wars from 1648 to 1792 but that they then came under pressure in the drift towards continental warfare, the concept of the nation in arms and the increasing destructiveness of weapons from 1792 to 1914.[5] So efforts had to be made in the middle of the last century to reimpose on war limits which up to that time had been based on custom and usage.[6]

The most celebrated attempt at codifying the customs and usages of war was the Lieber Code of 1863 issued by President Lincoln to the Union forces in the American Civil War. In the second half of the nineteenth century more reliance

[1] I. Detter de Lupis, *The Law of War*, Cambridge, 1987, pp. 121–3.
[2] See R. C. Algase, Protection of civilian lives in warfare: a comparison between Islamic law and modern international law concerning the conduct of hostilities, *Military Law and Law of War Review*, 1977, at p. 246.
[3] H. Grotius, *De Jure Belli ac Pacis*, 1642. A translation into English by F. W. Kelsey was published by Wildy & Sons in 1964.
[4] E. de Vattel, *Le Droit des gens*, 1758.
[5] United States, *International Law*, vol. II, Department of the Army, 1962, DA Pam 27–161–2.
[6] See further G. I. A. D. Draper, Humanitarianism in the modern law of armed conflict, in M. A. Meyer (ed.), *Armed Conflict and the New Law*, British Institute of International and Comparative Law, 1989, at p. 3. A useful summary of the historical development of the law of armed conflict is to be found in H. McCoubrey and N. D. White, *International Law and Armed Conflict*, Dartmouth, 1992, pp. 209–23.

was placed on codifying the rules of the law of war in treaty form, starting with the Geneva Convention of 1864, the St Petersburg Declaration of 1868 and continuing with the Brussels Conference of 1874 and the Hague Conferences of 1899 and 1907. It was during this period that some European states were developing powerful armies and navies and expanding their influence throughout the world. Some theorists, mainly German and notably Lueder, advanced the view that such military power should not be restrained by the uses and customs of war. These theorists influenced German thinking as late as 1914, when the chancellor is reported to have said of the invasion of Belgium, 'we are now in a state of necessity and necessity knows no law'.[7] Conversely, today, the less technologically advanced states sometimes see the law of war as an instrument for emasculating the mighty. One delegation at the CDDH even suggested that, where one nation in an armed conflict had an air force and the other had not, the nation with the air force should be prohibited from using it.[8]

The modern international law of war on land is to be found for the most part in treaties, notably the Hague Regulations of 1907, the Geneva Conventions of 1949, Protocol I of 1977 to those conventions and the various treaties dealing with weapons, culminating in the Conventional Weapons Convention of 1981.

That is not to say that customary law is replaced by treaty law. Treaties, of course, only bind the parties. Customary law continues to develop and binds all states. Treaty law may in two senses be helpful in interpreting customary law: in being in some cases a codification of customary law; in others, new treaty rules may by sufficient ratification become regarded as universally accepted and, therefore, indicative of customary law. They will not, however, if they have been subject to reservations.[9] Customary law cannot be excluded by treaty.[10] Treaty provisions which have never been applied in practice may, by custom, be rendered obsolete. The problem with customary law is ascertaining with any certainty what it is,[11] and here the opinions of writers may differ.

The tenuous nature of the law of war was admirably summarized by Professor Lauterpacht in the following words: 'If international law is, in some ways, at the vanishing point of law, the law of war is, perhaps even more conspicuously, at the vanishing point of international law.'[12] At the time he wrote this a consid-

---

[7]M. Walzer, *Just and Unjust Wars*, Pelican, 1980, p. 240.

[8]W. H. Parks, Air war and the law of war, 32 *Air Force Law Review* 1 (1990), p. 218.

[9]See, e.g., S. Kadelbach, Zwingende Normen des humanitären Völkerrechts, *Humanitäres Völkerrecht Informationsschriften*, 1992, No. 3, p. 118.

[10]Art. 53 of the Vienna Convention on the Law of Treaties.

[11]For an interesting article on this subject, see C. Bruderlein, Custom in international humanitarian law, *International Review of the Red Cross*, November–December 1991, p. 579. See also C. J. Greenwood, Customary international law and the First Geneva Protocol of 1977 in the Gulf conflict, in P. J. Rowe (ed.), *The Gulf War 1990–91 in International and English Law*, Routledge, 1993, pp. 66–9, who explains when the provisions of a multilateral treaty are to be treated as authoritative statements of customary law.

[12]H. Lauterpacht, The problem of the revision of the law of war, *British Yearbook of International Law*, 1952, p. 382.

erable effort had just been expended on bringing up to date the rules relating to the protection of the victims of war contained in the Geneva Conventions. Apart from the Wounded Convention, those conventions did not deal with law on the battlefield, or the law relating to the conduct of combat, which was to be found in principles derived from customary international law and in the Hague Regulations. Extending the Lauterpacht dictum, one could perhaps add that, if the law of war were at the vanishing point of international law, the law on the battlefield would be at the vanishing point of the law of war.

Early treatises[13] contained very little on the conduct of hostilities, but a lot of the rules relating to the conduct of combat are now codified in Protocol I. Some of the more important of those rules will be examined but first it is necessary to deal with general principles and with some expressions that will be used in the following chapters.

The great principles of customary law, from which all else stems, are military necessity, humanity, distinction and proportionality. According to the UK *Manual of Military Law*, the principles of military necessity and humanity as well as those of chivalry have shaped the development of the law of war.[14] Chivalry may, however, be classified as an element of the principle of humanity. These principles will dominate much of the discussion in later chapters, so need to be explained here.

Military necessity[15]

Views about military necessity vary. Some argue that too much emphasis has been placed on military necessity, to the detriment of the development of the law of war and the protection of war's victims. They say that 'the elasticity of the term "military necessity" under the laws of war has enabled belligerents to legally justify virtually any conduct otherwise available to the proponents of kreigsraison [*sic*]'.[16] Others, such as the writer, take a more pragmatic view. States are reluctant to give up anything that affords them a military advantage, so the search is always for common ground where states can agree on some measures which can afford a little protection for the victims of war. Although the results are often disappointing, every little gain helps. Even the critics seem

---

[13]See, e.g., J. Westlake, *International Law*, Part II (War), Cambridge, 1913, chapter IV of which devotes some sixty-four pages to law of war on land but very few pages to the conduct of combat.
[14]Part III, HMSO, 1958 (*Manual of Military Law*), para. 3. See Draper, Humanitarianism, p. 6, on the gradual elimination of the ideals of chivalry. See also R. W. Gehring, Loss of civilian protection, *Military Law and Law of War Review*, 1980, p. 14.
[15]For a more detailed treatment of the subject, see E. Rauch, Le concept de nécessité militaire dans le droit de la guerre, *Military Law and Law of War Review*, 1980, p. 209; H. McCoubrey, The nature of the modern doctrine of military necessity, *Military Law and Law of War Review*, 1991, p. 215.
[16]See C. Jochnick and R. Normand, The legitimation of violence: a critical history of the laws of war, *Harvard International Law Journal*, vol. 35, 1994, p. 64.

to accept this in the end: 'even minor limitations on belligerent conduct and marginal humanitarian gain are worth pursuing'.[17]

Dr Francis Lieber defined military necessity as long ago as 1863 as 'those measures which are indispensable for securing the ends of the war, and which are lawful according to the modern laws and usages of war'.[18]

The principle of military necessity is encapsulated in the preamble to the St Petersburg Declaration: that the only legitimate object which states should endeavour to accomplish in war is to weaken the military forces of the enemy and that for this purpose it is sufficient to disable the greatest possible number of men.

Whilst it was formerly argued by some that necessity might permit a commander to ignore the laws of war when it was essential to do so to avoid defeat,[19] to escape from extreme danger or for the realization of the purpose of war,[20] such arguments are now obsolete, since the modern law of war takes full account of military necessity. For example, the preamble to the Hague Regulations speaks of 'the desire to diminish the evils of war, as far as military requirements permit' and Protocol I, Art. 41, para. 3, prohibits the execution of prisoners of war whose presence would hamper or endanger special forces' operations.

Detter de Lupis[21] makes the following statement:

It is not only treaties and conventions that may be suspended in their application by dubious claims of military necessity, but also general uncodified rules on methods, including rules on targets and humanitarian rules. The legal position today, after a considerable body of case law has developed, appears to be that rules of the Law of War must be suspended only in case of 'clear military necessity'; that the burden of proof is increased for the suspension of any rules exempting targets from attack; and an especially enhanced burden of proof applies in the case of suspension from humanitarian rules. The degree of military necessity is also increased in proportion to violation of these three groups; the presumption exists that no military necessity can justify violations of rules of the Law of War.

This statement must be interpreted as referring only to the last vestiges of usages of war that have not been codified in treaty form: 'what may be ignored in case of military necessity are not the laws of war, but only the usages of war'.[22]

Now that practically all such usages have been codified in the Hague Regulations, Geneva Conventions and Protocols I and II, it is hard to see that this

[17]*Ibid.*, p. 416.

[18]Lieber Code, Art. 14.

[19]See Westlake, *International Law*, pp. 126–8, cf. J. S. Risley, *The Law of War*, Innes & Co., 1897, p. 125; L. Oppenheim, *International Law*, vol. 2, 7th ed., by H. Lauterpacht, Longman, 1952, pp. 231–3.

[20]Such arguments were mainly advanced by German theorists between 1871 and 1914 and are summed up in the maxim *Kriegsraison geht vor Kriegsmanier*—see United States, International Law, p. 9. For an interesting review of this doctrine, see G. Best, *Humanity in Warfare*, Methuen, 1983, pp. 172–9.

[21]*Law of War*, p. 337.

[22]See Oppenheim, *International Law*, p. 233.

exception has any practical significance nowadays. Although some treaties, such as Protocol I and the Weapons Convention, allow for denunciation by a party, the denunciations do not take effect until the end of an armed conflict in which the denouncing party is engaged.

Holland pithily summarizes the modern view in these words: 'military necessity justifies a resort to all measures which are indispensable for securing [the submission of the enemy]; provided that they are not inconsistent with the modern laws and usages of war'.[23]

De Visscher, writing in 1917, took the view that the old arguments could at best be applied to usages of war, but not to the law of war, whether in treaty or in customary form.[24]

References to military necessity are to be found in the Hague Regulations, which prohibit the destruction or seizure of the enemy's property, unless it be imperatively demanded by the necessities of war,[25] and which prohibit the use of weapons calculated to cause *unnecessary* suffering.[26]

Allowances for military necessity may be found in the Geneva Conventions, the Cultural Property Convention of 1954 and in Protocol I.[27]

Military necessity has been described as the principle that a belligerent is justified in applying compulsion and force of any kind, to the extent necessary for the realization of the purpose of war, that is, the complete submission of the enemy at the earliest possible moment with the least possible expenditure of men, resources and money.[28] Best comments that this approach is old-fashioned, which it is in the light of recent developments in the law of war, and provides 'no soothing syrup for civilians'.[29] The reference to the complete submission of the enemy, written in the light of the experience of total war in the Second World War, is probably now obsolete, since war can have a limited purpose, as in the termination of the occupation of the Falkland Islands in 1982 or of Kuwait in 1991. In the US Air Force manual[30] it is stated that the concept of military necessity has four basic elements:

1. That force is regulated.

2. That force is necessary to achieve as quickly as possible the partial or complete submission of the adversary.

---

[23] T. E. Holland, *The Laws of War on Land*, Clarendon, 1908, p. 12. See also G. Schwarzenberger, *International Law*, vol. II, Stevens, 1968, pp. 135–6; M. Greenspan, *The Modern Law of Land Warfare*, University of California Press, 1959, p. 314.

[24] C. de Visscher, Les lois de la guerre et la théorie de la nécessité, *Revue Générale de Droit International Public*, vol. 24 (1917), p. 74, at p. 99.

[25] Art. 23(g).

[26] Art. 23(e).

[27] Detter de Lupis, *Law of War*, pp. 334–6, lists various exceptions for military necessity. So does McCoubrey, Military necessity, pp. 229–37.

[28] *Manual of Military Law*, para. 3.

[29] G. Best, *Law and War since 1945*, Clarendon Press, 1994, p. 271.

[30] *International Law—the Conduct of Armed Conflict and Air Operations*, AFP 110–31, 1976, pp. 1–6.

3. That the force is no greater than needed to achieve this.

4. That it is not otherwise prohibited.

In other words, it is not possible for military commanders to do anything they like in war. What they do must be justified in every case by military necessity, that is, the military requirement to undertake the action in question.[31] The rule has been stated thus: 'in every case destruction must be *imperatively* demanded by the necessities of war, and must not merely be the outcome of a spirit of plunder or revenge'.[32] Attacking civilians is not normally a military requirement, because it does not weaken the military forces of the enemy. Destroying a cathedral or museum does not usually contribute to the defeat of the enemy's armed forces. McCoubrey[33] leaves open the possibility that military necessity may be a defence in cases of imperative military defensive need in response to an overwhelming threat. Schwarzenberger emphasizes, however, that the defence, which is of very limited scope, is personal necessity rather than the broader concept of military necessity.[34]

McCoubrey ends his study of military necessity[35] with the following definition:

Military necessity is a doctrine within the laws of armed conflict which recognizes the potential impracticability of full compliance with legal norms in certain circumstances and, accordingly, may mitigate or expunge culpability for *prima facie* unlawful actions in appropriate cases in armed conflict. Its precise effects in any given case will rest upon the combination of issues of circumstances, fact and degree and the strength of the claims of the norms concerned. The effect of the doctrine is limited to particular events and circumstances and does not have a general suspensory effect upon the law of armed conflict.

Military necessity has a threefold significance in the law of war. First, and foremost, no action may be taken which is not militarily necessary. Secondly, the law of war sometimes allows exceptions to its rules for good military reasons. Thirdly, it is an element of the rule of proportionality (dealt with below) in trying to achieve a balance between the sometimes conflicting aims of military success and humanitarian protection.

Humanity

The preamble to Hague Convention IV of 1907 respecting the laws and customs of war on land contains a clause, known, after its drafter,[36] as the Martens

---

[31]In fact, attacks must be directed at military objectives, see chapter 2.

[32]Oppenheim, *International Law*, p. 414.

[33]H. McCoubrey, *International Humanitarian Law*, Dartmouth, 1990, pp. 198–203.

[34]Schwarzenberger, *International Law*, pp. 129–30.

[35]McCoubrey, Military necessity, p. 240.

[36]Professor de Martens of the University of St Petersburg, legal adviser to the Russian imperial foreign ministry during the Hague conferences.

clause, which provides that in cases not covered by the attached regulations the belligerents 'remain under the protection and the rule of the principles of the law of nations' which, according to Martens, was derived from the usages established among civilized people, the laws of humanity and the dictates of the public conscience.[37]

The purpose of the clause was not only to confirm the continuance of customary law,[38] but also to prevent arguments that because a particular activity had not been prohibited in a treaty it was lawful. Humanity is, therefore, a guiding principle which puts a brake on undertakings which might otherwise be justified by the principle of military necessity. For example, a military commander might say that military necessity required him to put to death wounded enemy combatants in enemy-controlled hospitals on the grounds that when they recovered they would be able to continue fighting. The principle of humanity, however, intercedes on behalf of the wounded, recognizing that those *hors de combat* do not pose an immediate threat and requiring their lives to be saved.[39] They are, of course, protected under the Wounded Convention, which specifically applies the principle of humanity to the treatment of the wounded.

The rule of distinction

The idea of humanity comes most sharply into focus in the rule of distinction. It follows from the preamble to the St Petersburg Declaration that war is to be waged against the enemy's armed forces, not against its civilian population. Attacks are to be directed at military targets, not at civilian objects.

Civilians and combatants

Since military operations are to be conducted against the enemy's armed forces, there must be a clear distinction between the armed forces and civilians, or between combatants and non-combatants, and between things that may legitimately be attacked and things protected from attack.

Customary law has always drawn a distinction between combatants and the civilian population, or at least certain parts of it such as children and women and unarmed priests.[40]

---

[37]The clause is also found in the Geneva Gas Protocol, the Geneva Conventions of 1949, Protocol I and the Weapons Convention of 1981; see H. Spieker, Martens'sche Klausel, *Humanitäres Völkerrecht Informationsschriften*, October 1988, p. 46.

[38]Spieker, Martens'sche Klausel.

[39]See the Peleus case, 1 WCR 1; Best, *War and Law*, p. 253.

[40]See the authorities quoted by T. Meron in Henry the Fifth and the law of war, *American Journal of International Law*, 1992, at pp. 21–34. As late as 1897, Risley, *Law of War*, p. 108, wrote that 'old men, women, and children, and perhaps ministers of religion, are always regarded as non-combatants'.

By at least the eighteenth century the rule had emerged that non-combatants should not be directly attacked.[41] This principle was confirmed by the Lieber Code[42] and in the preamble to the St Petersburg Declaration.[43]

Non-combatants are not permitted to take part in hostilities and are at the same time protected from attacks and shielded from the indirect effects of war.

The current definition of a combatant is any member of the armed forces of a party to the conflict except medical personnel and chaplains.[44] All other persons are considered to be civilians.[45]

Only combatants are permitted to take a direct part in hostilities.[46] It follows that they may be attacked. Civilians may not take a direct part in hostilities and for so long as they refrain from doing so are protected from attack.[47] Taking a direct part in hostilities must be more narrowly construed than making a contribution to the war effort, and it would not include taking part in arms production or military engineering works or military transport.[48]

Nevertheless, civilians share the general dangers of war in the sense that attacks on military personnel and military objectives may cause incidental damage. It may not be possible to limit the radius of effect of an attack entirely to the objective to be attacked, a weapon may not function properly or may be deflected by defensive measures, or a civilian object may be attacked by mistake because of faulty intelligence. Similarly, civilians working in military objectives, though not themselves legitimate targets, are at risk if those objectives are attacked. Such incidental damage is controlled by the rule of proportionality, which is dealt with below.

Since combatants may be attacked, and to protect civilians, who may not, combatants are obliged to distinguish themselves from the civilian population while engaged in an attack or in a military operation preparatory to an attack.[49] They do so by wearing military clothing and equipment or at the very least by carrying their weapons openly at such times.[50]

Parks[51] complains that this reflects an extreme and unrealistic view of the rule of distinction as applied to personnel. He cites, as an example, the case of a civilian driving a military truck filled with ammunition. If the truck is attacked

[41]Oppenheim, *International Law*, p. 346. See also the review of the writers of the Age of Enlightenment in Best, *Humanity*, pp. 53–67.

[42]Art. 22.

[43]'. . . the only legitimate object which States should endeavour to accomplish during war is to weaken the military forces of the enemy'.

[44]Protocol I, Art. 43.

[45]*Ibid.*, Art. 50, para. 1.

[46]*Ibid.*, Art. 43, para. 2.

[47]*Ibid.*, Art. 51, paras. 2 and 3.

[48]F. Kalshoven, *Constraints on the Waging of War*, ICRC, 1987, p. 91.

[49]Protocol I, Art. 44, para. 3.

[50]For further discussion of this problem, see M. H. F. Clarke, T. Glynn and A. P. V. Rogers, Combatant and prisoner of war status, in Meyer, *Armed Conflict*, p. 120.

[51]Parks, Air war, at p. 134.

and the driver is killed, all is well; but if the truck driver is attacked directly, and killed, the soldier who fired at him has committed a grave breach of Protocol I. Parks says that 'some legal scholars', and the writer is probably one of them, 'have endeavoured to avoid the issue' by suggesting that the scenario in the example is perfectly logical. He takes the view that the current rules do not reflect history and suggests that an attack on a civilian ought to be lawful 'if his immunity from military service is based upon the conclusion that continued service in his civilian position is of greater value to a nation's war effort than that person's service in the military'.[52]

This is an extreme view. The idea that civilians should have a quasi-combatant status depending on the job they do seems to take little account of the confusion that it would cause. If there is to be any hope that the law will be complied with, the rules must be as simple and straightforward as possible.[53] At least the present law is clear: combatants may be attacked directly; civilians who are in or near military objectives run the risk of being killed as a side effect of attacks on those objectives.

In the example of the civilian driving the ammunition truck, it is the truck that is the target. Depending on the weapons available to him, the soldier attacking the truck may follow his training and fire at the centre of the target. If the truck driver is killed, it will be incidental to the attack on the target, proportionate and lawful. If, on the other hand, the attacking soldier is armed only with a sniper's rifle, his only way of stopping the truck may be to fire at the driver. In the unlikely event of the sniper knowing that the driver is a civilian—and if the truck is a military vehicle, the presumption of civilian status cannot realistically apply—it could be argued in the sniper's defence that the civilian is an unlawful combatant who has forfeited his protected civilian status by taking a direct part in hostilities by driving military supplies. The argument would be quite strong if the driving had been in the combat zone even if the vehicle had been a civilian vehicle. A grave breach would be committed only if the accused 'wilfully, in violation of the relevant provisions of' the Protocol made an individual civilian the object of attack.[54]

Civilian property and military targets

As with personnel, the attacker also has to distinguish between civilian property and military targets. The frequent use by commentators during the 1991 Gulf Conflict of the expression 'civilian target' indicates lack of understanding of this basic principle. The fact that civilians are killed as a result of mistaken attacks on civilian property, or as an incidental effect of attacking military targets, also leads to muddled thinking.

[52]*Ibid.*, p. 135.
[53]In this the writer agrees with Best, *Law and War*, p. 262.
[54]Protocol I, Arts. 43, para. 2, 51, paras. 2–3.

The preamble to the St Petersburg Declaration[55] placed great emphasis on attacks against military personnel. In the intervening years attacking military personnel has, in some conflicts, become less important.

Military objectives such as tanks, missile sites, munitions factories and dumps and communications installations have become correspondingly more significant, so that one could say in the last decade of the twentieth century that objects are militarily more crucial targets than personnel. During the course of this development the old-fashioned clear distinction between combatants and noncombatants seems, to some observers, to have become blurred. Perhaps more important now is the distinction between military objectives and civilian objects. That is not to say that the rule of distinction as applied to personnel has become obsolete. It remains in force, but no longer commands the dominant position it had in 1868.

Civilians and civilian objects protected

The Hague Regulations prohibit the unnecessary destruction of enemy property, attacking undefended towns, dwellings or buildings, and pillage. The parties to the conflict are also required to spare buildings dedicated to religion, art, science or charity as well as hospitals and other places where the wounded and sick are cared for.[56] Westlake commented as early as 1913 that, even in fortified towns, firing at homes, when it can be avoided, is cruel and useless and ought to be forbidden unless there is reason to suspect that the houses are occupied by troops or are being used as magazines.[57]

By 1938 the Prime Minister, Neville Chamberlain, was able to say in the House of Commons that:

1. The bombing of civilians as such and deliberate attacks upon civilian populations is against international law.

2. Targets which are aimed at from the air must be legitimate military objectives and must be capable of identification.

3. Reasonable care must be taken in attacking these military objectives so that by carelessness a civilian population in the neighbourhood is not bombed.[58]

These principles were confirmed in a resolution of the Assembly of the League of Nations later that year.[59]

State practice in the Second World War seemed to undermine this clear view

---

[55]'. . . for this purpose it is sufficient to disable the greatest possible number of men; . . . this object would be exceeded by the employment of arms which uselessly aggravate the sufferings of disabled men . . .'.

[56]Hague Regulations, Arts. 22–8.

[57]Westlake, *International Law*, p. 89.

[58]House of Commons Debates, vol. 337, col. 937.

[59]League of Nations paper A.69, 1938, IX, 28 September 1938, entitled 'Protection of Civilian Populations against Air Bombardment'.

of customary law.[60] It involved large numbers of civilian casualties and a tendency to bomb centres of population.[61] In brief,[62] this practice was due to the following factors.

1. Confusion over the concept of undefended towns. The Hague Regulations prohibited the bombardment of undefended towns but left open the question of what was defended and whether, if it were defended, the town itself could be bombarded or only military objectives in the town. Some thought that a town could not be regarded as undefended if it were defended by anti-aircraft guns or if it were behind the enemy front line and, therefore, not capable of unresisted occupation by ground troops. Some thought that undefended meant without military value or without military objectives.[63]

2. The concept of total war, where civilians worked in the armaments industry or in administrative or logistic capacities to release more soldiers for actual combatant duties.

3. The need to attack objectives supporting the war effort such as factories, ports, means of supply and communications, as well as purely military targets. This inevitably involved civilians who worked in those installations or who lived near by. Greenspan argued in 1959 that target area bombing could be justified on two grounds. First, that the area is 'so preponderantly used for war industry as to impress that character on the whole neighbourhood, making it essentially an indivisible whole'. The second factor must be that the area is so heavily defended from air attack that the selection of specific targets within the area is impracticable.[64]

4. The doctrine of belligerent reprisal[65] leads to confusion about legitimate targets. The doctrine allows a belligerent after a warning has remained unheeded to take proportionate measures which would ordinarily be unlawful in order to redress violations of the law of war by the enemy.[66] Such measures could include attacks on the enemy's civilian population. The German air attack on Coventry was said to be a reprisal for British attacks on German cities. Bomber Command retaliated by attacking the centre of Mannheim.[67] There are accusations and counter-accusations about who started the practice of target area

[60]H. M. Hanke, The 1923 Hague Rules of Air Warfare, *International Review of the Red Cross*, No. 292, January–February 1993, pp. 33–5, describes the gradual relaxation of the instructions on naval and air bombardment issued to the RAF in August 1935. See also Best, *Law and War*, pp. 199–205.
[61]For a brief summary of state practice during the Second World War, see E. Rosenblad, Area bombing and international law, *Military Law and Law of War Review*, 1976, p. 66.
[62]For a more detailed analysis, see Parks, Air war, p. 44.
[63]See Jochnick and Normand, Legitimation of violence, pp. 72, 76, 80.
[64]Greenspan, *Modern Law*, p. 336.
[65]For a more extensive treatment of the subject, see, e.g., C. J. Greenwood, Reprisals and reciprocity in the new law of armed conflict, in Meyer, *Armed Conflict*, n. 6, p. 227.
[66]Draper, Humanitarianism, p. 16, has expressed it much better as: 'a reprisal is an act, otherwise illegal, taken as a last resort to compel the enemy to desist from previous illegalities'.
[67]Rosenblad, Area bombing, p. 66.

bombing,[68] but the fact is that the German air force was primarily designed as a tactical arm in close support of the ground forces while the RAF concept had always been strategic.[69]

5. The allies found that the bombing of targets in Germany involved heavy losses of aircraft.[70] The RAF switched to night attacks, which increased the difficulty of identifying targets. Targets were attacked at increasing altitude to reduce the risks to the attacking forces but to the detriment of accuracy. This resulted in high civilian casualties. It is estimated that about 42,000 civilians were killed in Hamburg in August 1943 because of the fire storms which were impossible to bring under control.[71]

6. The reluctance of the attackers to accept risks means that they tend to rely on the information they have been given and presume that the object to be attacked is military rather than civilian. One author mentions a symposium in which officers were asked to discuss a hypothetical helicopter attack on a village they had reason to believe was undefended. Their response was that they would never allow themselves to get close enough to the target at a speed slow enough to tell whether the target was legitimate or not. They knew that if the village was defended they would be imperilled if they were to approach it too slowly or too close.[72] Such reluctance is offset by the greater sophistication of target intelligence, often by satellite, and of guidance and tracking systems. Reports of the accuracy of cruise missiles and guided bombs used by the United States in the Gulf conflict of 1991 are quite astonishing.[73] The responsibilities of the attackers in cases such as this will be examined in chapter 3.

7. There is also the theory, discussed by Walzer, that the decision to bomb German cities was taken at a time of supreme emergency when German forces were victorious everywhere and Bomber Command was the only possibility for offensive action to defeat those forces.[74] As noted above, there was an argument at the time that customs and usages of war could be suspended by military necessity. Parks makes the point with characteristic forcefulness that during the Second World War air planners were simply unable to ascertain what the law was. They would not have found a list of legitimate targets or a definition of the distinction between combatants and non-combatants; at best they 'would have

[68]The British directive of 29 October 1942, quoted by Gehring, Civilian protection, p. 34, seems to be based on the notion of reprisals.

[69]See Best, *Humanity*, pp. 271–2. However, Parks notes that the German air force also planned for strategic bombing—Parks, Air war, p. 54.

[70]Precision bombing raids caused severe losses, for example the British dam raids and the United States raid against the ball-bearing industry in Schweinfurt in 1943, see Rosenblad, Area bombing, p. 67.

[71]Rosenblad, Area bombing, p. 67. See also Best, *Law and War*, p. 280.

[72]P. Karsten, *Law, Soldiers and Combat*, Greenwood, 1978, at p. 93.

[73]See, for example, the report of a cruise missile attack on the Jumhouriyah bridge in Baghdad in the *Daily Telegraph* of 7 February 1991. Protocol I, of course, now re-establishes the presumption of civilian status, see Arts. 48 and 52, para. 3.

[74]Walzer, *Just and Unjust Wars*, pp. 255–63.

found considerable disagreement and confusion among scholars'. Similarly there would have been uncertainty about whether attacking civilians to lower morale and bring pressure to bear on their military leaders to surrender was a legitimate object of warfare, or whether undermining morale was simply a legitimate by-product of attacks on military objectives as they were then understood.[75] Best refers to the philosophical idea of double effect and concludes that hitting civilian morale was often as important as hitting military objectives and sometimes the principal purpose.[76] Parks adds that the law had failed to keep pace with technological developments.[77]

All these factors led to a generation of soldiers and civilians who were under the misapprehension that civilians and civilian objects might legitimately be attacked. While a delegate at the United Nations Conference on Conventional Weapons in 1979 the writer was told by a senior diplomat that it was only when the diplomat became involved in arms control matters two years previously that he had realized for the first time that it was not permissible to attack civilians. Even books written since Protocol I are not always entirely clear on the question of civilian immunity.[78]

Guerilla warfare has tended to cause confusion. During the Rhodesian civil war, for example, observation patrols watched a guerilla armed and in uniform disappear behind a bush and at the next sighting, five minutes later, appear in red shirt and dark trousers, having peeled off his uniform and hidden it with his weapon, leaving the patrol uncertain whether it was the same man.[79]

Media reports can also convey a misleading impression. If, quite rightly, they focus on civilian casualties caused, for example, by indiscriminate artillery fire or by a deliberate policy of terrorizing the civilian population, the uninformed may come to believe that attacks on civilians are a part of normal warfare.

Commentators who tried to rationalize these activities were, perhaps, led astray into thinking that the rule of distinction had changed. As has been pointed out elsewhere,[80] they might more profitably have concentrated on what was a legitimate target.[81] A military aircraft factory is clearly a legitimate target.[82] The factory may, of course, be manned entirely by civilians. However, it is only direct attacks on civilians that are prohibited.[83] Loss of civilian life caused by the destruction of the factory is incidental: civilians were not the object of the attack. It is here that the rule of proportionality, dealt with below, comes into

---

[75]See Jochnick and Normand, Legitimation of violence, pp. 78, 82, 86–9, 92.
[76]Best, *Law and War*, p. 280.
[77]Parks, Air war, p. 50.
[78]E.g. Detter de Lupis, *Law of War*. Contrast pp. 241 and 243.
[79]T. Arbuckle, Rhodesian bush war strategies and tactics, *Journal of the Royal United Services Institute*, 1979.
[80]A. P. V. Rogers, Conduct of combat and risks run by the civilian population, *Military Law and Law of War Review*, 1982, p. 295.
[81]This subject is dealt with, under the heading of military objectives, in chapter 2.
[82]Within the definition of military objective in Protocol I, Art. 52.
[83]*Ibid.*, Art. 51.

play. If the incidental casualties expected are out of proportion to the military gain anticipated, the attack becomes unlawful.[84]

The credibility of the concept of civilian immunity was stretched by the bombing techniques of the Second World War and steps had to be taken subsequently to reinforce that principle by making indiscriminate attacks unlawful. Whatever the legal position may have been in 1945, attempts have been made by the drafters of Geneva Protocol I of 1977 to restate and reinforce the customary rules protecting civilians. It is clear now that attacks on individual civilians or on the civilian population are prohibited.[85] Even reprisals against civilians and civilian objects are now prohibited by Protocol I.[86]

Rule of proportionality[87]

This rule is an attempt to balance the conflicting military and humanitarian interests (or to balance military necessity and humanity) and is most evident in connection with the reduction of incidental damage caused by military operations.[88] It has been described as the nub of the law of armed conflict, which may itself be regarded as a development of the rule.[89] It may be inferred from Arts. 15 and 22 of the Lieber Code and is to be found elsewhere, such as in the customary rules on reprisals and in the concept of self-defence in the *jus ad bellum*.[90] It is considered to be part of the customary law of armed conflict[91] and is reflected in the Hague Air Warfare Rules of 1923.[92]

An example of the application of the rule of proportionality is described by Masters.[93] In Iraq, in 1941, his battalion had just completed a successful assault on a feature known as the Big House. They saw wicker boats being launched on to the inland floods and were about to call up artillery fire when the CO told them to wait because there might be women and children in the boats. As the boats were setting out from a concealed village, this was quite possible. Masters protested that, whether or not the boats contained women and children, they

[84]See Protocol I, Art. 51, para. 5(b).

[85]Oppenheim, *International Law*, p. 346; Protocol I, Art. 51.

[86]Arts. 51 para. 6, 52 para. 1, 53 para. c, 54 para. 4, 55 para. 2, 56 para. 4, unless a reservation be entered to any or all of these paragraphs.

[87]For a more detailed essay on the subject, see F. Krüger-Sprengel, Le concept de proportionalité dans le droit de la guerre, *Military Law and Law of War Review*, 1980, p. 179.

[88]See D. Fleck, Die rechtlichen Garantien des Verbots von unmittelbaren Kampflandlung gegen Zivilpersonen, *Military Law and Law of War Review*, 1966, vol. I, pp. 98–9.

[89]D. H. N. Johnson, The legality of modern forms of aerial warfare, *Royal Aeronautical Society Journal*, August 1968, p. 685.

[90]The Caroline Case, 29 British and Foreign State Papers 1129.

[91]F. Kalshoven, The reaffirmation and development of international humanitarian law, *Netherlands Yearbook of International Law*, 1978, at p. 116; W. J. Fenrick, The rule of proportionality and Protocol I in conventional warfare, 98 *Military Law Review* (1982), p. 91, at p. 96.

[92]Art. 24.

[93]J. Masters, *The Road past Mandalay*, Michael Joseph, 1961, p. 35.

certainly contained enemy soldiers. Nevertheless, the CO gave the order not to fire. Disgusted at the time by his CO's attitude, on reflection Masters thought he had acted honourably. Strangely, the CO was not pleased with himself, because his character had prevented him from doing what a real ball-of-fire soldier would have done.

From the legal point of view, the CO acted correctly. He instinctively adopted the presumption that there were civilians in the boats as well as soldiers and concluded that to kill those civilians would have been out of proportion to the military gain achieved by killing the enemy soldiers, who posed no immediate threat to his unit.

A munitions factory is such an important military objective that the death of a large proportion of the civilians working there cannot be said to be disproportionate to the military gain achieved by destroying the factory. A more significant factor is the number of incidental casualties and the amount of property damage caused to civilians living near by if the factory is in a populated area. The explosion of a munitions factory may cause serious collateral damage, but that is a risk of war that would not infringe the proportionality rule.

Parks describes a US air attack, during the Vietnam War in 1972, on a hydroelectric plant at Lang Chi. It was estimated to supply up to 75 per cent of Hanoi's industrial and defence needs. On the other hand, it was thought that if the dam at the site were breached, as many as 23,000 civilians could die, presumably in the resultant floods. President Nixon's military advisers said that if laser-guided bombs were used there was a 90 per cent chance of the mission's being accomplished without breaching the dam. On that basis, the President authorized the attack, which successfully destroyed the electricity generating plant without breaching the dam.[94] This seems a good example of the proportionality rule at work.

Collateral damage may be even more severe if a factory produces nuclear, chemical or biological weapons. It is to be hoped that such factories will not be sited in populated areas,[95] but if they are the enemy must be entitled to attack them even though the consequences for the civilian population may be severe. What, therefore, does the rule of proportionality require of the attacker in the case of targets such as these? The answer is that the attacker must use precision weapons—for example, camera-guided missiles—aimed at the factory itself. If the attacking state does not possess such weapons, its obligations are to consider the feasibility of other methods or means of attack that would achieve the same result but reduce incidental damage as far as possible. In the Gulf War of 1990–91, for example, the Royal Air Force used Buccaneer aircraft fitted with laser target designators to pinpoint targets.[96] In certain situations it may be possible

---

[94] Parks, Air war, pp. 168–9.

[95] For the responsibilities of the defenders in such cases, see chapter 4.

[96] P. Hine, Despatch by the Joint Commander of Operation Granby, 2nd supplement to the *London Gazette*, 28 June 1991 (Despatch), p. G42.

to put targets such as these out of action by sabotage raids by commandos. Further, the attacker must, so far as possible, carry out the attack in such a way as to prevent the escape of dangerous substances, radiation, or chemical or biological contamination. An example of such a precision attack was the US air attack on vital equipment near the oil terminal at Al-Ahmadi during the Gulf conflict to prevent oil escaping into the Gulf.[97]

Attacking isolated targets in populated areas is one thing, but what of fighting between ground forces in densely populated areas? It is an unfortunate feature of war in populous areas that large numbers of civilians are killed. The death and destruction caused by artillery and mortar fire during the Yugoslav civil war of 1991–95 are all too obvious from media reports. Fenrick describes the capture of Manila in 1945 in the face of tenacious opposition by Japanese troops. US forces had frequently to resort to the use of artillery to protect the lives of their own soldiers. An estimated 100,000 civilians were killed, mainly in the cross-fire, compared with 17,000 soldiers on both sides. In Fenrick's words, 'No one wanted these people to die or derived any military benefit from their death. It just happened.'[98]

The rule of proportionality was first set out in treaty form in Arts. 51(5)(b) and 57(2)(b) of Protocol I.[99] The precise scope of the rule before that is not entirely clear, but it probably prohibited military acts that were grossly disproportionate to the object to be obtained.[100] The Pentagon put it thus: 'It prohibits military action in which the negative effects (such as collateral civilian casualties) clearly outweigh the military gain.'[101] This formulation has been criticized as more relaxed than the statements of the rule appearing in the US military manuals and in Protocol I.[102] But it seems to the writer that the Department of Defense report represents a reasonable attempt to articulate the rule of proportionality as it stood before the codification in Protocol I. Greenwood[103] comments that not too much significance should be attached to language in a report to the US Congress which was not a piece of precise legal drafting.

Despite its importance, no separate article of Protocol I is devoted to the rule of proportionality. It is to be found in two different places. First, it is merely given as an example of an attack which is prohibited because it is indiscriminate. The example is 'an attack which may be expected to cause incidental loss of civilian life, injury to civilians, damage to civilian objects, or a combination

---

[97] United States Department of Defense, *Conduct of the Persian Gulf War*, Final Report to Congress, April 1992 (Department of Defense Report), p. 625.

[98] Fenrick, Proportionality, p. 92.

[99] But had its roots in the ICRC draft rules of 1956, Art. 8.

[100] W. E. Hall, *A Treatise on International Law*, Clarendon Press, 8th ed. by A. Pearce Higgins, 1924, at p. 635.

[101] Department of Defense Report, p. 611.

[102] See R. K. Goldman, The legal regime governing the conduct of Operation Desert Storm, *University of Toledo Law Review*, vol. 23, 1992, No. 2, p. 337.

[103] Greenwood, Gulf conflict, p. 78.

thereof, which would be excessive in relation to the concrete and direct military advantage anticipated'.[104] Secondly, the proportionality rule is also to be found, in almost identical language, in the article dealing with precautions in attack. That article requires commanders to cancel an attack if it may be expected to offend the proportionality rule.[105]

As Kalshoven has pointed out, the word 'proportionality' does not even appear in these articles because of opposition by some delegations at the diplomatic conference at which Protocol I was negotiated (CDDH) to the very concept of proportionality.[106] They were reluctant to include any reference to the proportionality rule because of the difficulty of comparing things that were not comparable (i.e. military advantage and civilian losses) and because it precluded objective judgement, allowing military commanders to overemphasize the military advantage. Doswald-Beck sums it up well by saying that it is 'impossible to state that a factory is worth x civilians ... If, for example, the destruction of a bridge has a crucial importance for the success of a particular campaign, higher casualties will be tolerable to achieve this than, for example, the destruction of a munitions factory of secondary importance.'[107] The concept of excessive civilian loss was eventually accepted as a compromise.[108]

The rule is more easily stated than applied in practice, especially in a case where in adopting a method of attack that would reduce incidental damage the risk to the attacking troops is increased. The rule is unclear as to the degree of care required of the soldier and the degree of risk he must take. It is suggested, however, that the risk to the attacking forces is a factor to be taken into consideration when applying the proportionality rule. Nor is it clear what level of civilian casualties would be regarded as disproportionate. In the case of Manila mentioned above the ratio of civilian to military deaths was nearly 6:1. The problem is more acute nowadays, given the firepower available to relatively small units. Parks raises two interesting further points: first, that civilians working within a legitimate military target who are killed when it is attacked should not be regarded as collateral casualties and, therefore, should not be taken into account when applying the proportionality rule; and, secondly, that the attacking commander should be given credit for any civilian casualties caused through the failure of the defenders to take adequate precautions against the effect of attacks.[109] Both these points are valid, though there would still be an obligation on the attacker to take feasible precautions to minimize the risk to civilians working within the military target.[110]

[104] Art. 51, para. 5(b).
[105] Art. 57, para. 2(a)(iii) and (b); see further chapter 3.
[106] Kalshoven, Reaffirmation, p. 117.
[107] The value of the 1977 protocols, in Meyer, *Armed Conflict*, p. 156.
[108] Fenrick, Proportionality, pp. 103–6.
[109] Parks, Air war, p. 174.
[110] Protocol I, Art. 57, para. 2(a)(ii). See further chapter 3.

The ICRC *Commentary* contains the following passage:[111]

The idea has been put forward that even if they are very high, civilian losses and damage may be justified if the military advantage at stake is of great importance. This idea is contrary to the fundamental rules of the Protocol; in particular it conflicts with Article 48 (Basic Rule)[112] and with paragraphs 1[113] and 2[114] of the present Article 51. The Protocol does not provide any justification for attacks which cause *extensive* civilian losses and damage. Incidental losses and damages should never be *extensive*.

This passage introduces a new idea, of extensive damage, which cannot be supported by reference to Protocol I. Had the word 'excessive' been used for 'extensive' the last two sentences of the passage quoted above would be legally accurate. Otherwise this passage makes a nonsense of the rule of proportionality, the whole idea of which is to achieve a balance between the military advantage and the incidental loss. Clearly, the more important the military objective the greater the incidental losses before it can be said that the rule of proportionality has been violated. Greenwood[115] says that the above statements of the ICRC represent only the views of certain ICRC lawyers and that the comments of Air Vice-Marshal Wrattan are probably closer to the interpretation which most states would place on the proportionality principle. Air Vice-Marshal Wrattan said in evidence to the House of Commons Defence Committee that certain targets:

were not . . . in my judgement and that of the Americans of a critical nature. That is to say, they were not fundamental to the timely achievement of victory. Had that been the case then, regrettably, irrespective of what collateral damage might have resulted, one would have been responsible and had a responsibility for accepting those targets and for going against them.[116]

Another problem is whether the humanitarian and military limbs of the proportionality rule must be looked at in the longer or the shorter term. The answer probably is that it does not matter so long as the same time scale is applied to both limbs.[117]

The writer has made the following attempt elsewhere to summarize the practical application of the proportionality rule:

It is relatively easy to think of extreme situations such as the counter-attack on an enemy stronghold in a village. If the commander directs his attack at the stronghold, the risk of excessive incidental loss is minimal. If he destroys the whole village, there is a much greater risk of infringing the proportionality rule.

[111]Y. Sandoz, C. Swinarski, B. Zimmerman, with J. Pictet, *Commentary* on the Additional Protocols of 8 June 1977, ICRC, 1987 (ICRC *Commentary*), para. 1980.
[112]The rule of distinction.
[113]General protection of the civilian population.
[114]Civilian population and civilians not to be attacked.
[115]Greenwood, Gulf conflict, p. 78.
[116]House of Commons Defence Committee, Tenth Report, *Preliminary Lessons of Operation Granby*, HMSO, 1991 (Defence Committee Report), p. 38.
[117]Rogers, Conduct of combat, p. 311.

It is the commander who has to make the decision. He must weigh up the military advantages and the incidental loss. He must decide what steps are feasible to verify that the objects to be attacked are military objectives and what feasible precautions can be taken to minimize incidental loss. He may be able to make a comparison between different methods of attack, so as to be able to choose the least excessive method compatible with military success.

But his decision may be questioned later by a tribunal dealing with grave breaches under Art. 85 of the Protocol. It would seem that such a tribunal would have to look at the situation as it appeared to the military commander at the time, and then decide whether, in its opinion, the proportionality and feasibility tests were satisfied. If the tribunal found that the civilian object damaged was clearly separate, or that the military advantage was either nil or negligible, it might take the view that the commander had failed to do everything feasible or take all feasible precautions. The commander should, of course, be given the benefit of any doubt.[118]

Factors to be taken into account are numerous: for example, the military importance of the target or objective, the density of the civilian population in the target area, the likely incidental effects of the attack, including the possible release of hazardous substances, the types of weapon available to attack the target and their accuracy, whether the defenders are deliberately exposing civilians or civilian objects to risk, the mode of attack and the timing of the attack, especially in the case of a mixed target. If civilian workers are absent at night, that might be the best time to launch the attack so as to reduce civilian casualties.[119] In the Gulf War of 1991, allied attacks on dual-use facilities (i.e. military and civilian) were normally scheduled at night because fewer people would be inside or on the streets outside.[120] The rule of proportionality will be considered again in the context of precautions in attack in chapter 3.

Indiscriminate attacks

Having decided what the military objectives are, the military commander then has to consider whether they can be attacked jointly or whether they must be attacked separately. The rule of distinction, and possibly the rule of proportionality, is violated if the attack is indiscriminate.

Customary law

Whether there existed a customary rule prohibiting indiscriminate attacks is a debatable question. Probably only blind attacks were prohibited under customary law, since they would have violated the principle of distinction. Other,

---

[118]Rogers, Conduct of combat, p. 311. See Protocol I, Art. 75.4(d), on the presumption of innocence.
[119]ICRC *Commentary*, para. 2023.
[120]DOD Report, p. 100.

direct, attacks would have had to conform to the rule of proportionality.[121] It could be argued, however, that the rule of distinction implies that reasonable care must be taken to ensure that the military target is, in fact, attacked.[122] In 1919 the Committee of Imperial Defence expressed the view that it should be illegal to bomb the civilian population indiscriminately without attempting to attack military objectives. The drafters of the Air Warfare Rules obviously thought so too, because they provided that where military objectives were situated so that they could not be bombarded 'without the indiscriminate bombardment[123] of the civilian population, the aircraft must abstain from the bombardment'.[124] The rules were never adopted in treaty form, so the argument cannot be advanced with complete conviction, especially in the light of state practice in the Second World War, but it could be argued that the rule of distinction implies a third requirement, namely that the method or means selected for the attack must be such as to enable the target to be struck. Blix has described these three elements as follows.

1. Targets must be *identified* with some certainty as military objectives.

2. Attacks must be *directed* to such identified targets.

3. The weapons and methods must be such that the target may be hit with some degree of *likelihood*.[125]

Treaty law

The three elements identified by Blix are to be found in Protocol I, which prohibits indiscriminate attacks.[126] These are attacks which:

1. Are 'not directed at a specific military objective';

2. 'Employ a method or means of combat which cannot be directed at a specific military objective'; or

3. 'Employ a method or means of combat the effects of which cannot be limited as required' by the protocol;

'and consequently, in each such case, are of a nature to strike military objectives and civilians or civilian objects without distinction.'

The first of these elements would prohibit a missile attack directed at an area the size of a town such as the notoriously inaccurate Scud missiles used by Iraq in the Gulf War of 1990–91. The second might prohibit the area-bombing technique used to attack several military targets in a populous area. Green makes

---

[121] Rogers, Conduct of combat, p. 298.

[122] Hanke, Air Warfare, p. 24.

[123] In an earlier draft 'indiscriminate bombing' was rendered as 'bombing without distinction', see Hanke, Air Warfare, p. 25.

[124] Art. 24(3).

[125] H. Blix, Area bombardment: rules and reasons, *British Yearbook of International Law*, 1978, p. 31, at p. 48.

[126] Art. 51, para. 4.

the point[127] that just because a built-up area exists that does not mean that the larger area is no longer a military objective. He says that the civilian area within it should always be clearly defined and the rule of proportionality must be observed. It is difficult to know what to make of this statement. If civilian areas are defined, steps would have to be taken to avoid incidental damage in those areas, which might negate an area-bombing technique unless they were so small as to be insignificant in relation to the surrounding military objectives. The third element deals with two situations: where the attacker is unable to control the effects of the attack, such as dangerous forces released by it, or where the incidental effects are too great. In either case, the problem would seem to be covered by the rule of proportionality[128] and, of course, there is a specific article dealing with dangerous forces.[129]

The protocol goes on to give two examples of indiscriminate attacks. The first of these is 'an attack by bombardment which treats as a single military objective a number of clearly separated and distinct military objectives located in a city, town, village or other area[130] containing a similar concentration of civilians or civilian objects'. It has been pointed out that, whilst 'bombardment' was understood at the CDDH to mean bombardment by artillery as well as from the air, the meaning of 'clearly separated and distinct' was far less certain.[131] The second example is where the attack would violate the rule of proportionality.

In considering whether there has been a breach of the rule prohibiting indiscriminate attacks, it suffices if 1, 2 or 3 is violated provided the attack is 'of a nature' to strike military objectives and civilians or civilian objects without distinction. This is a curious provision because it takes no account of the *actual* consequences of an attack. On a strict construction, if the attack is indiscriminate by its nature it would seem to matter not whether any civilians are actually killed as a result. It is suggested that this would be an absurd and unintended result of the drafting. Certainly, to amount to a grave breach the indiscriminate attack must *affect* the civilian population.[132]

No hard-and-fast rules can be laid down, since so much depends on the facts of each case. If, for example, the military objective consists of widely scattered enemy tank formations in the desert, it would clearly be permissible to use weapons having a wider range of effects than would be possible were the attack to be directed at a single communications site in the centre of a heavily populated

[127]L. C. Green, *The Contemporary Law of Armed Conflict*, Manchester, 1993, p. 152. See also p. 184.
[128]Set out in Art. 51, para. 5(b).
[129]Art. 56.
[130]'Other area' covers refugee camps and columns—Kalshoven, *Constraints*, p. 94.
[131]G. Aldrich, New life for the laws of war, *American Journal of International Law*, 1981, at p. 780.
[132]Protocol I, Art. 85, para. 3(b).

area. Military objectives dispersed about densely populated areas would normally have to be treated as separate military objectives requiring separate attacks.[133] One commentator has adverted to the difficulty of getting information
about the exact location of enemy military objectives and the consequent use of
an area covering method.[134] Of course, there is nothing in the protocol to prevent the use of artillery covering fire or mine-laying to deny an area of land
to the enemy. That area of land is a military objective. Other rules of the protocol, such as the rule of proportionality, might, however, impinge on that
practice.

Another writer has referred to the difficulty in the choice of means when
attacking several targets by artillery fire. He concludes that it is not feasible to
separate artillery units below battery level.[135]

Aldrich expresses the view that 'if the objectives are sufficiently separated
so that they can feasibly be attacked separately with the weapons available
and if this degree of separation is evident to the attacker, then they must be
attacked separately in order to reduce the risks to the civilian population.'[136]

The first two points in the definition of indiscriminate attacks referred to
above and the first example of indiscriminate attacks may be regarded as a
development of the traditional rule which prohibited aimless attacks. In the
second example of indiscriminate attacks, elements of proportionality have
been introduced by the deeming as indiscriminate those attacks which would
cause excessive incidental damage. Although this is likely to cause confusion,
it may be regarded as simply a revised version of the customary proportionality
rule in another guise.

But Protocol I goes further in point 3 of the definition by prohibiting as
indiscriminate those attacks 'which employ a method or means of combat the
effects of which cannot be limited as required by the Protocol'.[137] This provision, which is new to international law, is unfortunately vague. There is no
provision of Protocol I that specifically limits the effects of methods and means.
It may be a reference to the rule of proportionality in Art. 57 (precautions in
attack). If so, it is superfluous, because Art. 57 applies anyway. If it is a
reference to Protocol I as a whole, it lacks the precision necessary for a
provision the breach of which may result in a person's being charged with a
war crime.[138]

---

[133]C. I. Skarstedt, Armed forces and the development of the law of war; R. Barras and S. Erman,
Forces armées et développement du droit de la guerre: *Military Law and Law of War Review*, 1982,
pp. 231, 261 and 270.
[134]Skarstedt, Armed forces, p. 231.
[135]E. L. Gonsalves, Armed forces and the development of the law of war, *Military Law and Law
of War Review*, 1982, p. 192.
[136]Aldrich, New life.
[137]Art. 51, para. 4(c).
[138]Compare Art. 85, para. 3(b).

The language of Protocol I is unsatisfactory because it confuses the distinction and proportionality principles. Parts 1 and 2 of the definition articulate the rule of distinction, but part 3 strays into considerations of proportionality.

The precise relationship between the rules in Protocol I of proportionality and prohibiting indiscriminate attacks has been closely scrutinized.[139] Some believe that indiscriminate attacks will be illegal even if the proportionality rule has not been offended.[140] Others believe that the proportionality rule prevails, so that even if an attack is actually indiscriminate there is no violation of the law if the proportionality rule has not been broken.

While it is difficult, applying the language of Protocol I, to come to the same conclusion as those in the second group, one has considerable sympathy with their argument. After all, who is concerned about the attack's technically being indiscriminate if no civilian is killed as a result?

Perhaps it is better to regard the various provisions of Protocol I as cumulatively requiring commanders to take care in their planning of an attack to ensure that separate military objectives are separately attacked, with incidental damage reduced as much as possible, and that if the incidental damage is likely to outweigh the military advantage the attack must be replanned. Basically, the commander will have to ask himself three questions before he proceeds with the attack.

1. Is the target a military objective?
2. Is the attack indiscriminate?
3. Is the rule of proportionality likely to be offended?[141]

The United Kingdom made a declaratory statement on signature of Protocol I to the effect that, in considering whether an attack is indiscriminate, the attack as a whole should be looked at, not merely isolated or particular parts of the attack, and that commanders must necessarily make their decisions on the basis of their assessment of the information from all sources which is available to them at the relevant time.[142] Doswald-Beck explains the need to look at the whole attack thus:

This approach should be acceptable if seen within the context of a given tactical operation: such an operation may necessitate, for example, the destruction of six military objectives, one of which, being particularly difficult to get at, might involve far greater casualties than the other five. The attack of that one objective on its own might be of no great use, but within the context of the operation as a whole, absolutely essential. The

[139]Krüger-Sprengel, Proportionalité, p. 179; Rauch, Necessité, p. 205.

[140]E. Rauch, Conduct of combat and risks run by the civilian population, *Military Law and Law of War Review*, 1982, p. 68. The precise view of Kalshoven on this point in *Constraints*, p. 43, is not entirely clear.

[141]Rogers, Conduct of combat, p. 303.

[142]A. Roberts and R. Guelff, *Documents on the Laws of War*, Clarendon Press, 2nd ed., 1989, p. 467.

yardstick, in this example, would be the number of casualties[143] overall in relation to the value of the operation as a whole.[144]

The responsibility of commanders is dealt with in chapter 7.

Definition of attack

The word 'attack' has already been used. It will be used many times in the course of this work. It would be useful, therefore, to define it now.

'Attack' is currently defined, for the purposes of the law of war, as any act of violence against an adversary, whether in offence or defence.[145] Kalshoven explains that 'act of violence' involves the use of means of warfare (i.e. weapons) and does not include taking prisoners of war, even though that may involve the application of force.[146] The words 'in offence or defence' ensure that forces which open fire to repel an attack or invasion are themselves engaged in an attack and equally responsible for compliance with all the rules of Protocol I dealing with attacks.[147]

Those rules apply to all attacks, even attacks in a party's national territory which is under adverse occupation,[148] and apply equally to sea and air warfare directed at targets on land.[149] The *a contrario* argument that, since the Protocol applies to attacks on national territory under the control of an adverse party, it does not apply to attacks on national territory not under the control of an adverse party is inadmissible, since it is clear from the wording that it applies 'to all attacks in whatever territory conducted'.

The definition of attack is wide enough to include a whole range of attacks, from that of a single soldier opening fire with his rifle to that of an army group's major offensive. However, Fenrick[150] points out that the context of certain provisions of Protocol I[151] is such that the attacks referred to cannot relate to the acts of a single soldier. He hazards the opinion that they can apply only to a formation the size of a division. On the other hand, Switzerland made a declaration on ratification that the provisions of Art. 57, para. 2, of Protocol I create obligations only for commanding officers at battalion or group level and above.[152] The Swiss authorities consider that commanders at lower levels do not

[143] This reference to casualties must, in the context, include collateral casualties.
[144] Doswald-Beck, The value of the 1977 protocols, pp. 156–7.
[145] Protocol I, Art. 49, para. 1.
[146] Kalshoven, *Constraints*, p. 87.
[147] The writer, perhaps obtusely, fails to follow Parks's contention that by so defining attacks maximum constraints were placed on a force engaged in offensive military operations—Parks, Air war, p. 115.
[148] Protocol I, Art. 49, para. 2.
[149] *Ibid.*, para. 3.
[150] Fenrick, Proportionality, p. 102.
[151] E.g. Arts. 51(5)(b) and 57(2).
[152] Roberts and Guelff, *Documents*, p. 467.

have the necessary means, in terms of reconnaissance, to comply with all the requirements of this paragraph.[153] The Swiss military manual places the responsibility on battalion and group commanders or higher commanders to ensure that civilians are warned if possible and that they are not injured and do not suffer harm and that the rule of proportionality is complied with.[154] However, it does not seem possible in practice to apply such a blanket rule, since so much will depend on the situation on the ground. The Swiss reservation may make sense in the context of a large-scale attack. The individual company or platoon commander will not have an overview of the tactical situation. That is why the United Kingdom approached the problem from a different angle and made a statement on signature of Protocol I that the commander must be judged in the light of the information available to him. A commander at a lower level, perhaps a corporal in command of a section, may be involved in an isolated attack when advancing through a town on, say, a small enemy position in a school.[155] In those circumstances the corporal would have to consider whether there were civilians (including children) in the school or whether it had been abandoned. In the former case, he would have to think very carefully about how and with what weapons he should attack the enemy or, indeed, whether he should attack at all if not fired upon. In the latter case, he would still need to consider the possibility of incidental injury being caused by his attack. The better view must be that the level of responsibility will depend on the precise circumstances of the incident under examination in its broader context.

An attack is an act of violence against the adversary, whether in offence or in defence.[156] It can consist of combined infantry, tanks, artillery, helicopters and other close support aircraft involving many combatants in many different but co-ordinated actions, each of which would fall within the definition of 'attack'. An offensive would amount to an attack, but so would all its constituent elements. A battle group[157] attack might contravene the provisions of Art. 57 and the question would arise as to whether the corps commander responsible for the whole offensive was also responsible for that small part of it.

Italy made a declaratory statement on ratification, as did other states, 'that the military advantage anticipated from an attack is intended to refer to the advantage anticipated from the attack considered as a whole and not only from isolated or particular parts of the attack'.[158] The United Kingdom made a similar

---

[153]Switzerland, *Botschaft über die Zusatzprotokolle zu den Genfer Abkommen*, Swiss Federal Council, 1981 (81.004), p. 52.

[154]Switzerland, *Gesetze und Gebräuche des Krieges*, Swiss Army regulation 51.7/lld, 1987.

[155]As postulated by G. J. Cartledge, *The Soldier's Dilemma*, Australian Department of Defence, 1992, pp. 171–3.

[156]Protocol I, Art. 49.1. The rules apply to both attackers and defenders and do not only apply to an invading power, as might be inferred from McCoubrey, *Humanitarian Law*, p. 116.

[157]Combined armour and infantry.

[158]See Roberts and Guelff, *Documents*, p. 465.

statement on signature.[159] What does this statement mean? The ICRC *Commentary* suggests that it is redundant and that 'it goes without saying that an attack carried out in a concerted manner in numerous places can only be judged in its entirety' but goes on to say that 'this does not mean that during such an attack actions may be undertaken which would lead to severe losses among the civilian population or to extensive destruction of civilian objects.'[160]

At first sight the Italian statement would seem to exculpate the corps commander where the battle group commander has acted outside his authority but it would also seem to exculpate the battle group commander, which would seem to go too far. The statement probably means that, when judging the responsibility of a commander or soldier at a particular level, one has to look at that part of the attack for which he was responsible, but in the context of the attack as a whole. The responsibility of the commander is dealt with in more detail in chapter 7.

[159]*Ibid.*, p. 467.
[160]ICRC *Commentary*, para. 2218.

2

Military objectives

Introduction

It follows from the rule on the protection of civilians and civilian objects that attacks must be limited to military objectives.[1] The word 'limited' does not mean that there must be no collateral damage. Limitation of collateral damage is dealt with in the rule of proportionality.[2]

The term 'military objective' is a relatively recent addition to the law of war. The St Petersburg Declaration merely referred to weakening 'the military forces of the enemy'. Even in military manuals published after the Second World War[3] the term is only obliquely referred to in connection with bombardments and is not defined; the emphasis of those manuals seems to be on defended and undefended localities.[4] However, even in the case of bombardment of defended localities, it is clear that the manuals envisaged such bombardments being directed against military objectives therein.[5] A definition of military objectives appeared for the first time in the Air Warfare Rules.[6] That definition was probably an attempt to rationalize the practice of states, but since the rules never became legally binding they were probably ignored by manual writers. It is necessary, therefore, to trace developments in state practice and treaty law before examining the current definition of the term.

Early texts such as the Lieber Code did not contain the concept of the military objective. Presumably, as indicated by the preamble to the St Petersburg

---

[1]Protocol I, Art. 52, para. 2.

[2]See M. Bothe, K. J. Partsch and W. Solf, *New Rules for the Victims of Armed Conflicts*, Martinus Nijhoff, 1982, p. 322.

[3]See, e.g., the UK *Manual of Military Law* Part III, HMSO, 1958, chapter VII; *The Law of Land Warfare*, US Department of the Army (FM 27–10), 1956, chapter 2, s. IV.

[4]See, further, chapter 4.

[5]See *Manual of Military Law*, para. 288. Para. 289 might mislead the reader into supposing that a defended town as such may be bombarded. This would be an erroneous deduction, since para. 289 must be read in the light of para. 288.

[6]Art. 24.

Declaration, it was assumed that war would be waged between the enemy armed forces.[7] The only exception to this was the rule that permitted the bombardment of fortified and defended places.[8] This, of course, involved the civilian population of those places. In the last century it was considered by some permissible to bombard civilian houses during a siege, since that might hasten the reduction of the enemy,[9] the inhabitants being considered temporarily to have lost their non-combatant status because of their close association with the garrison.

In modern wars, however, the enemy soldier has become a less important target than the weapons, such as tanks and aircraft, which he operates, the depots and lines of communication which keep the troops supplied and the civilian manufacturing industries which provide the raw materials, fuel and goods without which the armies cannot survive. In 1870 courts recognized the justification for destroying Confederate cotton during the American Civil War, since cotton sales provided funds for importing almost all Confederate arms and ammunition.[10] The importance of military objectives was recognized, first, in the Hague Naval Bombardment Convention of 1907, which for the first time acknowledged that the military significance of the target was a more relevant factor than whether a town or place was defended. The convention did not limit bombardment to purely military objects. It encompassed industrial objects of military value.[11] The convention permitted bombardment of military works, military or naval establishments, depots of arms or war *matériel* and certain workshops and plant.

The right of a belligerent to destroy the enemy's war *matériel*, railways and telegraphs has long been acknowledged, as well as barracks and accommodation for troops, military stores and factories and foundries manufacturing military supplies.[12]

Fauchille in 1917 considered that aerial bombardment was permitted against military works, military or naval establishments, depots of arms or war materials, workshops (*les ateliers*) and installations suitable for use by the enemy army or fleet, ships of war, the head of the government or his representative, soldiers and other persons officially attached to the army or fleet.[13]

According to Parks[14] the practice of the First World War showed that the following were regarded as legitimate targets: 'military and naval bases; ware-

---

[7]See L. Oppenheim, *International Law*, vol. 2, 7th ed. by H. Lauterpacht, Longman, 1952, paras. 105, 107. In fact, one looks in vain through Oppenheim for a definition of military objective.

[8]See, e.g., Arts. 15–16 of the Brussels Conference Draft Code of 1874 (Brussels Code).

[9]See, e.g., J. S. Risley, *The Law of War*, Innes & Co., 1897, p. 116; J. R. Baker and H. G. Crocker, *The Laws of Land Warfare*, Department of State, Washington, 1919, p. 199, who castigated this practice.

[10]US Department of the Air Force, *Commander's Handbook on the Law of Armed Conflict* (AFP 110–34), 1980, p. 2–1.

[11]See W. H. Parks, Air war and the law of war, 32 *Air Force Law Review* 1 (1990), p. 18.

[12]See J. M. Spaight, *War Rights on Land*, Macmillan, 1911, pp. 113 *et seq.*

[13]P. Fauchille, Le bombardement aérien, *Revue Générale de Droit International Public*, vol. 24 (1917), p. 73.

[14]Parks, Air war, p. 21.

houses, airfields and docks; lines of communication; and industrial targets that offered a contribution to the enemy's war effort'. In preparing the Hague Air Warfare Rules, according to Parks, the British delegation's draft included the term 'military objective' without defining it, while the US draft contained a list of objects that might be attacked without using the term 'military object-ive'.[15] The final text was obviously a compromise between the two approaches, because the Hague rules contained a definition which prepared the way for later, more comprehensive definitions: 'an object of which the destruction or injury would constitute a distinct military advantage to the belligerent'.[16]

The rules go on to give a list of military objectives. It is worth setting out the list in full:

military forces; military works; military establishments or depots; factories constituting important and well-known centres engaged in the manufacture of arms, ammunition or distinctively military supplies; lines of communication[17] or transportation used for military purposes.[18]

The preamble to the list states that aerial bombardment is legitimate only when 'directed exclusively at' the listed objects. The context in which the word 'ex-clusively' appears makes it ambiguous. Does it mean that only objects on the list may be attacked or that an attack on a listed object must be limited to that object and nothing else? Schwarzenberger seemed to think that the list was intended to be exhaustive,[19] while Rousseau refers to it as examples.[20] An examination of the remainder of the article does not help to resolve this ambiguity, but it does seem that it was the intention of the drafters that the list should be exhaustive.[21]

Art. 24(3) prohibits the bombardment of cities, towns, villages and dwell-ings not in the immediate neighbourhood of the operations of land forces, but does permit the attacking of the listed military objectives in such rear areas, provided the attackers are discriminate. The writer does not share the view of Parks[22] that Art. 24(3) 'specifically prohibited the attack of targets "not situated in the immediate vicinity of the operations of land forces"' or the similar view of Doswald-Beck.[23]

[15]Parks, Air war, p. 28.
[16]Art. 24(1).
[17]Detter de Lupis refers to various discrepancies between the English, French and German texts. For instance, the German text *Nachrichten and Vekehrsmittel* clearly refers to radio stations and other news media while the English 'lines of communication' is more vague, I. Detter de Lupis, *The Law of War*, Cambridge University Press, 1987, p. 236.
[18]Art. 24(2). This is similar to the list appearing in United States, *Law of Land Warfare*, at p. 19, of objects that may be attacked even if they are not defended.
[19]G. Schwarzenberger, *International Law*, vol. 2, Stevens, 1968, p. 153.
[20]C. Rousseau, *Le Droit des conflits armés*, Pedone, 1983, p. 130.
[21]H. M. Hanke, The Hague Rules of Air Warfare, *International Review of the Red Cross*, 1993, pp. 21–2.
[22]Parks, Air war, p. 138.
[23]The value of the 1977 protocols, in M. A. Meyer (ed.), *Armed Conflict and the New Law*, British Institute of International and Comparative Law, 1989, p. 143.

Article 24(4) relaxes the requirement of discrimination in the contact zone. It envisages the bombardment of cities, towns, villages and dwellings in the immediate neighbourhood of the operations of land forces but then goes on to add the proviso that 'the *military concentration*' must be sufficiently important to justify such bombardment, having regard to the danger thus caused to the civilian population. This was probably an attempt to adapt the defended town concept to air warfare.

This use of the words 'the military concentration' drives one to the conclusion that Art. 24(4) makes concessions to military necessity but does not enlarge the list of military objectives in Art. 24(2).

It does seem that the drafters of the rules, like the International Law Association in its draft convention of 1938 on the protection of civilian populations against new engines of war, did not envisage attacks on the broader manufacturing base of the enemy's industry. Of course, the rules were never adopted in treaty form, so they would have to be tested against customary law and state practice. In that light, the definition of military objectives cannot be regarded as anything more than an inexhaustive indication of what amounts to such objects. Spaight, as early as 1924, provided a long list of objects attacked during the First World War which fell outside the list in the Air Warfare Rules, including iron and steel works and oil production facilities.[24] The problem, as the Prime Minister, Neville Chamberlain, acknowledged, was that there was no agreed definition of military objectives.[25]

Stone[26] refers to the Anglo-French view during the World Wars that legitimate military objectives included:

docks and dockside warehouses; blast furnaces; iron works and foundries, steel works, coke ovens; power stations, gasworks, waterworks; motor and engineering works; oil wells, refining and oil storage depots; benzol works and depots; granaries.

But practice in the Second World War seems to have indicated a broader understanding of what amounted to a military objective. After the war a French court decided that a lighthouse attacked by German forces was a military objective because it could have provided navigational assistance to allied forces.[27] The strategic bombing concept decided upon at Casablanca in January 1943 envisaged the progressive disruption of the military, industrial and economic system of Germany, thereby enfeebling the German people to such an extent that the effectiveness of the German armed forces would be irreversibly undermined.[28] The resultant advent of target area bombing, of course, does not affect the contemporary understanding of what amounted to a military objective. In terms

[24] J. M. Spaight, *Air Power and War Rights*, Longman, 1924, pp. 233–5.
[25] J. M. Spaight, *Air Power and War Rights*, Longman, 1947, at p. 258.
[26] J. Stone, *Legal Controls of International Conflict*, Stevens, 1954, p. 624.
[27] See the case of Gross-Brauckmann, *Annual Digest*, 1948, Case No. 223.
[28] Rousseau, *Le Droit des conflits armés*, p. 366.

of accuracy it was merely an inefficient method of attacking military objectives. Parks, after an exhaustive review of the authorities, concludes that by the end of the Second World War the contemporary understanding of what was meant by 'military objectives' was as follows:

military equipment, units, and bases; economic targets;[29] power sources (coal, oil, electric, hydroelectric);[30] industry (war supporting manufacturing, export and/or import); transportation (equipment, lines of communication, and petroleum, oil, and other lubricants necessary for transportation); command and control; geographic;[31] personnel;[32] military;[33] and civilians taking part in the hostilities, including civilians working in industries directly related to the war effort.[34]

However, in the words of Blix,[35] 'if the view is taken . . . that practically the whole productive force of the belligerent is sufficiently relevant to justify attacks, the basic immunity of the civilian population is immediately placed in jeopardy'. An effort has to be made to draw a line somewhere.[36]

A US war crimes tribunal considered military objectives in the following passage:

A city is bombed for tactical purposes; communications are to be destroyed, railroads wrecked, ammunition plants demolished, factories razed, all for the purpose of impeding the military.[37]

The Geneva Conventions use the term 'military objective', but do not define it. Art. 18 of the Civilian Convention recommends that hospitals should be situated as far as possible from military objectives. The ICRC state[38] that although the concept of a military object was accepted, opinions differed widely as to what amounted to a military objective. Pictet[39] comments that military objectives must be understood in the strictest sense as clearly defined points of actual or potential military importance. The Prisoner of War Convention recognizes that metallurgical, engineering and chemical industries may be made the object of attack because prisoners of war may not be employed in those industries.[40]

Kalshoven, however, counsels caution in jumping to any conclusion that these

[29]Presumably, this should be a colon.
[30]Presumably, this should be a comma.
[31]Presumably this refers to areas of land.
[32]Presumably this should be a colon.
[33]Presumably this should be a comma.
[34]Parks, Air war, p. 55.
[35]H. Blix, Area bombardment: rules and reasons, *British Yearbook of International Law*, 1978, at p. 33.
[36]Spaight, *Air Power*, 1947, at p. 277, commented that it was 'the special, not the general, war potential of the enemy that is still the objective'.
[37]*US* v. *Ohlendorf (Einsatzgruppen case)*, IV *Trials of War Criminals before the Nürnberg Military Tribunals*, Washington, 1949, p. 467.
[38]ICRC *Commentary*, para. 2000.
[39]In his *Commentary* on the Convention (ICRC, 1958).
[40]Art. 50.

objectives may always be attacked, since the circumstances must be such that their elimination contributes to 'weakening the military forces of the enemy'[41] and thus represent a clear military advantage for the attacker.[42]

Another indication of what amounts to a military objective is to be found in treaty form in Art. 8 of the Cultural Convention,[43] which provides that refuges for cultural property are to be situated an adequate distance from:

any large industrial centre or from any important military objective constituting a vulnerable point, such as, for example, an aerodrome, broadcasting station, establishment engaged upon work of national defence, a port or railway station of relative importance or a main line of communication.

The ICRC draft rules of 1956[44] included a list of categories of military objectives which contained some objects of a civilian nature: war and supply ministries, lines of communication of military importance, broadcasting and television stations and telephone and telegraph exchanges of military importance, industries producing transport and communications material or metallurgical, engineering or chemical industries or installations producing energy (including gas and electricity) for mainly military purposes or use.[45]

The authors of the US Department of Defense report on the Gulf War of 1990–91 summarize the above treaties by saying, 'cultural and civilian objects are protected from direct, intentional attack unless they are used for military purposes, such as shielding military objects from attack'.[46] That summary may give a misleading impression. If, for example, the enemy were to hide their mobile missile launchers in a museum, one might have no alternative but to attack the museum, since the object of attack would be hidden from view; but if they placed a military helicopter close to a church, the helicopter would be the object of the attack, not the church, though the church might well suffer in the process.

The above examples are static objectives. But means of transport may be a military objective. The taxis commandeered by the military governor of Paris to transport reservists to the front in 1914[47] became military objectives when used for that purpose. Civilian oil tankers, lorries and railway wagons are not normally military objectives, but it is submitted that if intelligence reports suggest that the enemy plan to use such vehicles for military purposes, they can be attacked to prevent them being used for those purposes.

[41]Wording from the St Petersburg Declaration.
[42]F. Kalshoven, *Constraints on the Waging of War*, ICRC, 1987, p. 50.
[43]Dealt with in chapter 5.
[44]Sometimes known as the New Delhi draft rules.
[45]See Y. Sandoz, W. Swinarski and B. Zimmerman with J. Pictet, *Commentary on the Additional Protocols of 8 June 1977 to the Geneva Conventions of 12 August 1949*, Martinus Nijhoff, 1987 (ICRC *Commentary*), p. 632.
[46]United States, *Conduct of the Persian Gulf War*, Department of Defense Final Report to Congress, April 1992, p. 611.
[47]See Schwarzenberger, *International Law*, p. 112.

The term 'military objective' is not limited to inanimate objects. It also includes persons belonging to the enemy armed forces. It does not include members of the enemy civilian population. Even if the latter share the dangers of war, they are never in themselves military objectives. In this respect, McCoubrey's reference to the civilian work force actually working in military targets as military objectives is, in the writer's opinion, misconceived.[48] It is rather like Stone's attempt at rationalization with 'the work force of military objectives'.[49]

Another attempt at a definition which, because of its language, is obviously a precursor of the definition in Protocol I, is that adopted by the Institute of International Law in 1969:

There can be considered as military objectives only those which, by their very nature or purpose or use, make an effective contribution to military action, or exhibit a generally recognized military significance, such that their total or partial destruction in the actual circumstances gives a substantial, specific and immediate military advantage to those who are in a position to destroy them.[50]

Kalshoven has pointed out[51] that this definition falls into two disjunctive parts so that objectives qualify as military objectives if they either make an effective contribution to military action—and that presumably covers objects of a civilian nature—or they exhibit a generally recognized military significance. It is not clear from the drafting whether the last part of the definition qualifies both of the earlier alternatives (which it probably does) or only the second.

Current law

Military objectives[52] are now defined, so far as objects are concerned, as those which by their location, nature, purpose or use make an effective contribution to military action and whose total or partial destruction, capture or neutralization, in the circumstances ruling at the time, offers a definite military advantage.[53]

This abstract definition has been criticized as being not very constructive and it has been suggested that an abstract definition coupled with a non-exhaustive list of examples would be better.[54] However, it is clear from the definition that military objectives are not limited to those in the vicinity of the opposing armed

---

[48] See H. McCoubrey, *International Humanitarian Law*, Dartmouth, 1990, p. 115.

[49] As to which see Stone, *Legal Controls*, p. 627.

[50] See D. Schindler and J. Toman, *The Laws of Armed Conflicts*, Sijthoff & Noordhoff, 3rd ed., 1988, p. 265.

[51] F. Kalshoven, Reaffirmation and development of international humanitarian law, *Netherlands Yearbook of International Law*, 1978, p. 110.

[52] Military objective is used in the sense of the target rather than the overall military task—see ICRC *Commentary*, paras 2009, 2010.

[53] Protocol I, Art. 52, para. 2.

[54] E. Rosenblad, Area bombing and international law, *Military Law and Law of War Review*, 1976, p. 90.

forces; they include objects in the hinterland, and any remaining doubts on this issue have been dissolved.[55]

The United Kingdom made a statement on signature of Protocol I to the effect that an area of land could be a military objective.[56]

The writer analysed the definition of military objectives in 1982.[57] That analysis can now be brought up to date as follows.

At first sight the definition seems a very wide one. It does, however, have certain limitations:

1. The second part of the definition limits the first part, which otherwise would be limitless. The term 'definite' was eventually chosen from among various other suggestions such as 'distinct', 'clear', 'direct', 'substantial', 'obvious' and 'specific'. There seemed to be no special significance about the final choice,[58] but it has been suggested that 'definite' rather than 'relative' had the effect of excluding the rule of proportionality as a criterion for the interpretation of the term 'military objective', since an attack may offer a definite military advantage whether or not excessive collateral damage is caused by it.[59] Once it has been established that the object to be attacked is a military objective, one has to consider the rule of proportionality in respect of the incidental damage that the attack may cause. Having established that attacking the object concerned would confer a definite military advantage, the military commander, when considering the rule of proportionality, is then confronted with similar wording in that the collateral damage expected must not be excessive in relation to the concrete and direct military advantage expected.[60] 'Definite' also excludes a fanciful estimate of the military advantage or one which is not based on proper information;[61] or it means a concrete and perceptible military advantage rather than a hypothetical and speculative one.[62]

2. It must be read in conjunction with the prohibition on attacks against civilians and the civilian population in Art. 51, para. 2, of Protocol I. This rules out attacks directed against such civilians. But, subject to the rule of proportionality, it does not prevent attacks directed at military objectives which cause incidental damage to civilians.

[55]E. Rauch, Attack restraints, target limitations, etc., *Military Law and Law of War Review*, 1979, vol. 1–2, p. 55.

[56]A similar statement was made on ratification by Italy, the Netherlands and New Zealand, see A. Roberts and R. Guelff, *Documents on the Laws of War*, 2nd ed., Clarendon Press, 1989, at pp. 465–8.

[57]A. P. V. Rogers, Conduct of combat and risks run by the civilian population, *Military Law and Law of War Review*, 1982, p. 304.

[58]Kalshoven, Reaffirmation, pp. 110–12; ICRC *Commentary*, para. 2019. The German translation *eindeutig* (see, e.g., Switzerland, *Botschaft über dis Zusatzprotokolle zu den Genfer Abkommen*, Swiss Federal Council, 1981, p. 123, or F. J. Berber (ed.), *Völkerrechtliche Verträge*, 3rd ed., Beck, 1983, p. 451), meaning 'unequivocal', adds yet another dimension to the understanding of this term.

[59]E. Rauch, Conduct of combat and risks run by the civilian population, *Military Law and Law of War Review*, 1982, p. 67.

[60]See chapter 3.

[61]See ICRC *Commentary*, para. 2024.

[62]Bothe *et al.*, *New Rules*, p. 326.

3. There is no apparent reason for the inclusion of the words 'so far as objects are concerned' since the definition is sufficiently wide to include areas of land, enemy combatants and their equipment, which are quite clearly military objectives.[63] It could, of course, be argued that the word 'object' does not include combatant personnel.[64] The German manual lists the enemy armed forces separately from objects as military objectives.[65] The ICRC *Commentary*[66] states that 'object' means something tangible and visible, rather than something abstract like the object of a military operation. Rauch[67] hints at a difference between combatants and military objectives. If so, attacks on enemy military personnel would not be limited in any way by the definition, for example the need to show a definite military advantage by killing a single enemy combatant.

4. The words 'in the circumstances ruling at the time' are also a limiting factor.[68] A cathedral, for example, would not normally be an object of military importance and could not be attacked. If, however, the enemy moved its divisional headquarters into the cathedral, it would become a military objective in view of the circumstances ruling at the time, that is, the presence of the enemy headquarters.

5. The presumption of civilian status in Arts. 50 and 52 of Protocol I which applies even in the contact zone. This presumption was accepted despite some reservations in the negotiating committee to the effect that soldiers are unlikely to place their lives at risk because of the presumption, especially as in the front line civilian buildings may be incorporated in the defensive works.[69]

There are various key words in Art. 52. The first is *limited*. This word means that care must be used in directing attacks only against military objectives. Art. 52 does not deal with the question of collateral damage, which is regulated by Art. 57.[70]

The words *nature, location, purpose or use* need explanation. According to the ICRC, 'nature' refers to all objects directly used by the armed forces, e.g. weapons, military equipment, transports, headquarters, communication centres, etc.;[71] 'location' includes sites which are militarily important because they must be seized or denied to the enemy or because the enemy must be forced to retreat from them;[72] and 'purpose' means future intended use of an object, while 'use' means its present function.[73] It is hard to think of an example of a case where 'purpose' will be the deciding factor, especially given the limitation of 'in the

---

[63] CDDH, Report of Committee III, 2nd session, para. 64, under reference CDDH/215/Rev. 1. See also ICRC *Commentary*, para. 2017.
[64] Rauch, Conduct of combat; Kalshoven, Reaffirmation.
[65] *Humanitäres Völkerrecht in bewaffneten Konflikten,* ZDv 15/2, 1992, para. 442.
[66] Para. 2007.
[67] Attack restraints.
[68] Kalshoven, Reaffirmation, pp. 110–12.
[69] *Ibid.*
[70] See chapter 3.
[71] See ICRC *Commentary*, para. 2020.
[72] *Ibid.*, para. 2021.
[73] *Ibid.*, para. 2022.

circumstances ruling at the time'. If, for example, a military commander received intelligence that the enemy were about to use a school as a munitions depot, it is unlikely that he would want to attack it until the munitions had been moved in.

The words 'nature, location, purpose or use' are sufficiently wide to give the military commander considerable room for manoeuvre, but are subject to the qualifications later in the definition of *effective contribution to military action* and the offering of a 'definite military advantage'.

It has been suggested that there is no connection between effective contribution and military advantage. This means that it is permissible to attack bridges, fuel dumps and airfields in the rear areas, since these targets make an effective contribution to the enemy's military power in the area of operations. Similarly, diversionary attacks are permitted because by diverting enemy attention away from the point of attack they confer a definite military advantage on the attacker.[74] Industry producing goods used by the armed forces and facilities supporting those factories are military objectives, but the precise extent to which industry can be made the object of attack is far from clear.[75]

The term *military action* appears to have a wide meaning equating to the general prosecution of the war.

Meyrowitz, however, points out that while the definition of military objective in Protocol I allows more latitude than would be the case if the definition were based on a list of targets, the requirement that there should be a definite military advantage also imposes some limitations on the war aims of a party to the conflict.[76]

It has always been difficult to define military objectives with sufficient precision for military commanders and for some commentators[77] who feel that a non-exhaustive list would be useful. An annex listing such objectives was provided for in the ICRC draft rules of 1956 but never drafted.[78] There are so many variable factors. The only certainties are as follows.

1. A purely civilian object contains neither military personnel nor things of military significance.

2. A civilian object which contains military personnel or things of military significance is considered a military objective.[79]

Taking into account the practice of states and the attempts at codification,

---

[74]B. M. Carnahan, Protecting civilians under the draft Geneva protocol, 18 *Air Force Law Review*, 1976, p. 61.

[75]E.g. the Confederate cotton referred to above.

[76]See Buts de guerre et objectifs militaires, *Military Law and Law of War Review*, 1983, vol. 1–2, p. 108.

[77]See E. Rosenblad, Area bombing and international law, *Military Law and Law of War Review*, 1976.

[78]See Schindler and Toman, *Laws of Armed Conflicts*, p. 253.

[79]R. Barras and S. Erman, Forces armés et developpement du droit de la guerre, *Military Law and Law of War Review*, 1982, pp. 262, 271.

the following *examples of military objectives* may tentatively be given. It is important to stress that:

1. The list is by no means exhaustive.

2. The mere fact that an object is in the list, such as a railway or a main road, does not mean that it is necessarily a military objective. It must make an effective contribution to military action and its neutralization must offer a definite military advantage.[80]

military personnel and persons who take part in the fighting without being members of the armed forces;[81] military facilities, military equipment, including military vehicles, weapons, munitions and stores of fuel,[82] military works, including defensive works and fortifications,[83] military depots and establishments, including War and Supply Ministries;[84] works producing or developing military supplies and other supplies of military value, including metallurgical, engineering and chemical industries supporting the war effort;[85] areas of land of military significance such as hills, defiles and bridgeheads; railways, ports, airfields, bridges, main roads as well as tunnels and canals;[86] oil and other power installations; communications installations, including broadcasting and television stations and telephone and telegraph stations used for military communications.[87]

However, when attacking these targets the proportionality rule must be respected.

It follows from the general rule that attacks on certain types of targets are *prohibited*. These include:

cities, towns, villages as such;[88] buildings used by civilians such as dwellings, schools, museums, places of worship and other buildings without military significance;[89] foodstuffs and food producing areas; water sources for the civilian population.[90]

Doswald-Beck would add that commercial activity of no great importance for the opponent's defence would not be a military objective.[91] Special protection is, of course, given under various conventions to hospitals, internment and prisoner-of-war camps.

[80]See Protocol I, Art. 52, para. 2.
[81]ICRC *Commentary*, p. 632.
[82]See Bothe *et al.*, *New Rules*, p. 323.
[83]*Ibid.*, p. 323.
[84]See ICRC *Commentary*, p. 632.
[85]See ICRC *Commentary*, p. 632.
[86]See ICRC *Commentary*, p. 632.
[87]See ICRC *Commentary*, p. 632. The German manual *Humanitäres Völkerrecht*, para. 443, lists the following as military objectives: (1) the armed forces, (2) military aircraft and warships, (3) buildings and objects for combat service support, (4) economic objectives which make an effective contribution to military action (transport facilities, industrial plants, etc.).
[88]That means that the morale of the civilian population may not be used as a justification, see Doswald-Beck, The value of the 1977 protocols, p. 155.
[89]So long as they are not being used for military purposes.
[90]Food, food-producing areas and water are specifically dealt with in Art. 54 cf Protocol I. This prohibition does not include sustenance solely for members of the armed forces or objects used in direct support of military action.
[91]The value of the 1977 Protocols, p. 155.

In case of doubt about objects which are normally civilian, such as churches, houses or schools, they should be presumed to have civilian status.[92] Bothe *et al.*[93] point out that in the ICRC draft 'installations and means of transport' were also included in the presumption, but the phrase was later deleted because means of transport fell into a category where their use for military purposes could not be excluded by a presumption. Greenwood[94] comments that it is very doubtful whether the rule of doubt represents customary law. Green's statement that 'the location and surrounding situation may make the object a military objective, as would be the case of a dwelling-house in the centre of a combat area or in the event of street and house-to-house fighting'[95] needs to be treated with caution. Everything depends on the circumstances. It is not possible to lay down general exemptions.

One reporter has mentioned that drawing a distinction between military objectives and civilian objects often involves a lot of effort. If it calls for a disproportionate consumption of men, ammunition, or loss of time as a tactical factor, commanders, especially at lower levels, may be inclined to be less careful in their selection of targets.[96]

There continues in some quarters to be some inexplicable doubt about whether an area of land can be a military objective. Würkner-Theis[97] discusses these doubts by saying that to recognize an area of land as a military objective would be to legalize area bombardment and negate the principle of distinction; that the recognition of an area of land in the Mines Protocol might be regarded as limited to the purposes of that protocol; on the other hand the use of words like 'location' and 'neutralization' in the definition of military objectives seems to imply areas of land the denial of which to the enemy could be of considerable military importance; but since the precise effect of a mine cannot be forecast at the time of laying, it is difficult to say that there is a definite military advantage to be gained by laying a mine, unless the tactical situation is such that the enemy's manoeuvrability can be hindered by the laying of mines. After considering the authorities he comes to the conclusion that an area of land *can* be a military objective.[98]

A study of armed conflict reveals that areas of land have always featured very prominently in combat. The German official manual of the First World War laid down that it was permissible to bombard an area when it was intended to guard

---

[92]Protocol I, Art. 52, para 3.

[93]*New Rules*, p. 326.

[94]C. J. Greenwood, Customary international law and the first Geneva protocol of 1977 in the Gulf conflict, in P. J. Rowe (ed.), *The Gulf War 1990–91 in International and English Law*, Routledge, 1993, p. 75.

[95]L. C. Green, *The Contemporary Law of Armed Conflict*, Manchester, 1993, p. 147.

[96]E. L. Gonsalves, Armed forces and the development of the law of war, *Military Law and Law of War Review*, 1982, p. 192.

[97]G. Würkner-Theis, *Fernverlegte Minen und humanitäres Völkerrecht*, Lang, 1990, at p. 121.

[98]*Da die Neutralisation eines für die Bewegung des Gegners bedeutsamen Gebietes einen militärischen Vorteil bedeutet, ist ein Landgebiet daher ein militärisches Objekt.*

a passage, to defend approaches, to protect a retreat or to prepare or cover a tactical movement.[99] The US *Handbook*[100] confirms that it is permissible to deny an area to enemy troops by planting landmines on it, or destroy a mountain pass that is crucial to the enemy's lines of communication. The definition of 'attack' given earlier emphasizes this prominence. Denying land to enemy forces is often a principal consideration in military operations. Bothe *et al.* refer to the word 'neutralization' in the definition of military objective and point out that an area of land may be neutralized by laying mines on it.[101] In this respect Protocol I has changed nothing. If an area of land has military significance, for whatever reason, it becomes a military objective. This has been described as a reasonable interpretation: 'as no objection has been voiced against it either in the formal procedure by a State party to Protocol I or in literature, it is deemed to be generally acceptable'.[102] Such an area of land may be attacked or occupied. It would, therefore, be wrong to say[103] that 'civilian intervening areas' can never be a military objective. The ICRC *Commentary* seems to accept that an area of land may be a military objective provided it is of limited size and in the combat zone.[104] The reference to the combat zone is, in the opinion of the writer, an inadmissible restriction because it is not a limitation which appears in the definition of military objective itself. Art. 4 of the Mines Protocol to the Weapons Convention, for example, envisages the laying of mines outside the combat zone if certain precautions are taken. In these cases it is not the definition of military objective but the other rules of Protocol I that provide the necessary protection. If, for example, an area of land contains civilian objects, the military commander will be obliged to ensure that those civilian objects are not directly attacked and that precautions are to be taken to minimize incidental loss. If the rule of proportionality would be infringed the action would have to be replanned.

Detter de Lupis criticizes the 'subjective' approach adopted in Protocol I in the following terms:

How is [a party] expected to know the planned use of any particular installation? Surely objective criteria must be preferred rather than those which presuppose a detailed knowledge of enemy strategies. It is almost better to resort to large presumption of use and thus classify all industrial centres as military objectives.[105]

It is difficult, however, to see how objective criteria could be drafted without adopting the enumerative approach, which, first, can never be exhaustive and,

[99] See *Kriegsbrauch im Landkriege*, in the translation entitled *The German War Book*, by J. H. Morgan, John Murray, 1915, at p. 81.
[100] United States, *Commander's Handbook on the Law of Armed Conflict*, Department of the Air Force, Pamphlet 110-34, 1980, p. 2–1.
[101] *New Rules*, p. 325.
[102] H. P. Gasser, Some legal issues concerning ratifications of the 1977 Geneva protocols, in M. A. Meyer (ed.), *Armed Conflict and the New Law*, British Institute of International and Comparative Law, 1989, p. 87.
[103] Rauch, Conduct of combat, p. 68.
[104] ICRC *Commentary*, p. 2026.
[105] Detter de Lupis, *Law of War*, p. 238.

secondly, cannot adapt to changing circumstances and technological and other developments. At best, lists can be only illustrative. Objective criteria based on a non-enumerative approach would probably render almost nugatory the provisions for the protection of the civilian population which is assured, to some extent, by the 'subjective' definition of military objectives coupled with the rule of doubt and the principle of proportionality. As will be seen in the next section, the subjective approach seems to have caused no difficulty in the Gulf War of 1990–91.

Parks also criticizes the definition of military objectives in Protocol I, saying that it is intended to limit targets to objectives connected with a nation's military effort rather than its war effort and that this does not reflect state practice.[106] He says that if certain lines of communication used by enemy armed forces are destroyed, the enemy will simply transfer to other lines of communication; that electricity grids are so complex that it is impossible to ascertain whether a given power plant is supplying energy for national defence; that motorways may be used as airstrips for military aircraft; that nations export materials in order to pay for the purchase of weapons; that nations import raw materials to manufacture tanks, ships and aircraft; that dispersal of petroleum products or of the manufacture of parts for weapons systems adds to the problems of the attacker; that attacks of relatively slight military importance can have untold psychological value. He refers to the Doolittle raids on Japan in 1942 which caused Japan to switch aircraft to home defence and unleashed a chain of events which enabled the United States to stem the tide of Japanese conquests. Of course, that result may not have been foreseen by the Doolittle planners, who may have been concerned mainly with giving US forces a morale boost.[107]

The writer does not share all those concerns,[108] taking the view that the definition of military objectives is sufficiently wide to allow most of the above targets to be attacked. Obviously an attacker will wish to concentrate his efforts in such a way as to derive the maximum benefit. He will not attack a country's entire lines of communication, motorway system or electricity grid only because it may be used by the armed forces or to move supplies. He will attack those points which will give him the best advantage.[109] Dispersal of possible objectives makes things more difficult for the attacker, but that is not a problem which arises from the definition of military objectives. There is no difficulty about attacking raw materials used in the armaments industry, nor does the motive (i.e. the psychological advantage) for attacking a *military* objective matter.

The only potential area of difficulty is with regard to economic targets.[110] If

---

[106] Parks, Air war, p. 138.

[107] Parks, Air war, p. 142.

[108] Nor does G. Best, *Law and War since 1945*, Clarendon Press, 1994, pp. 274–5.

[109] This question will be discussed later in this chapter in the light of events in the Gulf War 1990–91.

[110] Such as the Confederate cotton previously referred to.

a country relies almost entirely on, say, the export of coffee beans or bananas for its income and even if that income is used to a great extent to support its war effort, the personal opinion of the writer is that it would not be legitimate to attack banana or coffee bean plantations or warehouses. The reason is that such plants would not make an *effective* contribution to *military* action, nor would their destruction offer a *definite* military advantage. The definition of military objectives thus excludes the general industrial and agricultural potential of the enemy. Targets must offer a more specific military advantage. Green puts it as economic targets that indirectly but effectively support enemy operations.[111] None of this, however, would prevent attacks on military objectives, such as means of transport or ports, which would indirectly affect the export of agricultural products.

The Gulf War of 1990–91

It is relatively easy to single out military objectives which are of a purely military nature. Before the Gulf War a leader writer urged allied forces to attack Iraqi military potential—'airfields, missile sites, military bases and factories producing chemicals or nuclear materials'—but also advised that they should not bomb 'dams, factories or centres of civilian population . . . or attempt the defoliation of the country'.[112]

In practice things are not so simple in a modern society. According to Roberts,[113] many of the objects attacked by the allies during the air campaign served the needs of both the armed forces and the civilian population, such as oil storage sites, power stations and factories, and it is difficult to neutralize the military effectiveness of such targets without simultaneously harming the civilian population. Schachter[114] comments that 'the hostilities revealed how difficult it can be to make a sharp separation between the military target and civilian objects, especially in an industrial society where their commingling is widespread'. Attacks on the electric power system meant that electric power was severely curtailed, resulting in shortages and contamination of the water supply.[115] Roads, railways, bridges, airports and ports are used for the deployment of military forces and the movement of military supplies as well as for civilian purposes. It has been pointed out that bombing to cut the enemy off from their supplies is more effective than attacking the enemy forces themselves, which, through

[111]Green, *Contemporary Law*, p. 183.
[112]*The Independent*, 11 January 1991.
[113]A. Roberts, Failures in protecting the environment, in Rowe (ed.), *Gulf War*, p. 139.
[114]O. Schachter, United Nations law in the Gulf conflict, *American Journal of International Law*, 1991, at p. 466.
[115]See report of the UN Secretary-General to the President of the Security Council of 20 March 1991, UN Document S/22366.

digging in and camouflage, can remain largely protected from air attack.[116] The attacks on bridges and supply lines were to prevent reinforcements and supplies reaching the Kuwaiti theatre of operations.[117] Microwave towers used for civilian communications can also be used as part of the military command and control system; and electric power grids can be used for civilian and military purposes simultaneously.[118] Some have been critical of the bombing of Iraq's electricity system[119] on the grounds that the civilian population suffered unduly as a result. But such a system is a military objective if by destroying it the enemy's military effectiveness is reduced.[120] Protection of the civilian population is provided by the rule of proportionality, see chapter 1.

In the Gulf War it was considered that because of the highly centralized Iraqi command arrangements the communications system was a very important target, since if it were rendered inoperative the Iraqi leaders would be unable to direct their forces. Bridges over the river Euphrates in Baghdad carried the fibre optic cables which provided communications with the forces. Destruction of the bridges served two ends: to sever those cables and to impede the deployment of Iraqi forces and their supplies.[121]

Targets actually attacked during the allied air campaign included the following.

1. Military targets—Iraqi military aircraft both in the air and on the ground,[122] some in hardened shelters,[123] air bases and runways, Scud missiles, naval vessels, tanks, military vehicles and artillery pieces, army and Republican Guard positions in the Kuwait theatre of operations,[124] barracks,[125] surface-to-air and anti-ship missile bases and their radars, military production facilities and ammunition storage areas, chemical weapon facilities, military headquarters and command posts[126] and minefields.[127]

2. Mixed targets[128]—leadership command facilities such as the Iraqi intelligence service headquarters,[129] refined oil production installations, nuclear, chem-

---

[116]E. Luttwak, Supplies, not troops, should be the main target of jets in Kuwait, *The Times*, 16 February 1991.

[117]See DOD Report, p. 98.

[118]See DOD Report, p. 612.

[119]E.g. Middle East Watch, *Needless Deaths in the Gulf War*, Human Rights Watch, 1991.

[120]Protocol I, Art. 52, para. 2, speaks of the object making an effective contribution to military action and whose neutralization, etc., offers a definite military advantage.

[121]DOD Report, p. 612.

[122]DOD Report, pp. 95–9.

[123]C. Allen, *Thunder and Lightning*, HMSO, 1991, p. 137.

[124]DOD Report, pp. 95–9.

[125]P. Hine, Despatch by the joint commander of Operation Granby, 2nd supplement to the *London Gazette*, 28 June 1991, p. G42; Allen, *Thunder and Lightning*, p. 137.

[126]DOD Report, pp. 95–9.

[127]Apparently, some were attacked with fuel-air explosive, see Hansard (Commons), 2 May 1991, at col. 484, and Hansard (Commons), 17 June 1991 at col. 16; and DOD Report, p. 196.

[128]These must, of course, be military objectives. Greenwood rightly emphasizes that there is no intermediate category of dual use objects: either something is a military objective or it is not. Greenwood, Gulf conflict, p. 73.

[129]Greenwood, Gulf conflict, states that ministries are not necessarily military objectives. It

ical and biological sites,[130] bridges,[131] communications towers, exchanges and lines, supply lines, including railway and road bridges between Baghdad and Basra, radio and television installations and electricity production facilities.[132]

According to media reports, mixed targets which might have been attacked but which were not for fear of the consequences for the civilian population included dams.[133] A dam is not necessarily a military objective.[134] It depends on its purpose. If it is purely to create a reservoir of drinking water it will not be a military objective. If it were only to provide hydro-electric power the situation would be different. It is more likely to provide both: water and electric power. There is, however, the danger from flooding to the civilian population to be considered if the dam is attacked. In the circumstances, it is better to attack the hydro-electric power installations with precision weapons rather than the dam itself.[135] According to Middle East Watch, other objects that were removed from the target list included statues of Saddam Hussein and triumphal arches.[136] According to one account, it seems that a statue was removed from the list mainly because of the fear of incidental damage.[137] Middle East Watch seem to assume that the definition of military objectives in Protocol I applied to the Gulf conflict[138] but, of course, Protocol I did not apply in that conflict. The less clear customary law understanding of the term which did apply may have permitted potential or indeterminate factors such as enemy morale to be taken into account.

In the Gulf War the US air warfare plan was to strike first at Iraqi command and control and communications facilities, secondly to gain air supremacy, thirdly to destroy the nuclear, bacteriological and chemical warfare capability, fourthly to eliminate Iraq's offensive warfare capability by attacking military production plants and fifthly to attack lines of communication to Iraqi forces in Kuwait. Only after that were enemy armed forces attacked.[139]

British aircraft attacked airfields, barracks, radar control centres, ammunition dumps, petroleum storage sites, power stations, Scud missile sites, bridges,

depends on the circumstances: what ministries they are and what contribution they make to the enemy's military action.

[130] DOD Report, pp. 95–9.
[131] Allen, *Thunder and Lightning*, pp. 113–16.
[132] DOD Report, pp. 95–9.
[133] *The Times*, 15 February 1991. The Secretary of State for Defence confirmed that the allies did not attack water supplies, see *Preliminary Lessons of Operation Granby*, House of Commons Defence Committee, Tenth Report, HMSO, 1991, p. 10.
[134] Special provisions protecting dams are to be found in Protocol I, Art. 56.
[135] See G. H. Aldrich, Prospects for US ratification of Protocol I, *American Journal of International Law*, 1991, p. 56, who points out that hydro-electric power stations are not themselves dams or dykes, but 'other military objectives located in the vicinity' thereof.
[136] See Middle East Watch, *Needless Deaths*, p. 156.
[137] T. P. Keenan, Jr, Die Operation Wüstensturm aus der Sicht des aktiven Rechtsberaters, *Humanitäres Völkerrecht Informationsschriften*, January–July 1991, p. 36.
[138] See, e.g., p. 159.
[139] DOD Report, p. 95.

hardened aircraft shelters, coastal defence positions, surface-to-air missile bat-
teries, supply depots, naval vessels, artillery positions and concentrations of
armour.[140]

The British army in the Gulf was not presented with the dilemma of how to
deal with mixed targets. The plan for the 1st (British) Armoured Division was
to defeat Iraq's tactical reserves in the area between the southern flank of the VII
US Corps and the Iraq–Saudi Arabia border. This involved ensuring that Iraqi
forces did not attack the flanks of the VII US Corps by destroying armour and
artillery in that area. In fact, all the objectives actually attacked were of a purely
military nature.[141] As Best comments, referring to the desert war of 1940–42 and
the absence there of civilians, the principles of restraint and discrimination are
observed 'not badly when men had will and space to observe them'.[142]

Allied targeting in 1991 has been criticized by some commentators[143] in
particular:

1. Food and grain warehouses, a dairy factory, flour mills and water treatment
facilities.
2. The electricity system.
3. Civilian vehicles on highways and Bedouin tents.
4. The oil sector.

They are correct with regard to food facilities not being military objectives
unless used exclusively by the armed forces or in direct support of military
action,[144] but there is no evidence that any of these facilities was deliberately
made the object of attack. Indeed, Parks comments that factories producing
textiles, foodstuffs, cement and household goods 'were *not* attacked *unless* they
also were of value to Saddam Hussein's defence of Kuwait or his CBW [chem-
ical and bacteriological warfare] programmes through dual use for military and
civilian purposes'.[145] Some damage to such factories may have been caused by
Iraqi surface-to-air missiles and anti-aircraft munitions.[146] Shotwell refers to the
effect of sanctions as well as air strikes on the morale of Iraqi troops during the
Gulf War of 1991 when increasing numbers of Iraqi soldiers reported dwindling
rations of food: some units were allocating only one piece of bread per day per
soldier.[147] There is evidence that the Iraqi regime used civilian installations as
a cover for military activities. For example, UN inspectors discovered chem-

[140] Hine, Despatch, p. G42.
[141] N. Pearce, *The Shield and the Sabre*, HMSO, 1992, pp. 90–121.
[142] Best, *Law and War*, p. 60.
[143] Middle East Watch, pp. 160 *et seq.*; C. Jochnick and R. Normand, The legitimation of violence: a critical history of the laws of war, *Harvard International Law Journal*, 1994, p. 402. For a different perspective, see Best, *Law and War*, p. 384.
[144] See Protocol I, Art. 54, para. 3. C.B.
[145] W. H. Parks, in a letter dated 22 December 1994 to the writer.
[146] G. Waters, *Gulf Lesson One: the Value of Air Power*, Air Power Studies Centre, 1992, p. 170.
[147] C. B. Shotwell, Food and the use of force, *Military Law and Law of War Review*, 1991, at p. 372.

ical bomb production equipment while inspecting a sugar factory in Iraq.[148] The most publicized incident in the allied bombing campaign was the attack on the al-Amariyah (or al-Firdos) bunker in Baghdad. This was a command and control centre in which, unbeknown to the allies, civilians had been allowed to take refuge.[149]

The modern military machine relies very heavily on electrical power, especially for command, control, communications and air defence systems. Take away that power and the enemy is severely handicapped and may be rendered blind and leaderless and vulnerable to air attack. The suggestion by Jochnick and Normand[150] that repeated attacks are not necessary where a war is going to be short is unrealistic. It was known that Iraq possessed very powerful armed forces with a nuclear, chemical and bacteriological capability, it was not known how long it would take to fulfil the UN mandate,[151] and the allies were fully entitled to take no risks in that respect. In these circumstances, power sources become military objectives. Electrical power is fundamental to the functioning of many industries, especially armaments and other war material. In the case of Iraq it was most urgent for the allies to neutralize Iraq's air defence and, more particularly, its nuclear, bacteriological and chemical warfare capability and its Scud missile system, and keep them neutralized by repeated attacks to prevent repair. However, steps were taken, for example by adopting a policy of attacking switching stations rather than generating stations, to enable repair of the electricity system after the war.[152]

Of course, the civilian population will be badly affected too. Integrated electricity grids are such that electricity used to power air defence computers or a biological weapons factory cannot be separated from that used to power electrical pumps for the water supply and to light homes. So the rule of proportionality applies.[153] It is estimated that ultimately allied air attacks rendered 88 per cent of Iraqi electrical generating capacity unavailable[154] but that by mid-1992

---

[148] DOD Report, p. 613.

[149] *Ibid.*, p. 615. See also Best, *Law and War*, p. 327; T. A. Keaney and E. A. Cohen, *Gulf War Air Power Survey, Summary Report*, US Government Printing Office, 1993, pp. 69, 249.

[150] Legitimation of violence, p. 404.

[151] The comment by Michael Howard in November 1990 that the war could be 'a bloody and prolonged business' (On balance, Bush must go to war, *The Times*, 5 November 1990) probably reflected the views of many at the time. Even as late as 24 December 1990 military planners acknowledged that the war could last six months, see *The Times* of that day.

[152] The writer is indebted to W. H. Parks for his assistance in dealing with these criticisms and for referring him to Keaney and Cohen, *Gulf War Air Power Survey, Summary Report*; D. T. Kuehl, Air power *v.* electricity: electric power as a target for strategic air operations, to be published in *Journal of Strategic Studies*, 1995; and various other authorities. He makes the valid point that in considering the post-war state of Iraq it is necessary to bear in mind the continuing UN sanctions and Saddam Hussein's failure to channel his resources into alleviating the conditions of the civilian population and refers in this respect to A. Dowty, Sanctioning Iraq: the limits of the new world order, *Washington Quarterly*, 1994.

[153] See chapter 1. Middle East Watch seems to accept that it is a question of proportionality rather than targeting.

[154] Not 96 per cent, as alleged by Jochnick and Normand, The legitimation of violence, p. 404.

capacity was back to 90 per cent of the pre-war level.[155] In this connection it is of interest that Middle East Watch quote a Harvard University group which visited Iraq in April and May 1991 and found that electricity was then supplied at 23 per cent of the pre-war figure. This may have been enough to support the needs of the civilian population and of agriculture, but not of industry, and may be regarded as proportionate. This is probably what General Schwarzkopf had in mind when, according to Middle East Watch, he said that some electrical power must be left for the civilians.[156] The writer would reject the allegation that repeated bombing of previously disabled electrical facilities served no military purpose. The purpose obviously is to prevent repair and keep the facility out of action. The fact that the allies did not bomb electrical facilities in Kuwait is really irrelevant.[157]

Civilian vehicles carrying military supplies for the benefit of the Iraqi armed forces would have been military objectives. The personal view of the writer is that civilian vehicles carrying Iraqi oil to Jordan would not. Some of the latter were attacked by mistake, having been mistaken for mobile Scud launchers. Some suffered incidental damage as a result of attacks on military vehicles using the same road.[158] It also appears that many of the objects attacked in the Scud launch areas were 'decoys, vehicles such as tanker trucks that had infra-red and radar signatures impossible to distinguish from those of mobile launchers'.[159] Jochnick and Normand's criticism of allied attacks on Iraqi oil facilities is effectively answered by Keaney and Cohen, who state that during the war allied air attacks rendered 90 per cent of Iraq's petroleum refining capacity inoperative but that by October 1992 it had returned to two-thirds of its pre-war level. Again, planners did not know how long the war would last and it was prudent to limit Iraq's ability to wage a protracted ground campaign.[160]

Legal opinion is divided on whether, in conflicts to which Protocol I does not apply, impairing civilian morale is a lawful aim of war,[161] but there seems to be no reason why it cannot lawfully be a by-product of attacks on legitimate military objectives. Remarks such as 'it is important that people understand that a war is going on'[162] must be seen in this context.

---

[155] Keaney and Cohen, *Gulf War*, pp. 73–5.
[156] Middle East Watch, p. 175.
[157] See Jochnick and Normand, The legitimation of violence, pp. 404–5.
[158] See DOD Report, p. 627.
[159] Keaney and Cohen, *Gulf War*, p. 83.
[160] *Ibid.*, pp. 76–7.
[161] See, e.g., Oppenheim, *International Law*, at pp. 528–9; Blix, Area bombardment, at pp. 44 *et seq.*
[162] Quoted by J. Campbell, Rings of disaster, London *Evening Standard*, 3 July 1991.

3

Precautions in attack

Introduction

Until Protocol I[1] there was no specific treaty provision dealing with the duty to take care to restrict the incidental damage caused by attacks. Even after Protocol I some of the authors of books and articles dealing with methods of warfare ignored the question of precautions altogether.[2] That such a duty existed may be inferred from the principles of customary law and from some of the treaty texts, but its precise scope was unclear. This chapter will be devoted to trying to discern the relevant customary and treaty law and to examining and explaining the rules of Protocol I on the subject.

It seems a well established principle of customary law that destruction of and damage to enemy property for the purpose of offence or defence is lawful, whether on the battlefield, in preparation for battle, in manoeuvring or reconnoitring, or in the transportation of military supplies, provided it is imperatively demanded by the necessities of war.[3] The reference to military necessity obviously requires an evaluation by the military commander contemplating such damage or destruction of whether it is really necessary and that implies a duty of care not to cause unnecessary damage or destruction. That duty must also imply the need to take precautions to avoid unnecessary damage, but failure to do so probably will not in itself be a basis for criminal responsibility under customary law, unless, as a result of such failure, unnecessary damage has been caused.

The Hague Regulations

The Hague Regulations introduced the following prohibitions which, to some extent, require precautions to be taken.

[1]Art. 57.
[2]E.g. I. Detter de Lupis, *The Law of War*, Cambridge University Press, 1987; or L. C. Green, The new law of armed conflict, *Canadian Yearbook of International Law*, vol. XV, 1977.
[3]L. Oppenheim, *International Law*, vol. 2, 7th ed. by H. Lauterpacht, Longman, 1952, at pp. 413–14.

1. To destroy or seize enemy property unless imperative military necessity so demands.[4]

2. To attack or bombard, by any means whatever,[5] undefended towns, villages, dwellings or buildings.[6]

They also introduced the following precautionary rules.

3. The requirement for the officer commanding an attacking force to do all in his power to give warning of an impending bombardment, except in cases of assault.[7] Some commentators of the time considered that the duty to give warning was the rule where the place threatened contained non-combatants.[8]

4. The requirement to take all necessary steps in sieges and bombardments to spare, as far as possible, buildings dedicated to art, science or charitable purposes, historic monuments, hospitals, and places where the sick and wounded are being collected, provided they are not being used for military purposes.[9]

Destruction or damage

The first of the above prohibitions was the subject of various war crimes trials after the Second World War[10] but the cases were concerned about whether there was any military need to cause the damage done, not about the duty to take precautions.

Non-combatants

It has been said that, as hostilities are to be directed against the enemy armed forces, 'non-combatants are not to be deliberately or carelessly subjected to attack. This principle underlies the Hague Regulations concerning sieges and bombardments.'[11] The use of the word 'carelessly' indicates a duty to take some care.

Warning

The warning is to enable non-combatants to leave or for them and their property to be moved to a place of safety;[12] the attacking commander cannot be held

[4] Art. 23(g).
[5] These words were added at the Second Hague Conference to cover bombardment by aircraft, T. E. Holland, *The Laws of War on Land*, Clarendon Press, 1908, p. 46; Oppenheim, *International Law*, p. 418; J. Stone, *Legal Controls of International Armed Conflict*, Stevens, 1954, at p. 621.
[6] Art. 25.
[7] Art. 26.
[8] See, e.g., J. R. Baker and H. G. Crocker, *The Laws of Land Warfare*, US Department of State, 1919, p. 205.
[9] Art. 27.
[10] Lingenfelder, IX WCR 67; Szabados, IX WCR 59; Holstein, VIII WCR 29; High Command trial, XII WCR 93; List, VIII WCR 66.
[11] H. Wheaton, *International Law*, 7th English ed. by A. B. Keith, Stevens, 1944, at p. 215.
[12] Wheaton, *International Law*, p. 216; Oppenheim, *International Law*, p. 420; Stone, *Legal Controls*, p. 622.

responsible for death, injury or loss if this does not happen. No period of notice between warning and attack is laid down or is apparent in practice,[13] but clearly it has to be sufficient to allow civilians to take shelter. Warning is not required in the case of assault, even if the assault is preceded or accompanied by a bombardment.[14] Further, a strict requirement to give warning is not imposed, since an officer is required only to 'do all in his power' to give a warning.[15] Clearly, he is not required to give a warning if he has not the means to do so, and sometimes military necessity[16] will preclude the giving of warnings. Stone adds that warning will rarely be possible in cases of aerial bombardment because of the risk of the loss of attacking aircraft and that it was not the practice to do so during the Second World War.[17] Greenspan agrees, saying that military exigencies and the necessity for surprise do not usually allow of prior warning in aerial bombardment.[18]

Assault

'Assault' refers to a surprise attack.[19] One author gives examples of cases where warnings were or were not given and of cases where civilians were not allowed by the attacking commander to leave, principally where it was decided to starve a town into submission rather than carry it by bombardment or assault.[20] According to Lauterpacht, assault, siege or bombardment on the battlefield is not prohibited; the rules impinge only on assaults, bombardments and sieges outside the battlefield.[21] Presumably by battlefield he meant areas which are not populated by civilians. Lauterpacht also expressed the view that undefended places may not be assaulted.[22]

Bombardment

According to the editor of Wheaton, there was 'no rule of law forbidding bombardment merely for destructive ends, and not as a measure to reduce a fortified place' but he criticized the long-range artillery bombardment of a town on the basis that the attackers would not be able to comply with the rule on protected

---

[13] Wheaton, *International Law*, p. 216.
[14] Oppenheim, *International Law*, p. 419.
[15] *Ibid.*, p. 420. The author refers to 'do all he can', which is slightly different.
[16] *C'est-à-dire quand la nécessité militaire ne le permet pas*, K. Obradovic, La protection de la population civile dans les conflits armés internationaux, in A. Cassese (ed.), *The New Humanitarian Law of Armed Conflict*, Naples, 1979.
[17] Stone, *Legal Controls*, p. 622.
[18] M. Greenspan, *The Modern Law of Land Warfare*, University of California Press, 1959, p. 339.
[19] Holland, *Laws of War*, p. 46.
[20] Wheaton, *International Law*, p. 216.
[21] Oppenheim, *International Law*, pp. 414–18.
[22] *Ibid.*, p. 418.

buildings.[23] He goes on to say that, if hospitals are deliberately set up in parts of the town which are of vital importance for the assailants to shell, the responsibility for damage to them and injury to the inmates must fall on the defenders. At first sight all this seems curious, but it must be subject to the qualification that the need to shell them is a matter of imperative military necessity, that undefended places are not to be bombarded and that warning is to be given except in cases of assault[24] and, of course, there can be no objection to the bombardment of enemy military positions and installations outside populated areas. Lauterpacht states that there is no rule of law that bombardment must be restricted to fortifications and also that the bombardment of private and public property is lawful as a means of 'impressing on the authorities the advisability of surrender'.[25] This statement, too, must be subject to the prohibition on attacks on undefended places and the requirement to protect certain installations.

Stone draws a distinction between:

1. The combat zone, where, he says, subject to the undefended places rule, liberty to bombard the whole area is quite plain, not restricted to enemy forces or installations, nor restrained by the presence of civilians in villages or towns usable for military purposes.

2. The hinterland of belligerent controlled territory, where the only common ground is that military objectives may be attacked.[26]

Necessary steps

Here a positive duty is placed on an attacking commander to take precautions to prevent damage to certain installations and a duty is also placed on the defenders to indicate those installations with signs. It has even been suggested that the signs must be visible from the point at which the besieging artillery carries out the bombardment.[27] While that may have been the case at the time of the Napoleonic Wars, it cannot have been right by the time of the First World War, when artillery was capable of engaging targets at a distance of several miles and no sign would have been visible.[28] It might, of course, have been visible to the artillery commander through the medium of reconnaissance aircraft. It would be totally impracticable to require the defenders to erect signs that would be visible at long range. It would seem, therefore, in those cases that some of the onus rests on the attacking commander to ascertain by reconnaissance and intelligence reports whether certain installations are protected.

[23] That is, Art. 27 of the Hague Regulations, see Wheaton, *International Law*, pp. 216–17.
[24] Arts. 25 and 26 of the Hague Regulations.
[25] Oppenheim, *International Law*, p. 421.
[26] Stone, *Legal Controls*, pp. 620–1; see also Greenspan, *Modern Law*, p. 333.
[27] Oppenheim, *International Law*, p. 421.
[28] For the difficulties of identifying the Red Cross emblem at a distance, see G. C. Cauderay, Visibility of the distinctive emblem on medical establishments, units and transports, *International Review of the Red Cross*, No. 277, July–August 1990.

Precautions

Apart from the duty to give warning and to take care to spare certain installations, there was no more general provision of the Hague Regulations requiring a commander to take precautions in attack. This omission may be contrasted with another treaty negotiated at the same time, the Naval Bombardment Convention. Article 2 lists various military objectives that may be bombarded, provides that in certain circumstances they may be attacked without notice and imposes a duty on the attacking commander to take 'all due measures in order that the town may suffer as little harm as possible'. This is clearly a requirement to aim fire at the military objectives and to reduce incidental damage as much as possible. According to Kalshoven it is possible to deduce from the older treaties, including the 1899 and 1907 Hague treaties, certain unwritten rules: the duty to identify a target prior to attack, a prohibition of area bombardment and the rule of proportionality.[29]

Air Warfare Rules

Although not legally binding on states, the Air Warfare Rules are a useful guide to contemporary thinking about the state of customary law and have been described as of persuasive authority in the context of land warfare.[30] They emphasize the need for directing attacks against military objectives and give a rather restricted definition of military objectives. It has been suggested that this definition of a military objective completely abandons the 1907 distinction between open towns and defended towns,[31] a distinction which is somewhat artificial in the context of air warfare, where targets hundreds of miles from the opposing ground forces are attacked. This point is considered more fully in chapter 2. The rules prohibit indiscriminate bombing but make a concession to target area bombing by permitting the bombardment of populated areas in the immediate vicinity of land force operations provided the military concentration is sufficiently important to justify the resulting danger to the civilian population.[32] However, there is no specific provision imposing a duty on the attacking commander to take precautions, only what can be inferred from the foregoing.

Greco-German Mixed Arbitral Tribunal

The tribunal was set up under the Peace Treaty of Versailles in 1919 to deal with claims arising out of the First World War. Two cases dealt with by the tribunal concerned precautions in air attack.

[29]F. Kalshoven, *Constraints on the Waging of War*, International Committee of the Red Cross, 1987, at p. 35.
[30]Greenspan, *Modern Law*, p. 334.
[31]C. Rousseau, *Le Droit des conflits armés*, Pedone, 1983, p. 362.
[32]Art. 24(3) and (4), an attempt to reduce the customary rule of proportionality to writing.

In *Coenca Brothers* v. *Germany*[33] Germany was held liable to pay damages for the destruction of coffee during an air raid launched without warning on Salonica in 1916. The tribunal recalled the generally recognized principle of international law that civilian life and property should, so far as possible, be respected and applied Art. 26 of the Hague Regulations by analogy.[34] According to Schwarzenberger, the tribunal was influenced in its decision by the fact that bombs were dropped from the considerable height of 3,000 m on a dark night when the lights of Salonica were switched off so that it was 'impossible to direct the bombs with the accuracy required to spare the private dwelling houses and the commercial establishments'.[35]

In the case of *Kiriadolou* v. *Germany*[36] the tribunal was concerned with the death of a civilian in an air raid on Bucharest in 1916 and applied by analogy not only Art. 26 of the Hague Regulations but also Art. 6 of the Hague Naval Bombardment Convention.

Schwarzenberger comments in respect of both decisions that:

the widespread resort to aerial bombardment without regard for the criteria laid down in Arts. 25 and 26 of the Hague Regulations during the First World War and, even more so, the Second World War has encouraged a critical, if not disparaging, attitude towards these decisions.[37]

He goes on to deal with the arguments deployed by the critics and concludes that the decisions command respect as lonely attempts to uphold the standard of civilization against wartime sovereignty at its most virulent and destructive.[38]

It does seem that the tribunals, and for that matter Schwarzenberger, seem obsessed with Art. 26 of the Hague Regulations and the need to give warning. That seems to the writer to be something of a side issue. More important is the reference in both cases to the failure of the bombers to take precautions to attack military objectives in a discriminate manner.

Second World War practice

The problem with unwritten or unratified rules is that opinions may vary as to their scope[39] and, worse, they tend to be ignored. There was not much evidence of compliance with these rules or of precautions being taken in attack in the Italy–Ethiopia war of 1935–36, the Spanish Civil War or the Sino-Japanese War.[40]

---

[33] *Annual Digest*, 1927–28, Case No. 389.
[34] Requiring 'the authorities' to be warned of impending bombardments.
[35] G. Schwarzenberger, *International Law*, vol. 2, Stevens, 1968, p. 145.
[36] *Annual Digest*, 1929–30, Case No. 301.
[37] Schwarzenberger, *International Law*, p. 146.
[38] *Ibid.*, p. 149.
[39] Blix, quoting Spetzler, says that there is a pressing need to dispel doubts through codification. H. Blix, Area bombardment: rules and reasons, *British Yearbook of International Law*, 1978, p. 38.
[40] See Rousseau, *Droit des conflits armés*, p. 363.

Air warfare

As has been noted above, the prohibition on the bombardment of undefended places also applied to bombardment from the air. As early as 1914 one author stated that it was forbidden to drop bombs on undefended towns or villages.[41] But apart from this there were no rules in place affecting aerial bombardment on the outbreak of war in 1939. A resolution of the League of Nations Assembly in 1938 called for prohibition of the intentional bombing of civilian populations, specified that only identifiable military objectives should be aimed at from the air and suggested that care should be exercised to avoid the bombing by negligence of the civilian population.[42] Stone comments that this resolution did not seek to prohibit damage incidental to attacks on military objectives and adds that, although it had no binding force, it was close to the views of the British government at the time, as evidenced by its reaction to Guernica and the Japanese attacks in China.[43] It was also based on a statement of the Prime Minister on 21 June 1938.[44] It is also remarkably close to the provisions now to be found in Protocol I.

At the beginning of the Second World War both sides declared the intention of sparing the civilian population, subject to reciprocity. In the early stages of the war there were indications that bombs were being dropped only if individual military objectives could be identified,[45] but as time went on practice did not conform to those declarations. A combination of various factors—the changing balance of air power and the capabilities of aircraft, an escalatory spiral of retaliation and reprisal, the use of target area bombing techniques against scattered and camouflaged objectives in populated areas,[46] the gradual extension of the concept of military objectives, the need to protect aircraft from anti-aircraft defences and the lack of sophisticated means of guiding bombs on to the target—led by 1943 to little discernible evidence of precautions being taken to protect civilians from attack.[47]

These practices tended to obscure the clear line of customary law and The Hague Regulations. Best has described it more graphically: 'The Second World War acted like an earthquake on the international law of war and left some of it in ruins.'[48] Afterwards international lawyers, especially Anglo-American

[41] T. Barclay, *The Law and Usage of War*, Constable, 1914, p. 1.
[42] D. Schindler and J. Toman, *The Laws of Armed Conflicts*, 3rd ed., Martinus Nijhoff, 1988, p. 222.
[43] Stone, *Legal Controls*, p. 625.
[44] Schindler and Toman, *Laws*, p. 221; Rousseau, *Droit des conflits armés*, p. 363.
[45] Stone, *Legal Controls*, pp. 625–6; and the Hague Air Warfare Rules seem to have had some influence on preventing indiscriminate bombardment—Blix, Area bombardment, p. 47.
[46] Greenspan, *Modern Law*, p. 335.
[47] Obradovic, Protection de la population, comments, at p. 140, that *il y a des cas, comme par exemple le siège de Varsovie en 1939, ou on bombarde une ville sans discrimination, à savoir sans tenir compte des précautions exigées par l'art. 27 du Réglement de la Haye.*
[48] G. Best, World War Two and the law of war, *Review of International Studies*, 1981. More soberly, Rousseau expressed it thus: *la régression ne pouvait être plus complète*—Rousseau, *Droit des conflits armés*, p. 367.

lawyers, struggled to rationalize the practices of the war and invented terms such as 'quasi-combatants'[49] or the 'workforce of the military objective',[50] but these terms did not take account of the many civilians who could not be termed quasi-combatants unless one regarded them as the victims of incidental damage caused by target area bombing of an area containing scattered military objectives.[51]

Monte Cassino

During the allied operations in Italy in 1943 various assurances were given by the allies that they would respect churches and religious institutions, provided they were not used for military purposes,[52] and the Benedictine abbey at Monte Cassino was included in the list of buildings to be protected. The German embassy at the Vatican gave an assurance that the abbey would not be used by German troops. On 29 December 1943 Eisenhower issued an order to all commanders drawing attention to the importance of cultural monuments in Italy, but saying that if there were a choice between buildings and men's lives the buildings would have to go. However, he added that in many cases monuments could be spared without any detriment to operational needs.[53]

The German forces included the ridge on which the abbey stood in their defensive plans, but gave instructions that the abbey itself was not to be used. When the allied attack began in January 1944 attempts to outflank Monte Cassino failed and a plan to conduct a wider, outflanking manoeuvre was abandoned because of lack of mules to carry supplies for the maintenance of the troops involved. Attention turned to a possible aerial bombardment of the abbey and its surroundings before an infantry attack.[54]

Alexander gave clearance for the bombing of the abbey 'if there is any reasonable probability that the building is being used for military purposes'. Although evidence has since come to light that the German forces were not using the abbey, intelligence reports received by the allies at the time included the reported capture of German soldiers from caves below the abbey foundations, reports of machine guns, aerials, telescopes and troop movements seen at the abbey (one from an Italian civilian that was probably highly exaggerated), and a report from an enemy prisoner of war that German troops were in 'the abbey on hill 468' (the abbey was actually on hill 516). Other intelligence reports, however, indicated no evidence of German presence or defences at the abbey.[55]

Nevertheless, it was decided to bombard the abbey. The decision was based

[49]J. M. Spaight, Non-combatants and air attack, (1938) 9 *Air Law Review*, p. 372.
[50]Stone, *Legal Controls*, p. 628.
[51]Oppenheim, *International Law*, p. 527.
[52]This reflected Art. 27 of the Hague Regulations.
[53]J. H. Green, The destruction of the abbey of Monte Cassino, *British Army Review*, December 1988, at p. 30.
[54]*Ibid.*, pp. 34–5.
[55]*Ibid.*, pp. 35–6.

on the intelligence reports and on supposition: the abbey made such a perfect observation point that surely no army could have refrained from using it. Other factors were that the walls of the abbey would provide shelter to troops outside it, the risk could not be run that the abbey might be used by the enemy for shelter once the infantry assault had been launched, and bombardment of the abbey would boost the morale of the attackers.[56] On 15 February 1944 the abbey was bombed and shelled,[57] leaving it a ruin and causing the death of an estimated 300 to 400 civilian refugees. But no Germans were killed.[58]

There is little doubt that the abbey was a military objective in the sense of being a dominant feature whose use to the enemy it was intended to deny. It is not clear whether the presence of the civilian refugees was known to the allies, but their deaths may not have been disproportionate to the value of the objective. As for precautions, unsuccessful efforts were made to bypass Monte Cassino or capture it by infantry attack and the bombardment itself seems to have been limited to the objective.

Events from 1945 to 1977

Warning of aerial bombardment was sometimes given by the UN forces during the Korean War of 1950–53.[59]

Fleck, writing in 1966, expressed the view that precautions to be taken in attack were left, in the main, to individual commanders, but that basic principles existed from which rules could be inferred: careful choice of targets, prior warning of the threatened civilian population, particular precautions in the carrying out of the attack and, finally, a duty to preserve proportionality between civilian damage and military success.[60] Fleck proceeds to analyse these duties in turn.

First, while emphasizing the duty to identify the object to be attacked, and excluding exceptions to this duty based on military necessity, on self-defence or on the basis of the overall military character of the area to be hit, he does not say of what this duty consists except roundly to condemn the target area bombing method.[61]

Secondly, although examples could be given of warning of air attacks,[62] and while the provisions of Art. 26 of the Hague Regulations have no place in air warfare, the attacker is under an obligation to consider whether the circumstances of a particular case permit a warning to be given.[63] Fleck considers that

[56]*Ibid.*, p. 36. See also Best, *Law and War*, p. 275.
[57]Some 442 tons of bombs and 266 artillery shells—*ibid.*, p. 36.
[58]Green, Monte Cassino, p. 36.
[59]Greenspan, *Modern Law*, p. 340.
[60]D. Fleck, Die rechtlichen Garantien des Verbots von unmittelbaren Kampfhandlungen gegen Zivilpersonen, *Military Law and Law of War Review*, 1966, p. 91.
[61]*Ibid.*, pp. 91–6.
[62]In this connection, perhaps, air superiority places a greater onus on the attacker to give warnings.
[63]Fleck, Die rechtlichen Garantien, pp. 97–8.

the rule on warnings is of only marginal importance even though it is the one express, rather than implied, rule of customary and treaty law having any application in connection with precautions in attack.

Thirdly, precautions to be taken in attack involve a choice of the methods, means and strength of the attacking forces and limitation of the measures of attack to the object to be attacked. Fleck suggests that particular care is required in attacking from the air military objectives in residential areas and moving objects and that attack by means of guns rather than bombs is to be preferred in such situations; and that railway lines should be bombed close to the military installations they serve rather than in the vicinity of residential areas.[64]

Fourthly, customary law imposes a general duty on a military commander to balance military success against the danger to civilians; armed forces therefore have a duty to develop standards for applying the proportionality principle when attacking military objectives.[65]

In its report to the Conference of Government Experts in 1971[66] the ICRC said that the need for precautions in attack 'has been affirmed by publicists for a long time, but without being expressed in a very precise manner in the provisions of international law in force'. The report may be summarized, in almost the same language as that used by Fleck, as follows. No express rules existed prior to Protocol I, apart from the rules on warning, and the need to take precautions could only be inferred from customary law and treaty language, especially the principles of proportionality, identification of the target (or the rule of distinction), warning and the choice of methods and means. Like Fleck, a majority of the experts consulted by the ICRC felt that the one principle that was enshrined in treaty language, that of warning, had fallen into disuse.[67]

Current law

Precautions in attack

Art. 57 of Protocol I endeavours to repair the harm done to international law by the practices of the Second World War and brings us back to the standards suggested in the Air Warfare Rules. According to Blix, the key elements are identification of the target with some certainty, directing the attack to that target and using methods and means that will hit the target with some degree of likelihood.[68] The protocol lays down for the first time in writing the duty of commanders, military planners and others responsible for military operations to ensure that the risk of loss of life among civilians and of damage to civilian property is kept to an absolute minimum. The rules may be paraphrased as follows.

---

[64] *Ibid.*, pp. 98–9.

[65] *Ibid.*, p. 100.

[66] Report to the Conference of Government Experts, III—*Protection of the Civilian Population against the Dangers of Hostilities*, ICRC, 1971, at p. 75.

[67] Fleck, Die rechtlichen Garantien, p. 81.

[68] Blix, Area bombardment, p. 48.

In the conduct of military operations, constant care must be taken to spare the civilian population,[69] civilians[70] and civilian objects.[71] According to the ICRC,[72] the conduct of military operations includes movement as well as attack, so a tank driver who unnecessarily drives his tank through a civilian house, demolishing the house in the process, would be caught by this provision. An attack may not be necessary if the overall military aim can be achieved in another way, for example by manoeuvre.

When planning or deciding on an *attack*,[73] *feasible precautions* must be taken to ensure that military objectives[74] are what they purport to be,[75] and to avoid and minimize incidental damage or loss to civilians.[76] Obradovic goes too far when he says 'le devoir d'être absolument sûr qu'il s'agit d'un objectif militaire'.[77] The French text of the protocol is the same as the English, i.e. 'faire tout ce qui est pratiquement possible pour verifier que les objectifs à attacquer sont . . . des objectifs militaires'. No commander could ever be absolutely sure that an objective to be attacked was a military objective unless he inspected it himself, which, of course, is quite impracticable. Mistakes based on faulty intelligence can be made.

Where an attack may be expected to cause incidental loss or damage to civilians or civilian objects which would be excessive in relation to the *concrete and direct* military advantage anticipated, the attack must not be carried out.[78] This is the proportionality rule.

An attack must be cancelled or suspended if it becomes apparent that the proportionality rule will be violated, or that the target is not a military objective or that it is subject to special protection.[79]

Effective advance *warning* of attacks which may affect the civilian population must be given, *unless circumstances do not permit*.[80]

Where there is a choice of targets offering the same military advantage, the attack which is expected to cause the least incidental damage is to be chosen.[81]

Article 57 has been criticized as employing wording that allows 'wide and at

[69]For definition, see Protocol I, Art. 50.2.
[70]For definition, see Protocol I, Art. 50.1.
[71]For definition, see Protocol I, Art. 52.1 and Art. 57.1.
[72]ICRC *Commentary*, para. 2191.
[73]For definition, see Protocol I, Art. 49.1.
[74]For definition, see Protocol I, Art. 52.2. For a full discussion of the concept of military objectives, see chapter 2. It must be remembered that, in cases of doubt, objects are to be presumed civilian—Protocol I, Art. 52.3.
[75]Protocol I, Art. 57.2(a)(i).
[76]Protocol I, Art. 57.2(a)(ii).
[77]Obradovic, Protection de la population, p. 154.
[78]Protocol I, Art. 57.2(a)(iii).
[79]Protocol I, Art. 57.2(b), for example, a nuclear power station protected under Protocol I, Art. 56.
[80]Protocol I, Art. 57.2(c).
[81]Protocol I, Art. 57.3. C. J. Greenwood, Customary international law and the first Geneva protocol of 1977 in the Gulf conflict, in P. J. Rowe (ed.), *The Gulf War 1990–91 in International and English Law*, Routledge, 1993, p. 83, considers that this provision may have gone beyond customary law.

times varying interpretations of the inferred standard' and as likely to confuse a commander in determining whether he has done everything feasible in identifying the target, in taking all feasible precautions for the safety of civilians, whether the proportionality rule has been complied with and whether the attack should be broken off, judgements which might be subjective and open to challenge by others, including subordinates.[82]

It seems to the writer that a lot of these points are matters which need to be dealt with in military manuals or by legal advisers when military operations are being planned. In military manuals the rules can be stated relatively simply, perhaps with explanatory examples.

Usually, compliance with the requirements of the law is assured by issuing troops with rules of engagement which indicate the level of force that may be applied in dealing with given eventualities. They can also include further restraints dictated by political considerations, or even military reasons such as economy of effort, to co-ordinate an attack or for the safety of friendly forces.[83]

Attack

The definition of attack is dealt with in chapter 1.

Feasible

Obviously, a military commander cannot always establish with certainty that the object to be attacked is a military objective. One version of the original ICRC draft article which laid down such an absolute standard[84] was rejected by the CDDH as unreasonable. The feasibility test is a fine balance because the commander will not wish to take precautions to such an extent as to reduce his chances of military success. On the other hand, military considerations cannot be overriding so as to render the protection for civilians useless. According to the ICRC, some delegations at the CDDH expressed the understanding that 'feasible' means 'that which is practicable or practically possible, taking into account all the circumstances at the time of the attack, including those relevant to the success of military operations'. A statement similar to that, with the omission of the words 'of the attack', was made by the United Kingdom on signature.[85] But the ICRC commentator felt that such statements were too broad because they seemed to neglect humanitarian considerations.[86]

[82]D. Craig, Should Australia ratify the 1977 Protocol I addendums to the 1949 Geneva Conventions? *Defence Force Journal*, May–June 1989.
[83]See the interesting article by G. R. Phillips, Rules of engagement: a primer, *Army Lawyer*, July 1993, p. 4.
[84]Draft Additional Protocols to the Geneva Conventions of August 12, 1949, ICRC, June 1973, Art. 50.1(a).
[85]A. Roberts and R. Guelff, *Documents on the Laws of War*, 2nd ed., Clarendon Press, 1989, p. 467.
[86]ICRC *Commentary*, para. 2198.

There were similar discussions at the conference which negotiated the Weapons Convention. These ended in consensus that feasible precautions 'are those which are practicable or practically possible taking into account all circumstances ruling at the time, including humanitarian and military considerations'.[87] The Italian statement on ratification of Protocol I is identical.[88]

Some consider that 'feasible' imposes a higher standard than customary law, which required only reasonable precautions.[89]

Precautions

Precautions include the type of weapons used and their means of delivery,[90] as well as factors such as the time of the attack. For example, an attack on a factory at night when it is known that civilian workers are not there would be a sensible precaution.[91]

Fighting in a town is always difficult, costly in lives and incidental damage. Tanks can be more easily attacked by the defenders.[92] The answer, sometimes, may be to bypass the town, leaving a blocking force to prevent enemy movement, or encircle it, cutting off the enemy's supply routes. Walzer refers to reports during the Korean War of artillery and air strikes being called up to assist advancing troops held up by automatic fire, observing that the strikes often did not work and that in the end the enemy position would have to be outflanked by an infantry patrol, with much less risk to the civilian population.[93] That is an example of an alternative method of warfare which proved not only more effective militarily, at some risk to the patrol, but also less likely to cause incidental damage.

Concrete and direct

According to the ICRC, 'concrete and direct' was intended to indicate that the advantage sought must be 'substantial' as opposed to 'hardly perceptible' and 'close' in time as opposed to 'long-term'.[94] Neither of these explanations seems to accord with ordinary English usage. It is noteworthy, therefore, that Solf's

---

[87]Protocol II to the Weapons Convention, Art. 3.4.

[88]See Roberts and Guelff, *Documents*, p. 465.

[89]E.g. D. L. Infeld, Precision guided missiles demonstrated their pinpoint accuracy in Desert Storm; but is a country obligated to use precision technology to minimize collateral civilian injury and damage? *George Washington Journal of International Law and Economics*, vol. 26, 1992, p. 118.

[90]See the discussion of the 1986 Libyan air strike in W. H. Parks, Air war and the law of war, 32 *Air Force Law Review*, 1990, p. 155.

[91]ICRC *Commentary*, para. 2200; United States, *Conduct of the Persian Gulf War*, Department of Defense final report to Congress, April 1992 (DOD Report), p. 100.

[92]As the Russian army found in its attempts to invade the Chechen capital in January 1995.

[93]M. Walzer, *Just and Unjust Wars*, Pelican, 1980, pp. 154–5.

[94]ICRC *Commentary*, para. 2209.

explanation is that 'concrete' means 'specific' or 'perceptible' (or even 'definite') rather than 'general' and that 'direct' means 'without intervening condition
of agency'.[95] This seems a sensible explanation of the term.

Warning

The requirement to give warnings of attacks is an echo of the Hague Regulations.[96] Carnahan comments that the protocol finally eliminates a conflict
between Art. 26 of the Hague Regulations, which required a warning in all
cases except assault, and the Hague Naval Bombardment Convention, which
provided only that a warning should be given when circumstances permit, and
imposes a single standard.[97] A similar provision appears in the Mines Protocol
to the Weapons Convention, which provides that effective advance warning is
to be given 'of any delivery or dropping of remotely delivered mines which
may affect the civilian population, unless the circumstances do not permit'.[98]
There is also a requirement, in respect of mines other than remotely delivered
mines used in populated areas which are not placed on or in the close vicinity
of a military objective under the control of an adverse party, to take measures
for the protection of civilians, and these include the issuing of warnings.[99]

It has been suggested that this provision of Protocol I is more restrictive
than Art. 26 of the Hague Regulations[100] but it is very difficult, comparing
the two texts, to discern any major differences between them, except for the
requirement of Protocol I that the warning must be *effective* and that the warning can be given direct to the population rather than to the authorities, although
a warning to the authorities would probably also suffice for the purposes of
Protocol I, provided it were effective.[101] On the other hand, it has also been suggested that Protocol I is less stringent than Art. 26 of the Hague Regulations,
which required warnings except in cases of assault.[102] It is, therefore, difficult

[95]M. Bothe, K. J. Partsch and W. Solf, *New Rules for the Victims of Armed Conflicts*, Martinus
Nijhoff, 1982, p. 365.
[96]Art. 26 of the Hague Regulations.
[97]B. M. Carnahan, Protecting civilians under the draft Geneva protocol, 18 *Air Force Law
Review*, 1976, p. 62.
[98]Art. 5.2.
[99]Art. 4.2(b).
[100]Obradovic, Protection de la population, p. 154. The Hague text is 'before commencing a
bombardment, except in cases of assault, do all in his power to warn the authorities', whereas the
protocol text is 'effective advance warning shall be given of attacks which may affect the civilian
population, unless circumstances do not permit'.
[101]Carnahan comments that the protocol is a more accurate reflection of state practice than the
Hague Regulations—B. M. Carnahan, Additional Protocol I: a military view, *Akron Law Review*,
vol. 19.4. L. C. Green, *The Contemporary Law of Armed Conflict*, Manchester, 1993, p. 148, says
that before the atomic bombing of Hiroshima the Japanese authorities were warned that named
towns would be heavily bombarded and that civilians should be evacuated, and that warnings were
occasionally given in the European theatre.
[102]Carnahan, Protecting civilians, p. 62.

to reconcile the two texts,[103] unless Protocol I is seen as an authoritative interpretation of the Hague warning requirements.[104]

Warnings include radio and television broadcasts as well as the dropping of
leaflets.[105] 'Effective' in this context is not defined and must be a matter of
common sense. Obviously, a broadcast in a language that the population does
not understand would not be effective. A warning to the authorities hundreds
of miles away and cut off from the place of the proposed attack might also
be considered ineffective.

Unless circumstances do not permit

The words 'unless circumstances do not permit', rather like 'except in cases of
assault', allow the commander a measure of discretion. The latter exception was
intended to preserve the element of surprise which may be essential to an attack.
The former formula will also cover the need to protect surprise, but the wording
seems to be of wider application. Solf[106] compares Protocol I with the Hague
Naval Bombardment Convention,[107] points out that there is a conflict between
the Hague Regulations, with the very narrow exception for cases of assault, and
the Naval Bombardment Convention, which allows the naval commander wider
discretion, and concludes that Protocol I[108] is an attempt to bring these conflicting provisions together.

But when, apart from the need to preserve surprise, would circumstances not
permit a warning to be given? Carnahan gives an example of Japanese soldiers
dressed as women engaged in moonlight by US marines in Okinawa in the
Second World War. Fire was opened on suspicion and no warning was given
because that would have been too dangerous. The suspicion proved to be correct, but Carnahan comments that, had the commander followed the rules as laid
down in Protocol I, the presumption of civilian status would have prevailed.[109]
It might be said in reply that it would not have been feasible in the circumstances to verify the status of the suspected Japanese soldiers nor would the
circumstances have permitted a warning to be given. Walzer gives an example
which is the antithesis of the Okinawa case. It relates to the bombing of 'dug-
outs', or cellars, during the First World War in a village where it was known that
there were civilians in some of the cellars. In one case two soldiers shouted

[103] Having regard to Art. 49.4 of Protocol I, which states that the rules of Protocol I are additional
to other rules of international law relating to the protection of civilians from hostilities.
[104] Carnahan, Protecting civilians, p. 62.
[105] For a description of the use of leaflets by Israel in the Lebanon in 1982, see Parks, Air war,
p. 165.
[106] Bothe *et al.*, *New Rules*, p. 367.
[107] Art. 6 of which provides that 'if the military situation permits, the commander of the attacking
naval force, before commencing the bombardment, must do his utmost to warn the authorities'.
[108] Art. 57.2(c).
[109] Carnahan, Additional Protocol I, p. 544.

down to make sure there were no civilians and, receiving no reply, were about to pull the pins out of their hand grenades when a young civilian woman came up the cellar stairs. She had been too frightened to answer the warning shouts. Walzer comments that the soldiers had accepted a certain risk in shouting warnings because if there had been enemy soldiers in the cellar they might have scrambled out, firing as they came.[110]

Sieges

Attacks and bombardments are not the only way of trying to achieve the submission of the enemy. Where enemy forces are surrounded, the surrounding force may decide to force the surrender of the enemy, and reduce the casualties it would sustain in an attack, by besieging the enemy forces, that is, cutting off all supplies and communications to the besieged locality. Siege has long been recognized as a legitimate method of warfare.[111] Siege has recently been practised in the Bosnian war, including the siege of the capital, Sarajevo. Under customary law a besieging commander was permitted to drive escaping civilians back into the besieged area to increase the pressure on the defending commander to surrender.[112] It is likely, however, that this rule of customary law has been rendered obsolete by Protocol I.[113] In fact the besieging commander would be better advised to allow all civilians and the wounded and sick to leave the besieged area.[114] He would then legitimately be able to prevent all supplies from reaching the enemy forces and bombardment and assault would be considerably eased. If the civilians elected to stay put, however, as Dinstein has pointed out,[115] that would put the besieging commander in a difficult position, because Protocol I[116] prohibits the starvation of civilians as a method of warfare, whatever the motive. Dinstein concludes that, in short, Protocol I prohibits siege warfare if civilians are affected but feels that such an injunction is untenable in practice, since no other method has been devised for bringing about the capture of defended towns.

The writer considers that, on a close analysis of Protocol I, the situation is not for a number of reasons as gloomy for the besieging commander as Dinstein suggests. First, starvation of civilians is not a grave breach of Protocol I.[117] Secondly, a clear intention would need to be expressed in a treaty to abolish

---

[110] Walzer, *Just and Unjust Wars*, p. 152.

[111] See Y. Dinstein, Siege warfare and the starvation of civilians, in A. J. M. Delissen and G. J. Tania (ed.), *Humanitarian Law of Armed Conflict, Challenges Ahead*, Martinus Nijhoff, 1991, p. 146.

[112] The High Command trial, 11 *Trials of War Criminals before the Nuremberg Military Tribunals*, Washington, 1950, at pp. 462, 563; *Manual of Military Law*, paras. 292, 296.

[113] Arts. 51, paras. 2 and 7; 54, para. 1. See also Bothe *et al.*, *New Rules*, p. 338.

[114] The suggestion by Best, *Law and War*, p. 258, to the contrary is not followed.

[115] Dinstein, Siege warfare, pp. 149 *et seq.*

[116] Art. 54, paras. 2–3.

[117] Art. 85.

such a well established practice.[118] Thirdly, the besieging commander would not need to violate Art. 54, para. 2, of Protocol I. There would be no need to 'attack, destroy or render useless' food supplies. He would simply prevent the supplies from getting through to the besieged area by turning them back. Fourthly, the provisions of Art. 54, para. 3, of Protocol I do not operate independently of those of Art. 54, para. 2. Fifthly, the besieging commander would not violate Art. 54, para. 1, of Protocol I if he guaranteed the safe passage of civilians (and the wounded and sick) out of the besieged area. Sixthly, given the terms of Art. 51, para. 7, last sentence, and Art. 58 of Protocol I, the besieged commander could not refuse such an offer. Seventhly, the relief actions referred to in Art. 70 of Protocol I can only take place with the agreement of the parties concerned.[119]

It is submitted that the interests of humanity are better served if the besieging commander proceeds as suggested above rather than attempting to take the besieged town by bombardment and assault. If the commander of the besieged town refuses to allow the evacuation of civilians and the wounded and sick, the blame for their subsequent starvation must rest squarely on his shoulders.

The Gulf War of 1990–91

This conflict showed some very sophisticated weaponry in use, some of it, like the Patriot missile, for the first time. Although of the main protagonists only Syria was a party to Geneva Protocol I of 1977,[120] early media reports indicated great efforts by the coalition forces to take precautions in attack to ensure that only military objectives were hit and that incidental damage was reduced to a minimum. It was reported that of eighty-four American Tomahawk cruise missiles launched on the first day of the war, eighty hit their targets.[121] RAF Tornado aircraft sustained heavy losses attacking Iraqi airfields by dropping JP 233 bombs from a low altitude above the target.[122] According to Infeld, 8.8 per cent of the bombs or missiles delivered were precision-guided missiles. They had an accuracy of 90 per cent compared with the rate of 25 per cent for conventional free-fall bombs and were used for attacking targets in heavily populated areas.[123]

---

[118]Bothe *et al.*, *New Rules*, p. 336, indicate that the intention was to prevent the destruction of foodstuffs, etc. Neither this commentary nor the ICRC *Commentary* (p. 652) refers to the practice of siege warfare.

[119]Bothe *et al.*, *New Rules*, p. 434, indicate that there may be refusal for valid and compelling reasons, including imperative considerations of military necessity.

[120]Iraq, the United States, France and the United Kingdom were not.

[121]*The Times*, 22 January 1991. By the end of the war 288 had been fired—DOD Report, p. 222 of the draft version of the report.

[122]P. Hine, Despatch by the joint commander of Operation Granby, 2nd supplement to the *London Gazette*, 28 June 1991, p. G42; United Kingdom, *Preliminary Lessons of Operation Granby*, House of Commons Defence Committee, Tenth Report, HMSO, 1991, p. xxi.

[123]Infeld, Precision guided missiles, pp. 127–8.

By contrast, Iraqi Scud missiles were notoriously inaccurate, reminiscent of the V1 rockets of the Second World War, and landed, when not shot down, for the most part in residential areas.[124] The accuracy of coalition air attacks was apparent from television footage shown at press briefings at the headquarters of the coalition commander, General Schwarzkopf, and from media reports: precision attacks using 'smart' bombs against military installations; the destruction of bridges on the road from Baghdad to Basra or in Baghdad itself;[125] or the precision attack on a fuel storage dump, leaving a neighbouring oil refinery unscathed.[126] Bombing by B52 aircraft, which by the nature of the means of delivery was likely to be less accurate, was directed in large part at Iraqi Republican Guard positions, obvious military objectives and unlikely to have been in populous areas.[127] Sometimes targets were not attacked because of the danger to civilians. The British air commander, Air Vice-Marshal Wrattan, had the power of veto over particular targets, which he used twice when severe collateral damage could have resulted from a weapon system malfunction.[128] Aircrew ordered to attack targets in populated areas were directed not to do so if they lacked positive identification of their targets.[129]

Infeld warns us that smart weapons are not a universal panacea. They are susceptible to deflection by heavy rain, thick cloud or fog or by smoke and other obscurants used by the defenders or by evading action taken by an attacking pilot. They are also extremely expensive. Smart bombs cost between $50,000 and $100,000 each and each Tomahawk cruise missile costs $1.35 million.[130]

Despite the efforts of coalition commanders, some incidental injury and damage was caused.[131] On the bare information available from media reports,[132] it cannot be said that these incidents would have been violations of Art. 57 of Protocol I had it applied.

Where orders are given to attack targets from a pre-selected list, there is a reasonably good prospect, faulty intelligence apart, of only military objectives being hit and of the best weapon system being chosen for that particular target, so that incidental damage will be reduced as much as possible. It is when orders are given for 'search and destroy' missions, which enable pilots to strike at opportunity targets, that central control diminishes and a greater responsibility is placed on the shoulders of individuals. Accepting at face value for the sake of legal analysis a press report of a pilot whose attack on an army lorry and a

---

[124] *The Times*, 23 January 1991.

[125] See *The Times*, 31 January 1991 or *The Daily Telegraph*, 7 February 1991.

[126] *The Times*, 5 February 1991, where General Horner, the US air commander, was reported to have said that 'these high-tech systems take war to a whole new level of efficiency'.

[127] *The Times*, 4 February 1991.

[128] Defence Committee Report, p. xi.

[129] DOD Report, p. 612.

[130] See Infeld, Precision guided missiles, pp. 126–33.

[131] *Ibid.*

[132] E.g. *The Times*, 4 February 1991.

busload of soldiers also killed a small boy in a civilian car,[133] this could not be said to have violated the proportionality principle. The same report refers to civilians having been killed in missile attacks on bridges. This raises an interesting point about long-range attacks. Even if cruise missiles accurately strike a military objective, the missile firer has no way of knowing whether there are civilians in the danger area, unlike the pilot who is guiding his missile on to the target by means of a television camera.

In fact the allied bombing campaign can be seen as a good example of the application in practice of the principles of Art. 57 of Protocol I.[134] Even critics admit that 'one claim has survived the tarnished aftermath of the Gulf War intact—namely, that the Coalition used modern military technology to comply with the fundamental legal requirement to distinguish between civilians and combatants more effectively than any belligerent in any past war'.[135]

Judging commanders and soldiers

General principles

Violation of Art. 57 of Protocol I may amount to a war crime. It will even amount to a grave breach of that protocol if an attack is launched in the *knowledge* that it will cause excessive incidental damage contrary to Art. 57.2(a)(iii). That, of course, is a provision which applies to those who plan and decide upon attacks.

There may be a temptation to judge a commander after an attack is over and with the benefit of hindsight.[136] Draper referred to this problem, saying:

the American Government said in effect, you must assess the acts of the commander in those circumstances, in the light of what is known to him at the time, not what the court knows afterwards from captured documents. But, of course, this is very difficult. You are then going to get very swiftly into the question of what he ought to have known? Now, negligence and war criminality do not run together any more than reprisals and humanitarianism do. By the time you are going to get negligence sufficient for war criminality, I think you are beginning to transcend the limits of justice in war crimes trials. Not everybody may agree with me.

To guard against these problems, some states have made statements on ratification of which the Italian statement is typical:

the Italian Government understands that military commanders and others responsible for planning, deciding upon or executing attacks necessarily have to reach decisions on the

---

[133] *The Times*, 8 February 1991.

[134] See Greenwood, Gulf conflict, pp. 83 *et seq.*

[135] C. Jochnick and R. Normand, The legitimation of violence: a critical history of the laws of war, *Harvard International Law Journal*, 1994, p. 387.

[136] G. I. A. D. Draper, The new law of armed conflict, *Royal United Services Institute Journal*, September 1979.

basis of their assessment of the information from all sources which is available to them at the relevant time.[137]

As Kalshoven has pointed out, the norm refers to the expected rather than the actual civilian loss and the anticipated rather than the actual military advantage.[138] In other words the test is subjective in the sense that in judging the commander's actions one must look at the situation as he saw it and in the light of the information that was available to him.

Even this understanding throws up other problems. What is meant by the information from all sources available to the commander? In one sense this is a useful qualification, because a junior commander may have very little information apart from what he observes, radio reports and the orders he receives. At the other end of the scale, a commander-in-chief may have masses of information available to him, much of which he will not have seen but which will have been digested for him by his staff. He will also have access to information held by others, such as allied forces and national ministries. The problem is exacerbated by modern information technology. Wortley comments that there may be a higher standard for the attacker with the more sophisticated means of information gathering.[139] How far does the commander-in-chief have to go in collating and assessing the available information before making a decision? Hampson asks the further questions 'How strenuous must the efforts be to obtain intelligence?' and 'How regularly must it be updated?'[140] In what circumstances is the commander criminally responsible for the mistakes of his staff? What is the liability of his staff officers? There are further problems when, for example, an officer is given authority, within certain parameters, to attack opportunity targets. He may have to call for permission, but is the commander giving permission responsible if the officer does not give a truthful or accurate description of the target?

Kalshoven refers in this connection to the *Queenfish* case, where in 1945 the commander of a US submarine torpedoed a Japanese ship which had been granted safe conduct by the United States. Although information about the safe conduct had been received on board the submarine, the commander was unaware of it. But the court-martial found him guilty nevertheless because he was responsible for the inefficient internal procedures which resulted in his not being informed.[141]

The test must be reasonableness and will depend to some extent on the amount of information readily available, the staff available to deal with it, whether the

[137] Roberts and Guelff, *Documents*, p. 465.

[138] Kalshoven, Reaffirmation, p. 117.

[139] B. A. Wortley, Observations on the revision of the 1949 Geneva 'Red Cross Conventions', *British Yearbook of International Law*, 1983, p. 153.

[140] F. J. Hampson, Means and methods of warfare in the conflict in the Gulf, in P. J. Rowe (ed.), *Gulf War*, p. 93.

[141] Kalshoven, Reaffirmation, p. 118, quoting US Naval War College, *International Law Studies*, 1966.

information raises questions that require further research into other sources of information. This must be what Kalshoven is referring to when he says that a commander may be responsible if, although information about the potentially indiscriminate nature of a projected attack is not available within his unit, it could have been made available but the commander neglected to take the necessary steps to acquire it—a requirement, he argues, of the obligation to verify that the target is a military objective.[142] Perhaps the most important factor of all is the time available for making the decision.

The question of the information available to a commander will also be relevant to the question of criminal intent for, and defences to, war crimes. An order to attack may seem perfectly reasonable and lawful to the officer with limited information who is ordered to carry out the attack, but not to a higher commander ordering the attack who has information which would indicate that, if the attack is carried out, there will be a serious breach of the proportionality rule. It would be unjust in such circumstances to hold the subordinate officer criminally responsible.

The view has been expressed elsewhere by the writer that any tribunal dealing with the matter would have to look at the situation as the soldier making the decision saw it before assessing his guilt.[143]

The situation could arise where the commander came to one conclusion on the information, but the tribunal trying him, even looking at the information available to him and as he saw it, comes to a different conclusion. If the test is reasonableness, as suggested above, it is not entirely subjective. The court will look at the situation as the commander saw it but then apply the standards of international law to that perceived situation. Kalshoven has described it thus: 'decisive is whether a normally alert attacker who is reasonably well informed and who, moreover, makes reasonable use of the information could have expected the excessive damage among the civilian population'.[144] One might describe such an attacker as the man in the Chobham tank! In a borderline case the tribunal might give the accused the benefit of the doubt.

Levels of responsibility

Those who plan or decide upon an attack seem to have more responsibilities than those who carry them out. The former must verify the target, minimize the risk of incidental damage and respect the rule of proportionality while the latter only have a responsibility to break off the attack if the objective turns out not to be military or if the rule of proportionality would be breached. The ICRC, introducing the text in the first place, stated that it was for the party concerned

---

[142] Kalshoven, Reaffirmation, p. 119.

[143] A. P. V. Rogers, Conduct of combat and risks run by the civilian population, *Military Law and Law of War Review*, 1982, p. 311. See the Hostages trial, VIII WCR at p. 58.

[144] Kalshoven, *Constraints*, p. 100.

to decide upon the precise level of responsibility, depending on the organization of its armed forces.[145]

Taken at face value, Art. 57.2(a) would appear to apply to commanders at all levels. A platoon or company commander may be involved in planning and carrying out an attack on a specific objective within the overall framework of a directive from higher authority. Similarly, he may have to carry out defensive measures involving the use of the firepower available to him if his position is attacked by the enemy, sometimes without the time to consult higher authority. Kalshoven oversimplifies the matter when he states of the commander: 'in the event of a major operation this will be the commanding general with his staff, in the case of a minor action, say, of a few men on a patrol or a small group of guerilla fighters it will be the leader (or the collective leadership) of the unit'.[146]

As was mentioned in chapter 1, Switzerland made a reservation on ratification that the provisions of Art. 57, para. 2, of Protocol I create obligations only for commanding officers at the battalion or group level and above. Others have expressed the view less formally that the obligations apply to commanders at brigade level and higher[147] or even, as suggested by Austria, at high-command level.[148] Kalshoven appears to lend some support to the Swiss position by saying that the provisions of the protocol 'are so intricate, both in language and in train of thought, that full implementation may probably be expected only at higher levels of command'. He points out that the small unit may be limited in the means of combat at its disposal and its capacity 'to evaluate all relevant aspects of the situation'.[149]

Solf supported this approach, saying that in a

co-ordinated military operation, the relative importance of the military objective under attack in relation to the concrete and direct military advantage anticipated is not a matter that can be determined by individual tank leaders, the commanders of lower echelon combat units or individual attacking bomber aircraft . . . they must assume that an appropriate assessment has been made . . . Thus, in this situation, the decision to cancel will have to be made at the level at which the decision to initiate the attack was made.[150]

But these formulations may be too rigid. They look at the situation from the point of view of the commander. Suppose, however, a ground attack aircraft pilot is flying over the area of operations and attacking opportunity targets. Obviously, the tasking commander is under a responsibility to lay down certain

[145] W. J. Fenrick, The rule of proportionality and Protocol I in conventional warfare, *Military Law Review*, 1982, p. 107 (quoting Levie).

[146] Kalshoven, *Constraints*, at p. 98.

[147] See Rogers, Conduct of combat, p. 309. Fenrick, Proportionality, p. 108, considers that the proper level will not be below a divisional or equivalent headquarters.

[148] Fenrick, Proportionality, p. 108.

[149] Kalshoven, *Constraints*, p. 100.

[150] Bothe et al., *New Rules*, p. 366.

parameters, but within those parameters the pilot will have to make a decision to attack, and will be subject to the constraints of Art. 57.[151]

What of the responsibility of the officer under a duty to carry out the attack? As Kalshoven indicates, he may not have the weapons available to carry out the attack within the rule of proportionality,[152] especially if unexpected factors, not taken into account in the plan of attack, arise. His responsibility must be to break off the attack and report back to higher authority or call up an attack using other means. Those carrying out attacks at long range would probably be unaware of a change of circumstances or new factors on the ground and would, no doubt, rely implicitly on what they had been told by the planners. Since the change or new factors would not 'have become apparent' to them, they would not be caught by Art. 57.2(b) of the protocol. This provision is more likely to affect those attacking at shorter ranges who may well have a greater choice of means available to them.

Conclusions

The general requirement to take care obviously applies to everybody involved in military operations from the ministry of defence planning staff, through the commander in the field to the tank commander.

The requirement to take precautions in attack applies to military planners and commanders who give the orders for the execution of those plans.

The duty to suspend or cancel an attack applies not only to those ordering it but also to those who carry it out. Pilots who, during the Gulf conflict of 1991, returned to base with full bomb racks because they were unable to identify the target[153] acted in accordance with this principle.

As Roberts has said, developments in military technology have made it far more likely that suitable precautions are now taken in attacks because the means have become available. Writing at the beginning of the conflict in the Gulf in 1991, he said:

there may be better prospects than in previous wars of the coalition partners focusing their air attack on military targets. The accuracy of their intelligence, the open nature of the terrain, and the huge improvements in the design of delivery systems, all make the restriction of the assault to military targets possible in a way that it was not in the Second World War.[154]

The operator's responsibilities under Art. 57 may be summarized in military manuals on the following lines. He must:

[151] See ICRC *Commentary*, para. 2220.
[152] Kalshoven, *Constraints*, p. 99.
[153] DOD Report, p. 612.
[154] A. Roberts, The laws of war and the Gulf conflict, *Oxford International Review*, vol. II, No. 2, 1990/91, at p. 52.

1. When planning military operations always take into account the effect they will have on the civilian population and civilian objects, including the environment.

2. Do everything feasible to verify that the target is a military objective.

3. Take all feasible precautions to reduce incidental damage and loss. This will involve a careful choice of weapons as well as care in preparing the plans for carrying out the attack.

4. Observe the rule of proportionality. This requires a calculation of the likely casualties, both military and civilian, and damage compared with the expected military advantage. It is probably too early to say whether it also involves an assessment of the risk and effect of weapons malfunctioning or of human error[155] but it certainly does not include matters over which the attacker has no control, such as the effect of enemy action.[156] Obviously, factors such as air supremacy or the availability of smart weapons will weigh heavily in favour of taking precautions to protect the civilian population.

5. Be ready to cancel or suspend an attack, if necessary. This also involves weighing military against humanitarian considerations.

6. Give warnings, unless the circumstances do not permit.

7. Consider carefully his choice of targets in terms of what offers the best military advantage with the least incidental loss or damage.

8. Ensure that target lists are kept constantly under review in the light of changing circumstances.[157]

---

[155] These matters were taken into account by allied planners during the Gulf War of 1991, see the evidence of Air Vice-Marshal Wrattan, Defence Committee Report, p. 38, q. 74.

[156] See Hampson, Gulf conflict, pp. 92–3.

[157] *Ibid.*, p. 94.

4

Precautions against the effects of attacks

Introduction

The early law of war treaties and writings seem hardly to have addressed the problem of how to protect the civilian population from the effects of attacks. Prior warning of bombardments was perceived as giving the authorities of the besieged town an opportunity to evacuate non-combatants, especially women and children.[1] Although it was accepted that direct attacks on civilians were prohibited, it was recognized that civilians were at risk from attacks conducted against legitimate targets. But attention was mainly concentrated on regulating the conduct of the attackers. Very little thought was given to the responsibilities of the authorities of the place or country under attack to ensure the safety of its civilian population.

By 1907 the only positive rule relating to precautions against the effects of attacks was the requirement to mark hospitals and religious edifices with distinctive signs.[2] An early, but nugatory, attempt to improve matters was the Draft Convention for the Protection of the Civilian Populations against the New Engines of War adopted by the International Law Association in 1938. This included quite detailed rules for setting up safety zones under the supervision of an independent controlling authority for the protection of a very limited section of the population: those under fifteen or over sixty, expectant or suckling mothers or persons too infirm to be able to carry out any war work. Such zones were to be immune from attack or bombardment.

Van Dongen,[3] echoing the ICRC, criticizes the draft convention on the grounds that it gives belligerents an excuse not to take any precautions for the protection of the civilian population outside such zones. This is not a very cogent argument, given the clear requirement to take precautions outside safety zones in

---

[1] See, e.g., the Lieber Code, Art. 19.
[2] Hague Regulations, Art. 27.
[3] Y. van Dongen, *The Protection of Civilian Populations in Time of Armed Conflicts*, Groningen University, 1991.

Arts. 2–5 of the draft convention. As is discussed below, the concept of safety zones is retained in the modern law of war.[4]

For the rest it was left to the good sense of the authorities of a place under attack to provide shelter for its citizens, and, with the advent of aerial bombard-ment, air raid warning systems and air raid shelters were usually provided. Rousseau adds the practice of issuing gas masks and the possibility of evacuat-ing part of the population to a neutral country, but underlines that effective plans would require enormous resources, especially in transport, which are more likely to be devoted to the military effort.[5] During the Second World War plans were drawn up and executed to evacuate civilians, especially children, from towns or from the vicinity of military objectives. Children of foreign nationality can now be evacuated to a neutral country only in the limited circumstances laid down by Protocol I, Art. 78.

Current law

Precautions against the effects of attacks

The parties to a conflict are obliged by Art. 58 of Protocol I, to the maximum extent *feasible*, to:

1. *Remove civilians and civilian objects* from the vicinity of military object-ives.

2. *Avoid* locating military objectives in *densely populated areas*.

3. *Protect civilians and civilian objects* from the dangers of military opera-tions.

This provision, which involves longer-term planning,[6] seems to be addressed primarily to the civil authorities but the military authorities will also have a role to play, especially with regard to 2 and 3 above, or where the military authorities are effectively in control, as when opposing forces are in contact. As for 1, the military authorities may be asked to assist the civil authorities. Roberts warns the UK authorities that on ratification of Protocol I they will have to review their policy of leaving civil defence on a 'care and maintenance' basis.[7] The extent to which a state can be forced to comply with its obligations to its own citizens, an area in which international law has in the past, with the exception of human rights, been slow to intervene, is a moot point. According to Parks—who reminds readers that some states have made statements on signature or ratification that this provision is not to be regarded as a restriction on meas-ures for the defence of their national territory—this provision is not obligatory.[8]

[4]Civilian Convention, Art. 14.
[5]C. Rousseau, *Le Droit des conflits armés*, Pedone, 1983, p. 82.
[6]L. Doswald-Beck, The value of the 1977 protocols, in M. A. Meyer, *Armed Conflict and the New Law*, British Institute of International and Comparative Law, 1989, p. 142.
[7]A. Roberts, Civil defence and international law, in Meyer, *Armed Conflict*, pp. 187, 193.
[8]W. H. Parks, Air war and the law of war, 32 *Air Force Law Review*, 1990, p. 159.

Understandings of what is meant by 'to the maximum extent feasible' will vary. Systematic provision of shelters is expensive, although Switzerland introduced the requirement some years ago for certain new buildings to be equipped with shelters. Some states would argue that with limited budgets other priorities are more urgent and that, in any event, Protocol I applies only in armed conflicts and, therefore, that the only peacetime obligation is to undertake the necessary planning for war. From the military point of view, however, it is obviously easier to wage war in the knowledge that one's own civilian population is adequately protected and that military resources do not have to be diverted from the conduct of military operations in order to support the civil authorities in protecting the civilian population.

Remove civilians and civilian objects

Although the first priority must be to avoid locating military objectives in populated areas, where that is not possible efforts have to be made to evacuate civilians and civilian objects from the vicinity of obvious military objectives.

The first obligation seems a tall order, especially as regards immovable civilian objects, but even in respect of civilians, who, compared with objects, are mobile, it may be difficult to apply in practice, since what may be a military objective today because of the prevailing circumstances may not be tomorrow because of a change of circumstances. Evacuation itself will cause hardship, especially if it is for an extended period, there is a shortage of housing and the weather makes tented accommodation unsuitable, and probably would only be undertaken when there is an immediate threat, for example if the enemy had complied with its obligation to give warning of an impending attack on a military objective in a populated area,[9] though citizens might, as a general precaution, be advised to send their children away from industrial centres to relatives in areas thought to be remote from danger. Here the second obligation overlaps the first.[10]

Measures are likely to be undertaken only in time of war but, bearing in mind, as Fleck has pointed out,[11] that they are likely to be carried out under great time pressure and against a background of panic, it is in the interests of the military authorities that civilians should be evacuated in a controlled and orderly way, otherwise the deployment of the armed forces may be adversely affected.[12] During

---

[9]The question of warning is discussed in chapter 3.

[10]Evacuation within the borders of a state is governed by the law of that state, D. Fleck, *Die rechtlichen Garantien des Verbots von unmittelbaren Kampfhandlungen gegen Zivilpersonen, Military Law and Law of War Review*, 1966, p. 103. Evacuation into occupied or foreign territory is controlled by Art. 49 of the Civilian Convention and Art. 78 of Protocol I. In occupied territory the special provisions of Art. 49 of the Civilian Convention apply. In the case of children the special provisions of Art. 78 of Protocol I must also be complied with.

[11]*Ibid.*, p. 103.

[12]See also ICRC *Commentary*, para. 2248.

long-range aerial bombardment civilians may stay put if adequate air raid warnings are given and shelters are available, but even so they may be tempted to
move to relatives or friends in country areas. On the other hand, the approach
of enemy ground forces is likely to result in panic and a serious refugee problem.[13]
So evacuation plans must be drawn up in peacetime and resources earmarked
to execute them. In Germany, for example, a whole range of emergency laws
have been passed, some of them amending the basic law, covering business
and finance, the supply of food and water, the building of shelters and the movement and location of the civilian population.[14] This obviously involves close
co-operation between the civil and military authorities.

Avoid densely populated areas

Solf commented that there was a consensus at the Diplomatic Conference
that 'to avoid placing military objectives in populated areas is a goal to be
achieved if feasible which must, however, give way to military requirements
if necessary'.[15]

There may be little the authorities can do in any event, especially where the
war industry is closely bound to the civilian population. If a bridge across a
river is a military objective because it is on a route for the transport of military
supplies, nearby civilian buildings[16] cannot be moved although clearly in danger
if the bridge is attacked. The use of smart bombs, however, may mean that the
other end or the centre of the bridge can be destroyed if that lessens the risk to
civilian objects. In planning the location of new military installations, of course,
the rule would have to be taken into account and mobile military units would
have to take care about where to position themselves. Military units are frequently stationed in barracks in towns in peacetime. Because their location is
likely to be known to an enemy, however, they may well deploy out of these
locations in wartime if there is a possibility of their being attacked. But, when
deployed into the countryside, units are often based in villages where soldiers
can be billeted in houses and vehicles put under cover in barns and use can be
made of local power and water supplies.[17] It is submitted that these tactics have
not been affected by Protocol I because it may not be feasible for the forces
concerned to do otherwise. Commanders will, nevertheless, have to ask themselves before locating troops in a populated area whether it would not be feasible to locate them somewhere else. So much depends on the circumstances at
the time: the urgency or otherwise of the moment, the tactical situation, the level

---

[13]The conflict in Yugoslavia had by July 1992 led to 2,300,000 people fleeing the fighting—see
International Review of the Red Cross, July–August 1992, p. 389.

[14]Fleck, Die rechtlichen Garantien, p. 103.

[15]M. Bothe, K. J. Partsch and W. Solf, *New Rules for the Victims of Armed Conflicts*, Martinus
Nijhoff, 1982, p. 372.

[16]Like the cathedral and museum next to the railway bridge over the Rhine at Cologne.

[17]This is the experience of the writer on exercises in Germany. See also Parks, Air war, p. 160.

and density of the civilian population, the overall deployment or battle plans and many other factors.

The meaning of 'densely populated' is not defined. Interpretation is left to the good sense of the authorities concerned, whether military or civil.

As Fleck has pointed out,[18] this rule of Protocol I is partly a matter of planning in peacetime, since it should be possible when deciding on the location of headquarters, barracks and supply depots as well as armaments factories to ensure that they are located at a suitable distance from centres of population. But even if new headquarters are set up in the middle of nowhere they will soon attract an assembly of civilian bars and second-hand car salesrooms. Consideration should also be given to moving existing military installations away from populated areas, but it is unlikely, on grounds of cost, that this can be done on a systematic basis, though when the opportunity arises it should be taken. Roberts[19] underlines the difficulty of moving such potential military objectives as Heathrow airport and the Ministry of Defence in London.[20] As he rightly says, though, more could be done in this matter, for example a thorough review of potential military objectives, to see what can be done about their relocation. To this might be added a legislative requirement for both the Crown and local government to consider the provisions of Art. 58 of Protocol I when concerned with the siting of potential military objectives and when drawing up development plans.

Fleck comments that the removal of potential military objectives from populated areas is to be preferred to attempts to camouflage them.[21] Attempts to camouflage military objectives by trying to make them look like something else can lead to accusations of bad faith and of trying to protect military objectives by locating them close to civilians.

The provisions of Art. 58 pose something of a dilemma, since moving military objectives out of populated areas may make them more readily identifiable by the enemy. Furthermore, if it is not possible to move a fixed installation in a populated area, the defenders will inevitably wish to camouflage it and that will increase the risk to civilians in the vicinity.

In this connection the following passage in a newspaper report is salutary:

In some cases the Iraqis have only themselves to blame for the loss of civilian life. Their policy of re-locating staff from government offices to schools and other civilian buildings and of moving military hardware out of their barracks to better camouflaged wooded areas in the countryside near farms and villages frequently exposes non-combatants to attack.[22]

---

[18]Fleck, Die rechtlichen Garantien, at p. 101.
[19]Roberts, Civil defence, p. 195.
[20]However, plans to rusticate sections of the ministry would be consistent with the requirements of Protocol I.
[21]Fleck, Die rechtlichen Garantien, p. 102.
[22]R. Beeston, Civilian casualties take on a key role . . . *The Times*, 11 February 1991. Of course, if barracks are in towns, the danger to the civilian population is probably greater.

Protect civilians

The last obligation covers a wide range of possibilities, from the provision of shelters, firefighting, provision of equipment to protect civilians from nuclear, chemical or biological attack, the enforcement of a blackout, an evacuation service, co-ordination of the emergency services and taking other adequate civil defence measures, a civil responsibility, to the broadcasting of warnings such as air raid warnings, a shared responsibility, and the fencing of minefields or the provision of military engineer support, a military responsibility.

Feasible

The word 'feasible' appears again here. It was included on the insistence of the densely populated countries, which felt that Art. 58 would adversely affect their ability to defend themselves, and of countries worried about the expense of complying with the provision.[23] Its meaning is also discussed in chapter 3. There does not seem to be any significant difference between 'to the maximum extent feasible', used in Art. 58, and 'everything feasible' or 'all feasible precautions', used elsewhere in the Protocol.[24] Kalshoven comments that the words 'to the maximum extent feasible' merely reflect the fact that the obligations of Art. 58 'will often be extremely difficult, if not impossible, to realize'.[25] Gasser sums up the obligation well by saying that 'the law does not expect the impossible, but it asks the commander or the staff officer to do what he can do'.[26]

The need for close co-operation between military and civil authorities is clearly vital, with the exchange of all necessary information. In Belgium, in all cases short of a state of siege (martial law), there is an interdepartmental committee responsible for co-ordinating the civilian and military efforts.[27]

Own territory

In some respects, despite the provisions of Article 49, para. 2, of Protocol I, which applies the rules on attacks to all attacks in whatever territory, the rules of the protocol are more relaxed in respect of a state's acts on its own territory. Switzerland anticipated difficulties, for geographical and population structure reasons, in evacuating its civilian population from heavily populated areas and in removing military objectives from residential areas. In addition, its infantry

[23]Bothe *et al.*, *New Rules*, pp. 372, 374.

[24]A. P. V. Rogers, Conduct of combat and risks run by the civilian population, *Military Law and Law of War Review*, 1982, p. 313.

[25]F. Kalshoven, *Constraints on the Waging of War*, International Committee of the Red Cross, 1987, p. 101.

[26]H. P. Gasser, Some legal issues concerning ratification of the 1977 Geneva Protocols, in Meyer, *Armed Conflict*, p. 88.

[27]A. de Smet, General Report on Civilian Support to the Armed Forces, 1991, to be published in the *Military Law and Law of War Review*.

were dependent on the defence potential of populated areas and, although good protection was available to the population through civil defence measures, it was thought that Switzerland might be accused of violating Arts. 58(a) and (b) of Protocol I. Relying on the words 'to the maximum extent feasible', and on the special circumstances of Swiss defence plans, Switzerland entered a reservation to Art. 58 in the following terms:

Inasmuch as Article 58 contains the expression 'to the maximum extent feasible', paragraphs (a) and (b) will be applied subject to the requirements of the defence of the national territory.[28]

Failure by defenders; position of attackers

Protection of the civilian population is not only a matter for the attackers, because the defenders share the responsibility for putting civilians in danger by using them in war production or by placing military objectives in their midst.[29] Art. 58 of Protocol I seems to be based on the assumption that a state will wish to protect its own civilian population and will, therefore, take steps to separate civilian and military activities. The US Air Force pamphlet reinforces this assumption by saying that a party to the conflict which places its own citizens in danger by failing to separate civilian and military activities necessarily accepts collateral damage caused as a result of attacks on military objectives.[30] But this is an overoptimistic statement. What of the ruthless leader for whom protection of the civilian population is subordinate to his war aims?

As is clear from such terms as *to the maximum extent feasible*, *endeavour* and *avoid*, the requirements of Art. 58 of Protocol I are not absolute. A defender may be tempted to ignore his obligations under this article so as to make things more difficult for the attacker. Why, he might ask, should I ease my opponent's task and lose the propaganda victory which I would achieve if my civilian population were attacked?[31] Sometimes a party to a conflict may provoke massive retaliation by the enemy so as to evoke sympathy from the world's media for the resultant losses among that party's civilians.[32]

During the Gulf War of 1990–91 it was alleged that Iraq pursued a deliberate policy of placing military objectives near protected objects, for example, near mosques, medical facilities and cultural property. Examples included dispersing military helicopters in residential areas, storing military supplies in mosques, schools and hospitals, including a cache of Silkworm missiles in a school in

---

[28] See Switzerland, *Botschaft über die Zusatzprotokolle zu den Genfer Abkommen*, Swiss Federal Council, 1981, p. 53.
[29] See M. Walzer, *Just and Unjust Wars*, Pelican, 1980, p. 158.
[30] United States, *International Law—The Conduct of Armed Conflict and Air Operations*, Department of the Air Force, Pamphlet 110–31, 1976.
[31] Parks, Air war, p. 166, refers to his experience of deliberate attempts by the PLO to use the civilian population of Beirut as a shield against attacks by the Israeli forces.
[32] A graphic example of this in the Vietnam War is given by Parks, *Air war*, p. 160.

Kuwait City, placing fighter aircraft near the ancient temple of Ur, and the discovery by UN inspectors of chemical weapon production equipment in a sugar factory in Iraq.[33] It was also alleged that Iraq used hostages, some of them civilians, as a 'human shield' to protect military objectives.[34] There was also some ambiguity in the Iraqi approach. Using a facility for both military and civilian purposes such as the al-Amariyah bunker bombed by the allies on 13 February 1991 is to court disaster.[35]

According to the US Department of Defense, Iraq also adopted a deliberate policy of not moving civilians away from military objectives, not evacuating civilians from Baghdad and providing air raid shelters for only a very small percentage of the population. The fact that the Iraqis were capable of carrying out evacuation plans was demonstrated by the civil defence exercise carried out in the month preceding the allied air campaign, in which over a million civilians were evacuated from Baghdad.[36]

Such tactics might lead to deaths among the civilian population which would be disproportionate to the military gain achieved by the attackers. Are the attackers, therefore, relieved of their responsibility because of the failure of the defenders to comply with their obligations under Protocol I? It may be inferred from Kalshoven that this question should be answered in the negative. He points out that the use of civilians to shield military objectives does not release the attacker from the requirement to take precautions in attack[37] and comments that 'the above precautions against the effects of attacks have not been introduced to facilitate military operations'.[38]

An attack which causes excessive loss of life to civilians may be a grave breach of Protocol I.[39] Failure to take precautions against the effects of attacks is not a grave breach. Nor is a failure by a party to distinguish at all times between civilian objects and military objectives,[40] an obligation which applies to defenders as well as attackers.[41] It seems that a state could almost with impunity[42] carry out a policy of using the civilian population as a shield, especially on foreign territory where its forces were deployed, and yet this would be no defence to an attacker charged with causing excessive loss of civilian life. At most it would amount to mitigation.

---

[33] United States, *Conduct of the Persian Gulf War*, Department of Defense final report to Congress, April 1992, (DOD Report), p. 613.

[34] *Ibid.*

[35] *Ibid.*, p. 615, where it is stated that part of the bunker was a 'C2 center', a command and control centre, and that, unbeknown to the allied authorities, it was also used as a shelter for civilians.

[36] *Ibid.*, pp. 614–15.

[37] Protocol I, Art. 51, para. 8.

[38] F. Kalshoven, Reaffirmation and development of international humanitarian law, *Netherlands Yearbook of International Law*, 1978, p. 121.

[39] Art. 85, para. 3 (b).

[40] Protocol I, Art. 48.

[41] Bothe *et al.*, *New Rules*, p. 282.

[42] It would still be a war crime, though not carrying the stigma of a grave breach.

This is an area where Protocol I fails to achieve an objective balance between the rights and duties of attackers and defenders and, perhaps, encourages the defenders to violate the law of war. This is a point made with force by Parks,[43] who thinks that there was a deliberate attempt to shift responsibility on to the shoulders of the attacker only; and in the Department of Defense report,[44] where it is stated that this problem is exacerbated by the presumption of civilian status in Art. 52, para. 3, of Protocol I and that media attention is likely to focus on the incidental loss and damage caused by the attacker rather than on the perfidious activities of the defender, a point that public relations staff and psychological warfare experts would do well to remember. The justification by Adler of target area bombing on the basis that the enemy concealed and camouflaged its war industry and made no real attempt to separate military targets[45] might be inapplicable to parties to Protocol I[46] unless it could be argued that the targets were not 'clearly separated and distinct'.

Nevertheless, a tribunal considering whether a grave breach had been committed would be able to take into account when considering the rule of proportionality the extent to which the defenders had flouted their obligation to separate military objectives from civilian objects and to take precautions to protect the civilian population. State practice suggests that the attackers are unlikely to be deterred from attacking military objectives sheltering in populated areas. As Schwarzenberger commented in connection with the Hague Air Warfare Rules:

it assumed—incorrectly, as events proved—that governments would accept or act upon a rule which would make it possible for the belligerent to gain immunity for objectives of the highest military value by resorting to the device of placing them in centres of population outside the zone of military operations.[47]

It is submitted that the proportionality approach by tribunals should help to redress the balance which otherwise would be tilted in favour of the unscrupulous.

Civil defence

The provisions of Art. 58 of Protocol I overlap to quite an extent with those of the protocol dealing with civil defence.[48] Civil defence falls outside the scope of this work,[49] which is concerned with the law as it affects the military commander, but Art. 61 of Protocol I contains a list of civil defence measures that can be taken for the protection of the civilian population. The list is useful in

[43]Parks, Air war, p. 163.
[44]Page 616.
[45]G. J. Adler, Targets in war: legal considerations, *Houston Law Review*, 1970, at p. 36.
[46]Since such attacks would amount to indiscriminate attacks—Art. 51, para. 5(a).
[47]G. Schwarzenberger, The revision of the law of war, *British Yearbook of International Law*, 1952, at p. 367.
[48]Arts. 61 to 67.
[49]For a detailed treatment of this subject, see Roberts, Civil defence, p. 175.

indicating to the military commander where the responsibilities of the civil authorities towards the civilian population lie, namely in:

1. Warning.
2. Evacuation.
3. Management of shelters.[50]
4. Management of blackout measures.
5. Rescue.
6. Medical and religious services.
7. Firefighting.
8. Detection and marking of danger areas.
9. Decontamination.
10. Emergency accommodation and supplies.
11. Emergency assistance in restoring and maintaining order.
12. Emergency repair of public utilities.
13. Emergency disposal of the dead.
14. Assistance in preserving objects essential for survival.

The military authorities may be able to assist the civil authorities of their own, friendly or occupied territory with points 1, 2, 5, 6, 8, 9, 10, 11, 12, 13 and 14 above by providing information, transport, medical personnel and facilities,[51] decontamination equipment, tents and rations, engineering equipment, support for police patrols and the facilities of the military burial service. Such assistance will depend on the tactical situation and availability of resources. The primary duty will, in any event, rest with the civil authorities. The appointment to the commander's staff of a civil liaison officer would be of immense benefit in ensuring that a party's obligations under Protocol I were complied with.

In a fluid battlefield, or where territory is still being fought over, it is unlikely that the military authorities will be able to assist except, possibly, in treating civilian wounded and, of course, there will be no or little contact with the civil authorities.

Zones

The provisions of Art. 58 of Protocol I cannot be viewed in isolation. There are other provisions designed to protect civilians and others from the effects of attacks. They may conveniently be grouped under the heading of zones. The underlying idea of providing sanctuary for civilians was put into practice to good effect in the Sino-Japanese conflict of 1937–38 when troops, munitions factories and military establishments were removed from Shanghai, Hankow

---

[50] The civil authorities would also be responsible for the provision of shelters.

[51] Although Art. 15, para. 2, of Protocol I envisages help being supplied to the civilian medical services by a party to the conflict, where that help is provided by the military authorities, care must be taken to ensure that the protected status of the civilian services is not compromised, see Art. 13, para. 2, of Protocol I.

and other cities.[52] There have been many examples since 1945 of zones being set up by agreement between the parties at the instigation of the United Nations or the International Committee of the Red Cross.[53] Recent examples include the safety zone in Port Stanley in the Falkland Islands in 1982, the safe havens for the Kurds in Iraq in 1991 and safe havens in Bosnia in 1993. The types of zones may be briefly summarized as follows.[54]

1. Hospital zones and localities to protect the wounded and sick of the armed forces and medical personnel.[55]

2. Safety zones for wounded and sick civilians, old people, children, expectant mothers and mothers of small children.[56]

3. Neutralized zones. These are larger in scale than safety zones and possibly encompass whole towns. They are intended to protect the wounded and sick, both combatants and civilians, and also civilians who are taking no part in hostilities.[57]

4. Civilian hospitals are also immune from attack and may display the protective emblem.[58]

5. Non-defended localities may be created where opposing forces are in contact. All combatants and movable military equipment must be evacuated. The locality may not be attacked, but may be occupied by the adverse party.[59]

6. Demilitarized zones. These are similar to non-defended localities but may not be occupied, so are likely to be set up in rear areas.[60]

Open or undefended towns

According to the Hague Regulations, attacks on or bombardment by any means whatsoever of undefended towns, villages, dwellings or buildings is prohibited.[61] Since these objects are undefended, they can be occupied by ground troops without opposition or casualties, rendering attack or bombardment unnecessary.

Some authors have reflected upon whether the presence of supplies of military value to the enemy, or the presence of railway establishments, telegraphs or bridges in a town constitutes sufficient excuse for bombarding it.[62] Again, the answer is probably in the negative if the town is open to occupation by troops.

---

[52]See J. Stone, *Legal Controls of International Armed Conflict*, Stevens, 1954, p. 631.

[53]See, e.g., Rousseau, *Le Droit des conflit armés*, p. 131.

[54]A more detailed analysis can be found in L. C. Green, *The Contemporary Law of Armed Conflict*, Manchester University Press, 1993, pp. 95–8.

[55]Wounded Convention, Art. 23.

[56]Civilian Convention, Art. 14.

[57]*Ibid.*, Art. 15.

[58]*Ibid.*, Art. 18.

[59]Protocol I, Art. 59.

[60]*Ibid.*, Art. 60.

[61]Hague Regulations, Art. 25.

[62]See J. W. Garner, *International Law and the World War*, Vol. I, Longman, 1920, p. 421; J. M. Spaight, *War Rights on Land*, Macmillan, 1911, p. 170.

Of course, the situation is different in respect of military objectives such as munitions factories in undefended towns behind the enemy front line which cannot be occupied without opposition.

As long ago as 1920, Garner came to the conclusion that the distinction between defended and undefended places had no place in air bombardment.[63] Rousseau[64] seems to be of the same opinion, expressing the view that by the time of the static First World War the concept of the open town had become archaic, that it was inappropriate in the context of aerial warfare and that the modern trend was to provide protection by means of zones of special protection. It may be inferred from the Tokyo district court decision of 1963 that the open town concept applies only to towns capable of being occupied by enemy forces and does not apply to towns in rear areas.[65] This decision is consistent with military practice[66] and with naval practice, since the Naval Bombardment Convention permits the bombardment of military objectives in undefended towns.[67]

Writers may have fallen into the trap of thinking that the concept of the open town had fallen into disuse because the matter was not addressed in the Air Warfare Rules.[68] The reason why it was not addressed was probably that a town could not be occupied by air forces. In the words of Doswald-Beck, the 'notion of "defended" or "undefended" had no sense whatever for bombardments behind enemy lines'.[69] While there is no doubt that the addition in the Hague Regulations of the words 'by whatever means' was intended to include aerial bombardment, their inclusion seems to have left doubt in the minds of commentators whether it is possible to apply the concept of the open town to towns in the rear areas which are accessible to bombing from the air but not accessible to occupation by ground troops.[70] As the principle of the open town was based on the notion that, since such towns were open to unopposed occupation, bombardment was unnecessary, it ought to be evident that an open town cannot exist in rear areas.[71]

---

[63] Garner, *International Law*, p. 469. The US Air Force seems to take the view that refugee camps are also capable of being open towns, see United States, *Commander's Handbook on the Law of Armed Conflict*, Department of the Air Force, Pamphlet 110-34, para. 3-6a.

[64] Rousseau, *Le Droit des conflits armés*, at p. 128.

[65] The Shimoda case, 1965, 32 *International Law Reports* 626, at p. 631.

[66] United States, *Air Operations*, pp. 5–12; *Manual of Military Law*, para. 290. See also Doswald-Beck, The value of the 1977 protocols, p. 142.

[67] Art. 2.

[68] See, e.g., I. Detter de Lupis, *The Law of War*, Cambridge University Press, 1987, p. 234. It is true, however, that a vestige of the open town concept appears in the Rules. As Doswald-Beck, The value of the 1977 protocols, p. 143, rightly indicates, they permitted the bombardment of towns only in the 'immediate neighbourhood of the operations of land forces'.

[69] Doswald-Beck, The value of the 1977 protocols, at p. 142.

[70] See, e.g., H. Lauterpacht, The problem of the revision of the law of war, *British Yearbook of International Law*, 1952, p. 366.

[71] See H. Blix, Area bombardment: rules and reasons, *British Yearbook of International Law*, 1978, p. 41. So Green's question about a place defended by anti-aircraft guns is probably academic. See Green, *Contemporary Law*, p. 97.

However, in a mobile war fought by ground forces the concept could still be usefully applied to allow towns to be occupied to prevent unnecessary damage. As Green has pointed out, however, if enemy troops hold a line in front of a city, it cannot be regarded as an undefended town, since it is not open to occupation.[72] It may be concluded that the provisions of the Hague Regulations about attacks on and bombardments of undefended places have been overtaken by the provisions of Protocol I on attacks, military objectives and precautions in attack. The only relevance now of the undefended place concept is to allow the occupation of such places by advancing troops without a fight.

It is likely in future practice that, rather than relying on the Hague Regulations, parties to Protocol I will avail themselves of the provisions of that protocol dealing with non-defended localities.

[72]Green, *Contemporary Law.*

5

Cultural property

Introduction

The siege of Dubrovnik during the Yugoslav civil war of 1991–95 directed attention to the vulnerability of cultural property during war. Dubrovnik was one of the most perfectly preserved walled cities in Europe and a world heritage site.[1] Yet, according to press reports, on 6 December 1991 it was hit by more than 500 rockets which damaged 45 per cent of the buildings in the old city and destroyed 10 per cent. The fifteenth-century Rector's Palace and St Saviour's Church were badly damaged.[2]

According to Rousseau, the protection of cultural property is based on the notion that it forms part of the common property of mankind.[3]

As McCoubrey has pointed out,[4] there are two main problems concerning the protection of cultural property in war: damage to cultural monuments, for example by bombing as in the case of Dresden, and the looting of art treasures, as in the case of the Rosetta Stone, which passed from Egypt through French to British hands and now rests in the British Museum.

The German military instruction manual,[5] outlining the history of the protection of cultural property, gives numerous historical examples which amount to a sad litany of the destruction and looting of cultural property from antiquity through the Middle Ages, the Crusades and the Thirty Years War to the World Wars of this century. Perhaps attitudes to the need to protect cultural property

[1] P. J. Boylan, *Review of the Convention for the Protection of Cultural Property in the Event of Armed Conflict*, UNESCO, 1993, p. 19.

[2] M. Binney, Dubrovnik's scars laid bare, *The Times*, 8 February 1992. In a letter to *The Times* of 6 October 1993, P. Cormack and others draw attention to the destruction of mosques in Banja Luka and monasteries at Zitonislic and Kraljeva Sutjeska in Bosnia as well as important collections of manuscripts and works of art.

[3] C. Rousseau, *Le Droit des conflits armés*, Pedone, 1983, p. 132.

[4] H. McCoubrey, *International Humanitarian Law*, Dartmouth, 1990, p. 119.

[5] Germany, *Der Schutz von Kulturgut bei bewaffneten Konflikten*, ZDv 15/9, Ministry of Defence, July 1964, p. 35.

are beginning to change. The plan of the army of the former German Democratic Republic for the invasion of West Berlin (Operation Centre, 1987) included plans to occupy and protect a number of sites of significant cultural heritage: the Egyptian Museum, Schloss Bellvue, Schloss Charlottenburg, the State Library, the National Gallery, the Museum of Antiquity and the Prussian Heritage Foundation.[6]

It was only after the Napoleonic Wars that a different perception started to develop: that cultural property was common property and, therefore, that it should not be transferred from one country to another. This principle was recognized at the Congress of Vienna in 1815.[7] After that commanders started to protect art treasures, as in the case of the French commander, Oudinot, in Rome in 1849.[8]

By the time of the Lieber Code it was accepted that the protection previously reserved for churches extended to 'classical works of art, libraries and scientific collections' even if they were contained in fortified places being besieged or bombarded,[9] and at the Brussels Conference of 1874 a draft declaration was drawn up which protected 'buildings dedicated to art, science, or charitable purposes' provided they were not being used for military purposes. The drafters, perhaps encouraged by the adoption of the red cross emblem at the first Geneva Convention of 1864, also envisaged the use of protective emblems communicated to the enemy beforehand.[10] This approach was reflected in the Oxford manual, prepared by the International Law Commission in 1880, on the laws and usages of war.[11]

Protected property

The Hague Regulations

The Hague Regulations require 'buildings dedicated to religion, art, science, or charitable purposes and historic monuments'[12] to be spared so far as possible during sieges and bombardments, provided they are not being used for military purposes.[13]

There is a duty on the besieged to indicate protected buildings by distinctive

[6] A. D. Meek, Operation Centre, *British Army Review*, No. 107/1994.
[7] *Ibid.*, p. 9.
[8] Referred to by J. R. Baker and H. G. Crocker, *The Laws of Land Warfare*, US Department of State, 1919, p. 211; H. Wheaton, *International Law*, 7th English ed. by A. B. Keith, Stevens, 1944, p. 217.
[9] Art. 35.
[10] Art. 17.
[11] Art. 34.
[12] Historic monuments were included at the suggestion of the Greek delegation, see Baker and Crocker, *Laws of Land Warfare*, p. 209.
[13] Art. 27.

and visible signs, notified to the enemy beforehand.[14] Parks[15] points out that the language of the regulations is neutral and, therefore, imposes obligations concerning the protection of cultural property on both attackers and defenders. The defenders can, for example, place sandbags around statues or evacuate movable cultural property such as the contents of libraries and art treasures.[16]

In occupied territory the Hague Regulations provide protection from seizure, destruction or damage for 'institutions dedicated to religion, charity and education, the arts and sciences as well as historic monuments and works of art and science'.[17]

Despite the provisions of the Hague Regulations and the efforts of the French and German cultural protection organizations,[18] there were many instances of the destruction of or of damage to protected property during the First World War.[19] At Strasbourg 400,000 volumes and 2,400 manuscripts in the library were destroyed by artillery fire.[20] At Rheims the cathedral was virtually destroyed by artillery fire which, according to the German general headquarters, was bombarded by light artillery when an observation post was discovered in one of the towers. This was denied by the French.[21] Similar claims and counter-claims were made in respect of the destruction of the Cloth Hall at Ypres, which dated back to 1304.[22] It has been suggested that allegations of the destruction of cultural property are often denied by the enemy or justified on the basis that it was being used for military purposes.[23] It is more likely, though, that such destruction is in the main incidental to attacks on military objectives, caused by mistake when the wrong target is attacked from a distance by artillery fire, or is done at junior level by someone who is either ignorant or reckless of or indifferent to the protection of cultural property.

Air Warfare Rules

The Air Warfare Rules[24] contain provisions similar to those of the Hague Regulations in the context of bombardment by aircraft. The basic Hague provision is extended to meet the special circumstances of air warfare by requiring:
  1. Protective signs to be visible from the air and at night.

[14] *Ibid.*
[15] W. H. Parks, Air war and the law of war, 32 *Air Force Law Review*, 1990, p. 60.
[16] This was done in Leningrad in 1941, *ibid.*
[17] Art. 56. This differs from Art. 27 in protecting institutions rather than buildings and adding 'education' to the list.
[18] Germany, *Der Schutz*, p. 9.
[19] Wheaton, *International Law*, p. 217.
[20] See Baker and Crocker, *Law of Land Warfare*, p. 210.
[21] A full account of this incident is given in J. W. Garner, *International Law and the World War*, vol. 1, Longman, 1920, pp. 441 *et seq.*
[22] *Ibid.*, p. 448.
[23] L. Oppenheim, *International Law*, vol. 2, 7th ed. by H. Lauterpacht, Longman, 1952, p. 421.
[24] These were drafted by a Commission of Jurists but never put into treaty form.

2. The use of a protective emblem for buildings (other than military hospitals and the like, protected by the Red Cross emblem) of a 'large rectangular panel divided diagonally into two pointed triangular portions, one black and the other white'.[25]

The rules also envisage the setting up of published and marked neutralized zones around historic monuments and neutral inspection committees to ensure that such monuments and zones are not used for military purposes.[26]

Roerich pact

Most states of the American continent are parties to the Roerich Pact of 1935. This confers a neutral status in peace and war on 'historic monuments, museums, scientific, artistic, educational and cultural institutions'.[27] They and their personnel are to be respected and protected. There is a protective flag.[28] States party are required to send to the Pan American Union[29] lists of the property to be protected under the pact.[30] It is not clear whether this is a prerequisite of protection. Property made use of for military purposes loses its protection.

Draft convention of 1939

A draft convention on the protection of historic buildings and works of art in time of war was prepared in 1939 under the auspices of the League of Nations. Although never implemented, the draft was evidently a forerunner of the Cultural Convention of 1954. Apart from the requirement to respect historic buildings and works of art and to punish people looting or damaging them, the draft provides for a protective emblem, special rules on refuges, special provision for notified monuments, an obligation not to use them for military purposes, shelter in another country and international commissions of inspection to ensure that no breaches occur. The draft was enhanced by draft implementing regulations.

Second World War practice

Things did not improve during the Second World War. Commenting that the City of London suffered severe losses of historic churches and other buildings, Boylan points out that since the accuracy of long-range night bombers at the

[25] Art. 25.
[26] Art. 26.
[27] This differs from Art. 56 of the Hague Regulations by specifically mentioning museums, though these are probably covered by the Hague Regulations anyway.
[28] A red circle containing a triple sphere on a white background.
[29] The predecessor of the Organization of American States.
[30] Boylan, *Review*, p. 30, states that only Mexico has prepared such a list.

time was plus or minus five kilometres, no part of the city was safe from attacks directed at the docks.[31] Even places like Peckham suffered badly from attacks directed at the docks. The British bombing of Lübeck resulted in reprisal attacks, known as the Baedeker raids, on English cathedral cities.[32] The allied bombing very late in the war of Nuremberg on 2 January 1945 and of Dresden on 13–14 February 1945 resulted in the destruction of irreplaceable cultural property.[33]

The bombing of towns like Dresden and Hamburg is very well documented, but they are only examples of the extensive damage to cultural centres in Germany during the war. Another example is that of Brunswick, which had aspirations to be the cultural capital of Lower Saxony. Brunswick had to endure forty bombing raids between August 1940 and March 1945. Of these the most severe were those which started in 1944 and culminated in the raid of 14–15 October 1944, when 90 per cent of the historic town centre was destroyed. It included the cathedral and most of the medieval churches, the ancient castle, the ducal palace, guild houses and no fewer than 800 timbered houses. A town whose appearance had hardly changed since the fifteenth century was reduced to ruins.[34]

On the other hand, examples can be given of care being taken to protect important cultural property, especially during the campaign in Italy in 1943–44. The allied commander-in-chief, General Eisenhower, sent out an order to all allied commanders requiring them to respect cultural monuments so far as war allowed, saying that he did not want military necessity to cloak slackness or indifference and requiring commanders to determine the location of cultural property through the allied military government.[35] From 1944 the allies had cultural advisers on their staff to assist in identifying property to be protected.[36] On 19 June 1944 all military installations were removed from Florence by order of the German authorities and the historic centre was not permitted to be used by military transport.[37]

The international military tribunal at Nuremberg dealt with the systematic plunder of works of art in occupied territory.[38] The only war crimes trial relating to cultural property seems to have been the case of Lingenfelder,[39] who was convicted by a French tribunal of the wanton destruction of public monuments.

[31] Boylan, *Review*, p. 35.

[32] *Ibid.*

[33] Germany, *Der Schutz*, p. 10.

[34] R. Moderhack, *Braunschweig—das Bild der Stadt in 900 Jahren*, vol. 1, Städtisches Museum Braunschweig, 1985, pp. 101–3.

[35] See Parks, Air war, p. 61. For a discussion of the attack on Monte Cassino, see chapter 3.

[36] Boylan, *Review*, p. 37.

[37] Germany, *Der Schutz*, para. 906.

[38] Trial of the Major War Criminals before the International Military Tribunal, Nuremberg, 1948, vol. XXII, p. 481 onwards.

[39] IX WCR 67. The IG Farben case (X WCR 1) was concerned with the plunder of public and private property.

Cultural property

Cultural Convention[40]

In the light of experience in the Second World War, attempts were made to improve the protection of cultural objects, hence the Hague Convention of 1954 on the Protection of Cultural Property in the Event of Armed Conflict (the Cultural Convention). This places an equal obligation on defenders and attackers by requiring states party to refrain from uses of cultural property that would expose it to danger in armed conflict and to refrain from acts of hostility against cultural property.[41]

The United Kingdom and most English-speaking countries are not parties to the Cultural Convention.[42] Most continental European countries are parties to the convention and within the NATO framework British forces may be fighting on the territory of a contracting party and should understand the principles of the convention.[43]

Although the obligation to protect cultural property is a requirement of customary law, it is not true to say that the Cultural Convention is part of customary law.[44] It may well be that the requirement to respect cultural property (along with all civilian property) is a principle of customary law, but by no stretch of the imagination can all the detailed provisions of the Cultural Convention be regarded as customary law.

Scope of application

The Cultural Convention contains an article equivalent to common Art. 2 of the Geneva Conventions which applies the convention to wars and armed conflicts between the high contracting parties and to the occupation of the territory of one party by the forces of another.[45] The provisions of the Cultural Convention that deal with the protection of cultural property must also be respected in civil war.[46] Parties are required to take measures in peacetime to protect cultural property against risks foreseeable in the event of an armed conflict.[47] This would

[40] An important new work on the Convention is J. Toman, *La Protection des biens culturels en cas de conflit armé*, UNESCO, 1994. Unfortunately, it reached the writer after he had revised this chapter for publication.

[41] Art. 4, para. 1.

[42] Although the United States is not a party because of objections by the Joint Chiefs of Staff, the US army has included the convention in its doctrine and the details of the convention are taught in law of war courses—Parks, Air war, p. 59.

[43] The *Manual of Military Law* contains no narrative chapters dealing specifically with cultural property but does contain the text of the Cultural Convention.

[44] Boylan, *Review*, pp. 7, 104, misquotes the DOD Report, United States, *Conduct of the Persian Gulf War*, Department of Defense final report to Congress, April 1992.

[45] Art. 18.

[46] Art. 19.

[47] Art. 3.

include identifying property, earmarking shelters, allocating transport and personnel[48] and giving appropriate instructions in military regulations.[49] Even after the end of hostilities parties to the Protocol to the Cultural Convention (the Cultural Protocol) have a residual obligation to return cultural property removed from occupied territory.

Definition

Cultural property is defined as 'movable or immovable property of great importance to the cultural heritage of every people', and includes:

monuments of architecture, art or history, whether religious or secular; archaeological sites; groups of buildings which, as a whole, are of historical or artistic interest; works of art; manuscripts, books and other objects of artistic, historical or archaeological interest; as well as scientific collections and important collections of books or archives or of reproductions of the property defined above.

The term also covers buildings in which such objects are collected and refuges intended to shelter such property during armed conflict.[50] It also extends to cultural centres,[51] being those containing a large amount of cultural property or the buildings housing it, and transports.

It is immediately apparent that the definition in the Cultural Convention is both wider and narrower in scope than that of the Hague Regulations. While the categories of property are wider, they do not include charitable and educational institutions (unless of historic, etc., importance). Furthermore, the property must be of significance going beyond national boundaries. It must be property of great importance to the cultural heritage of every people. This may involve delicate decisions about whether, for example, an original manuscript by a minor composer, say Spohr, was of great importance to the cultural heritage of every people, perhaps not. The situation would be different if it were an original manuscript by one of the great composers, say Schubert.

Ordinary protection

The scope of ordinary protection is to be found in Art. 4, where the parties agree to refrain from:

1. Using cultural property, its immediate surroundings and appliances for its protection for purposes which are likely to expose it to damage in the event of armed conflict.

---

[48] Germany, *Der Schutz*, p. 31.
[49] Art. 7, para. 1.
[50] Art. 1.
[51] According to Rousseau, *Le Droit des conflits armés*, p. 133, this would include the historic parts of certain towns such as Florence, Venice, Ghent, Cambridge and Carcassonne. As the United Kingdom is not a party to the Cultural Convention, Cambridge can be included only as an indication of the sort of cultural centres that are covered by the convention.

2. Acts of hostility directed against cultural property.

3. Reprisals against cultural property, even if the enemy has unlawfully attacked cultural property.

This prohibition of reprisals is, presumably, based on the notion that cultural property is the common heritage of mankind and must be preserved at all costs. It is a prohibition that cannot be waived on grounds of military necessity. Military necessity can never justify recourse to reprisals, since reprisals are not actions taken in the conduct of military operations, they are actions taken to redress violations of the law of war. In any event, Art. 4.2 of the Cultural Convention, which allows waiver of protection of cultural property, refers only to the general protection of that property under Art. 4.1, not to the protection from reprisals in Art. 4.4.[52]

The parties are obliged to prevent theft, pillage, misappropriation and acts of vandalism against cultural property[53] and undertake to respect cultural property in their own territory and in the territory of another party, especially in occupied territory.[54]

Cultural property normally displays the single protective emblem.[55] According to Carcione[56] protective emblems are not displayed on Italian cultural monuments, unlike those in Belgium.[57]

Waiver of protection. Ordinary protection can be waived, by defender or attacker, only in cases of imperative military necessity by a commander at whatever level.[58] The meaning of 'military commander' in this context must be the person who gives the order for the attack upon the cultural property in question. In the ordinary course, fire should not be directed at protected property in any event. There is, however, no provision of the convention dealing with incidental damage. This must mean that, while precautions must be taken to prevent incidental damage in the usual way, incidental damage to protected property is not a breach of the convention, subject to the rule of proportionality.[59] Imperative military necessity permitting waiver implies that there is no other way the military aim can be achieved than by attacking the protected property. If, for example, enemy snipers are operating from protected property, it may be possible simply to bypass that property. The German manual[60] gives two

[52] See also F. J. Hampson, Belligerent reprisals and the 1977 Protocols, (1988) 37 *International and Comparative Law Quarterly*, at p. 826.

[53] Germany, *Der Schutz*, p. 17, refers to the vandalism involved in the breaking of the vases in a valuable collection at Schloß Stolpe by Soviet troops in May 1945.

[54] For occupied territory, see Art. 5.

[55] Art. 17, para. 2.

[56] M. M. Carcione, Protection des biens culturels en cas de conflit armé, International Institute of Humanitarian Law, September 1991 (sixteenth Round Table).

[57] Or, as the writer has seen, in Austria and Germany.

[58] Art. 4, para. 2.

[59] A commander waiving protection would still be bound by the provisions of Protocol I, e.g. Art. 51, para. 5(b).

[60] Germany, *Der Schutz*, p. 16.

examples of imperative military necessity permitting the destruction or military use of cultural property:

1. A cultural bridge which is the only means of access across a river for enemy forces.

2. An artillery position close to cultural property if that is the only position from which an enemy stronghold dominating the battlefield can be attacked.

Special protection

The parties to the Cultural Convention agree in respect of specially protected property to refrain from:

1. Any act of hostility directed against such property.

2. Any use of such property or its surroundings for military purposes.[61]

Contrasting ordinary and special protection reveals certain anomalies in the drafting of the convention. In the case of specially protected property there is no mention of appliances for the protection of cultural property, of reprisals or of protection from theft and so on. It can only be assumed that the larger category includes the smaller and that the provisions of Art. 4 apply to all cultural property.[62] If that construction is correct, there seems little point in having a separate article dealing with the immunity of specially protected property.

Specially protected property falls into one of three categories:

1. Refuges for sheltering cultural property such as the Oberrieder Stollen in the Breisgau district of the Black Forest.[63]

2. Centres containing monuments. The Vatican City has been so registered, but it is the only one.[64]

3. Immovable cultural property of very great importance. No property in this category has been registered.[65]

It bears a triple protected emblem and is registered in an international register of cultural property under special protection. It has to be at an adequate distance from potential military objectives,[66] unless it is in a bomb-proof shelter, and must not be used for military purposes.[67] A cultural centre is deemed to be used for military purposes if it is used for the movement, even the transit, of military per-

[61] Art. 9.

[62] That is the position taken in Germany, *Der Schutz*, p. 20.

[63] Germany, *Der Schutz*, para. 912. The Netherlands has registered six such shelters (on 12 November 1969) and Austria one—Boylan, *Review*, p. 77.

[64] Carcione, Protection de biens culturels. An application by Cambodia to register Angkor Wat was suspended because of objections from countries that did not recognize the regime in Cambodia—Boylan, *Review*, pp. 79–80.

[65] Boylan, *Review*, p. 79. He complains, at p. 17, that this category does not include the world's great museums. They would, of course, be protected by the Hague Regulations and Protocol I in any event.

[66] For example, large industrial centres, aerodromes. broadcasting stations, defence establishments, ports, important railway stations or main lines of communication—see Art. 8, para. 1(a).

[67] Art. 8.

sonnel or supplies, activities directly concerned with military operations, the sta-
tioning of military personnel or the production of war material. The guarding of
cultural property by specially appointed 'armed custodians' or by ordinary police
officers does not amount to military use.[68] The position of the armed custodian who
kills a member of an occupying force who is smashing priceless vases is rather
awkward. It is submitted that, at a trial by the occupying power for murder, the
tribunal would have to consider the circumstances, the heat of the moment and
whether the custodian could reasonably have resorted to other methods to protect the property in his care. Unlike medical installations, which can be guarded
by military personnel, it does seem that cultural property may not be guarded by
military personnel even if assigned to civil defence duties, since, according to
Protocol I, Art. 61, guarding cultural property is not a civil defence task.[69] Even
when cultural property is close to a military objective, special protection can still
be afforded if an undertaking is given not to use that objective.[70]

Boylan points out that some states are reluctant to register shelters, as they
regard the information as secret. He quotes the case of Vukovar, where a shelter
for cultural property was identified from official records and the contents were
removed to Belgrade.[71]

Waiver of protection. Immunity can be waived in exceptional cases of unavoidable military necessity by an officer commanding a force the equivalent
of a division or larger.[72] Whenever circumstances permit, the enemy are to be
informed a reasonable time in advance of the decision to withdraw immunity.[73]
While this provision applies to both attackers and defenders, it is difficult to
imagine cases where attacking commanders will admit that circumstances permit a warning to be given, at least not where the element of surprise is an
important factor in the success of the attack. In one case, though, prior notification has to be given, and that is where immunity is to be withdrawn because
of the violation of the protection of cultural property by the enemy.[74] This is
most likely to occur where the enemy is using specially protected property for
military purposes. Although at first sight a decision to waive the immunity of
very important cultural property can be made at a relatively low level of command, in practice it is likely that approval at government level will be needed
because of the requirement to report in writing to the commissioner-general for
cultural property as to why immunity is being withdrawn.[75] It is submitted that
there is no difference between imperative and unavoidable military necessity.

[68] Art. 8, para. 4.
[69] Art. 8, para. 3.
[70] Art. 8, para. 5. In the case of ports, railway stations and aerodromes, traffic is to be diverted
elsewhere.
[71] Boylan, *Review*, p. 79.
[72] Art. 11, para. 2. Parks, Air war, p. 62, reminds us that this is a lower level than that at which
the decision to bomb Monte Cassino was taken.
[73] Art. 11, para. 2.
[74] Art. 11, para. 1.
[75] Art. 11, para. 3.

Rousseau refers to the insistence of the 'Anglo-Saxon' states that there should be this reservation for military necessity which was passed by twenty-two votes to eight with eight abstentions.[76] Carcione[77] goes further and says that the threat by the 'Anglo-Saxon' states not to ratify the convention unless provision were made for military necessity turned out to be a pretext.

Whenever circumstances permit, the enemy must be notified of the intention to withdraw immunity from specially protected property and a written report giving the reasons for doing so must be delivered to the commissioner-general for cultural property.

Occupation

In addition to the other rules on the protection of cultural property, when occupying enemy territory the occupying forces are obliged to support the authorities of the occupied territory in protecting cultural property and provide assistance where those authorities are unable to take measures to preserve cultural property. There is even an obligation on parties to the convention to remind recognized resistance movements of their obligation to respect cultural property.[78] The German manual refers to textbook action by Israeli forces when they occupied Sinai in 1956–57 in assisting in the running of the monastery of St Katharine, looking after visitors, supplying the monks with food and investigating an attempted break-in to the treasury of the monastery church.[79] The Cultural Protocol requires parties, on pain of payment of an indemnity, to prevent the exportation of cultural property from territory they occupy.[80] Other parties are required to preserve and return at the end of hostilities property so exported. It may not be retained as war reparations.

Transports

The Cultural Convention and Cultural Regulations contain detailed provisions for the transport of cultural property. Basically there are two possibilities:[81]

---

[76]Rousseau, *Le Droit des conflits armés*, p. 133; Alexandrow refers to the unwillingness of the United States, Great Britain and 'other imperialist states' to provide radical solutions for the protection of cultural property—E. Alexandrow, *International Legal Protection of Cultural Property*, Sofia Press, 1979, p. 57.

[77]Carcione, Protection de biens culturels.

[78]Art. 5.

[79]Germany, *Der Schutz*, p. 21. The suggestion by Boylan, *Review*, p. 58, that the authorities in the various parts of the former Yugoslavia should control the various fighting factions would apply only in the case of occupation of territory.

[80]The Hague Regulations and Protocol I do not contain a corresponding provision, but the expropriation and export of cultural property may still be a war crime and any 'consent' obtained by threats a nullity, see the IG Farben and Krupp trials, X WCR 1 and 69, abstracted at XV WCR 125–30.

[81]And it matters not whether the property transported is under ordinary or special protection—Germany, *Der Schutz*, p. 23.

1. Special protection where specific arrangements have been made with the commissioner-general for cultural property.[82] In that case the distinctive emblem is to be displayed, attacks against such transports are prohibited and there is no waiver for military necessity.

2. Urgent cases where there is not time to make these arrangements. Notification should, so far as possible, be made to opposing parties and the distinctive emblem may be displayed within, but not outside,[83] the territory of the state arranging the movement. Other states are required to take 'so far as possible, the necessary precautions to avoid acts of hostilities directed against the transport . . . displaying the distinctive emblem'.[84]

The distinctive emblem to be displayed in the case of all transports is that applicable to immovable cultural property under special protection.[85] That makes it difficult to distinguish transports under special protection and transports in urgent cases.[86]

Personnel

Persons engaged in the protection of cultural property have a status rather like that of military medical personnel: they must be respected, and if they fall into the hands of the enemy they must be allowed to continue their cultural duties if the property for which they are responsible also falls into enemy hands.[87] They will, of course, be protected by the Prisoner of War Convention if they are members of the armed forces or by the Civilian Convention if they are civilians. They carry a special identity card and wear a special armband.[88]

Protective emblem

The distinctive emblem is a blue and white shield displayed singly for property under ordinary protection and cultural personnel, or as a group of three shields (the triple emblem) for immovable property under special protection, transports and refuges.[89]

Carcione[90] criticizes the regime of the convention in that it is left to the discretion of the parties to the convention whether to display the protective

---

[82] Art. 12; and Art. 17 of the Cultural Regulations. The latter sets out the detailed provisions for the application to the commissioner and the movement of property.

[83] Art. 31, para. 1, states that a transport conveying cultural property to the territory of another country may not display the distinctive emblem unless immunity has been expressly granted to it. This seems to be a reference to the special immunity under Art. 12.

[84] Art. 13, para. 2.

[85] That is, the triple emblem, see below, Arts. 16–17.

[86] Germany, *Der Schutz*, p. 25.

[87] Art. 15.

[88] Reg. 21 of the Cultural Regulations.

[89] Art. 17.

[90] Carcione, Protection de biens culturels.

emblem (except in the case of specially protected property) and then only during armed conflicts. This leads to insufficient knowledge of the emblem. Further confusion is caused by the fact that different emblems are prescribed by the Hague Regulations and the Roerich Pact. He feels that the display of the emblem on specially protected property in peacetime should be mandatory, and that display[91] of the emblem on property under ordinary protection should be actively encouraged.[92] This would be an aid to recognition of the emblem.

Supervision

It is envisaged that the convention will be applied with the assistance of the protecting powers and of UNESCO.[93] Parties are to nominate to the Director-General of UNESCO persons qualified to act as commissioner-general for cultural property. Once an armed conflict occurs, a commissioner-general is to be accredited to each party to the conflict by agreement between the recipient party and the protecting powers. In the absence of agreement, the President of the International Court of Justice may arbitrate. If there is no protecting power, the commissioner-general exercises its functions. The parties to the conflict are also to appoint representatives for cultural property who act as a liaison between the commissioner-general and the authorities of the state appointing him[94] and the protecting powers are to appoint delegates.[95]

This elaborate structure seems to suffer the weakness that it depends for its efficacy on the efforts of the protecting powers. So far as the writer is aware, no protecting powers have been appointed for any purposes in recent conflicts,[96] certainly not by the United Kingdom during the Gulf War of 1990–91. It is not clear what is to happen in the absence of protecting powers, especially where the parties to the conflict, as is likely, have broken off diplomatic relations and are not in communication with each other. Perhaps the Director-General of UNESCO could lend his good offices in persuading the parties to accept his proposals for commissioners-general.[97]

As Carcione[98] has stated, unlike the Geneva Conventions, which depend to a large extent on the activities of the ICRC and the national Red Cross societies to ensure compliance by the parties, the Cultural Convention gives only a minor role to an outside supervision agency. The parties may turn to UNESCO for assistance but UNESCO is not given a positive role in the protection of cultural

[91] It must be capable of being seen to afford protection.
[92] Boylan, *Review*, p. 85, is of the same opinion.
[93] Arts. 22–3.
[94] Germany, *Der Schutz*, p. 28.
[95] Cultural Regulations, Regs. 1–6.
[96] Boylan, *Review*, p. 85, mentions the absence of protecting powers in the Iran-Iraq conflict of the 1980s and the Yugoslav conflict of 1990 onwards.
[97] Boylan, *Review*, p. 87, also complains about serious problems of appointing commissioners-general where there are no protecting powers.
[98] Carcione, Protection de biens culturels.

property,[99] save for making proposals,[100] or in the dissemination of information about the convention.[101] Reports are submitted to UNESCO by parties about the steps they have taken to comply with the convention[102] and UNESCO may, and must if one-fifth of the parties so request, convene meetings of the parties to discuss the implementation of and amendments to the convention.[103]

Almost in despair, Carcione calls for a 'Red Cross for cultural property'. A study of the feasibility of such a proposal is being undertaken by the International Council for Museums and Sites. It is too early to say whether anything will come of this proposal, but the precedent of the ICRC seems to indicate that states are more willing to deal with a non-governmental body because it does not necessarily mean official recognition that a particular state of affairs exists. It would certainly be helpful to have a body that is more pro-active than the role assigned to UNESCO under the Cultural Convention. However, it is counterproductive to have a multiplicity of bodies active in the same field. UNESCO already has a leading role and it might be better to strengthen its position than introduce something new. Financial considerations will probably militate against a new organization, in any event.

Enforcement

It is left to the parties to introduce penal legislation to punish breaches of the convention.[104] Reprisals against cultural property are prohibited.[105]

Duty of defenders

The Cultural Convention, like the Hague Regulations, imposes a duty on defenders, as well as on attackers. They must, so far as possible, avoid siting shelters for specially protected cultural property near potential military targets,[106] avoid the use of cultural property and its surroundings for military purposes[107] and may unilaterally declare a waiver of use for military purposes of what might otherwise be military objectives in the vicinity.[108] Of course, effective protection of cultural property involves much more than compliance with the treaty obligations. It requires comprehensive listing of property, co-ordination between ministries, local government and the armed forces, plans for the protection of

[99] Art. 23.
[100] According to Boylan, *Review*, p. 88, the Director-General of UNESCO has intervened to good effect on several occasions in relation to Cyprus (1972) and Tyre (1980) and, more recently, Dubrovnik.
[101] Art. 25.
[102] Art. 26.
[103] Art. 27.
[104] Art. 28.
[105] Art. 4, para. 4.
[106] Art. 8.
[107] Art. 4. That would preclude the placing of military aircraft near to cultural property.
[108] Art. 8, para. 5.

cultural property in peacetime, including establishing refuges, duplicating important archives and the protection of electronic data.[109]

Measures for compliance

It is instructive to see what measures states party have taken to implement the
Cultural Convention. Under Art. 26 parties are required to submit a report of
such measures to UNESCO every four years.[110]

An example is Germany.[111] The convention entered into force for Germany
on 11 November 1967 and the text was published in the *Federal Law Gazette*.
A German translation of the text was distributed to the competent federal, state
and local authorities, schools, universities, museums, art galleries, churches and
the press in 1966 and again in 1973. The text was also published in military
regulations, reinforced by leaflets and posters and the inclusion of the subject
in military training programmes and the production in 1964 of a training
pamphlet and other training aids. In 1975 the Federal Ministry of the Interior
published a first list of cultural property worthy of protection and a map has
been produced showing all important immovable cultural property in Germany.
A commissioner-general for cultural property has been appointed and steps
have been taken to include the following offences in criminal law:

1. Damaging or pillaging cultural property.
2. Misuse of and damage to the protective emblem.
3. Obstruction, violence, insults and threats to those responsible for the protection of cultural property.

The Netherlands have comprehensive arrangements for the protection of cultural property in place in peacetime, including inter-ministerial co-operation and
the listing of cultural property. Of interest to the armed forces in this respect is
the appointment of army reserve officers as cultural protection officers whose
role is to prevent damage to or theft of cultural property or its use for military
purposes.[112]

Sending and receiving states

What is the position of the troops of a sending state that is not party to the
Cultural Convention on the territory of a receiving state that is a party? That is
the situation in respect of British troops assigned to NATO on German soil.

[109] See Boylan, *Review*, p. 72.
[110] Submission of reports has been somewhat erratic. Some states have submitted regular reports
(Germany six, Poland five) but thirty-nine states have submitted none—Boylan, *Review*, p. 89.
[111] Report of the Federal Republic of Germany concerning the execution of the Cultural Convention, Bonn, September 1977, published in *Military Law and Law of War Review*, 1978, vol. 4,
p. 718.
[112] Boylan, *Review*, p. 68.

Under Art. II of the NATO Status of Forces Agreement[113] it is the duty of the force 'to respect the laws of the receiving state'. In Germany the Cultural Convention is part of German law, following ratification and approval by the federal parliament. It cannot, of course, be binding on states not party, but the duty to respect German law does place an obligation on the troops of the sending state to respect the principles of the Cultural Convention when planning military deployments and operations on German soil. It would be incumbent on them to respect any lists of cultural property supplied by the German authorities.

Discussion

Carcione contrasts the differences in definition between the broad concept of cultural property in the preamble, the main definition in Art. 1, which speaks of property of 'great importance', and Art. 8, dealing with special protection, which refers to property of 'very great importance', and considers that these differences may give rise to difficulties of interpretation on the part of military commanders. This is especially true of property under ordinary protection, where the display of the protective emblem is not mandatory.

Carcione is also very critical of the language of the convention. He points out that Art. 8, para. 1, uses terms which give rise to fine shades of interpretation, such as: cultural property 'of very great importance', 'important' military objectives and, in his words, the almost grotesque railway station of 'relative importance'. Then the articles permitting derogation on grounds of military necessity are different. Art. 4 (property under ordinary protection) speaks of 'military necessity' while Art. 11 (property under special protection) speaks of 'exceptional cases of unavoidable military necessity'. It seems absurd to have shades of military necessity. He is of the opinion that the special rules of the convention do not affect the normal application of the principle of military necessity. This must be because of the rather cavalier manner in which the term is used in the Cultural Convention. It should not affect the way the term is understood outside the context of the Cultural Convention. Carcione thinks that much is left to the good sense and linguistic skill of commanders. He wonders whether the movement of military units or supplies in the vicinity of specially protected property would amount to a violation of Art. 9, which requires the high contracting parties to refrain from using the property or its surroundings for military purposes. This is because Art. 8, para. 3, specifically states that the movement of military personnel or material through a cultural centre would be regarded as using it for military purposes. The answer would depend on whether one applied a strict construction of the text or tried to implement the spirit of the convention.

[113] Agreement regarding the Status of Forces of Parties to the North Atlantic Treaty, London, 1951, UK Treaty Series No. 3 (1955), Cmd. 9363 (HMSO).

A further curiosity, according to Carcione, is Art. 8, para. 2, which makes a violation of the protection of specially protected property the standard by which it is decided whether protection can be afforded!

The main advantage of the Cultural Convention is not so much the protection it affords, which can be waived by officers at a relatively low level, as the discipline it imposes on states in peacetime with regard to the identification, marking, registration and siting of cultural property.

Under Arts. 27 and 39 of the convention meetings of the parties can be arranged and proposals made for amendment but, although such a meeting was called by UNESCO in 1984, nothing much has happened,[114] despite a further meeting arranged by the Dutch government in 1993.

Cultural property and places of worship

Protocol I

Protocol I also prohibits acts of hostility against, or the use in support of the military effort of, or reprisals against 'historical monuments, works of art or places of worship which constitute the cultural or spiritual heritage of peoples'.[115] In one sense Protocol I is stricter than the Hague Regulations. It prohibits acts of hostility against cultural property, while the earlier rule was more exhortatory in requiring steps to be taken, so far as possible, to spare cultural objects. On the other hand, Protocol I applies only to a limited class of objects: those constituting the cultural or spiritual heritage of peoples.[116]

Protocol I, while prohibiting the use of cultural property in support of the military effort, is also stricter in not repeating the principle of customary law, confirmed in the Cultural Convention, that protected property used for military purposes loses its immunity. It is not clear whether that was thought so obvious as not to require stating or whether a conscious decision was made to afford protection to cultural property at all times. The summary records throw no light on the matter, apart from an oblique reference by Brigadier-General Wolfe of Canada to the corresponding provision of draft Protocol II in which he said (in reported speech): 'to the extent that the Hague Convention provided certain exceptions, his delegation interpreted that reference as giving those exceptions validity in the Protocol'.[117] Some states decided to put the matter beyond doubt

---

[114] Carcione, Protection de biens culturels.

[115] Protocol I, Art. 53.

[116] See F. Kalshoven, Reaffirmation and development of international humanitarian law, *Netherlands Yearbook of International Law*, 1978, p. 124. The Swiss understanding is that the protocol applies to property of considerable historical value and of international importance. The report of the Swiss Federal Council, *Botschaft über die Zusatzprotokolle zu den Genfer Abkommen*, 1981, put it as follows: *Es handelt sich folglich um Objekte mit erheblichem, historischem Wert, deren Bedeutung über den lokalen oder nationalen Rahmen hinausgeht.*

[117] Official Records of the CDDH, vol. XV, Swiss Federal Political Department, 1978, p. 110.

by making statements on ratification along the lines of the statement by Italy that 'if and for so long as the objectives[118] protected by article 53 are unlawfully used for military purposes, they will thereby lose protection'.[119] Commentators would avoid confusing people if they stopped saying 'objective' when they mean 'object' and, as so often in the media during the Gulf War of 1990–91, 'civilian target' when 'civilian object' is meant.

Further, Protocol I does away with the derogation for military necessity to be found in the Cultural Convention. This is surprising, given the insistence of the English-speaking states on the inclusion of such a derogation in the Cultural Convention. Was it an oversight, or have the attitudes of those states changed?[120] The answer may be that there is no need to attack cultural objects unless they are used by the enemy for military purposes. In the words of Parks,[121] the 'burden essentially shifted entirely to the attacker despite clear evidence that many nations in the intervening years regularly used hospitals, cultural objects, civilian objects and the civilian population to shield lawful targets from attack'.

Protocol I does not specify any protective emblems for cultural property.[122] However, making clearly recognized cultural property the object of an attack is a grave breach of Protocol I if the property is subject to special protection (for example, under the auspices of a competent international organization), extensive destruction is caused and the object is not in the immediate proximity of a military objective.[123]

If a monument or work of art is marked with the protective emblem under the Cultural Convention, that must be regarded as *prima facie* evidence that it may also be protected under the Hague Regulations or under Protocol I and puts a military commander on notice. It would be useful for military planners to be given details of property listed under the World Heritage Convention of 1972.[124]

However, the precise nature of the property which is protected defies analysis.[125] The Hague Regulations,[126] at least in sieges and bombardment, cover in very general language 'buildings dedicated to religion, art, science' and 'historic monuments', provided they are not used for military purposes. The Cultural

---

[118] *Sic.*

[119] See A. Roberts and R. Guelff, *Documents on the Laws of War*, 2nd ed., Clarendon Press, 1989, p. 465. The legal adviser to the Directorate at the ICRC comments that 'so long as it remains clear that the limits set by articles 48 *et seq.* of Protocol I remain applicable, in particular the rule of proportionality, it is difficult to object to the Dutch and Italian reservation'—H. P. Gasser, Some legal issues concerning ratification of the 1977 Geneva Protocols, in M. A. Meyer (ed.), *Armed Conflict and the New Law*, British Institute of International and Comparative Law, 1989, p. 91.

[120] Again, the summary records of the CDDH, vols XIV and XV, do not provide illumination.

[121] Parks, Air war, p. 62.

[122] Kalshoven, Reaffirmation, p. 125.

[123] Protocol I, Arts. 53 and 85, para. 4(d).

[124] According to Boylan, *Review*, p. 110, some 378 sites and monuments have been listed.

[125] Boylan, *Review*, p. 50, also complains that there are considerable variations in the wording used for identical categories of property in twelve UNESCO texts.

[126] Art. 27.

Convention[127] deals with property 'of great importance to the cultural heritage of every people'. Protocol I[128] protects 'historic monuments, works of art or places of worship which constitute the cultural or spiritual heritage of peoples'. Detter de Lupis[129] refers to the discussions at the CDDH as to whether all churches were protected under Protocol I or only those which constitute the cultural heritage of peoples and concludes, rather obviously, that Protocol I implies the more limited protection.[130] Nevertheless, the more general protection of churches is provided by the Hague Regulations, which reflect customary international law.[131] The result may be that, if the United Kingdom were a party to Protocol I, St Nicholas' Church, Shepperton, would have the limited protection in sieges and bombardments of the Hague Regulations while Westminster Abbey would have the more general protection of Protocol I.

Reprisals against the important cultural property protected by Protocol I are prohibited. That is not to say that reprisals may be taken against other cultural property, because Protocol I prohibits reprisals against civilian objects.[132]

Discussion

It seems at first sight that an officer who took advantage of the Cultural Convention and withdrew protection would be caught by Protocol I.[133] However, Solf considered that, since Protocol I is expressed to be without prejudice to the Cultural Convention and all other relevant instruments, 'it must be inferred that loss of . . . protection . . . is an appropriate defensive (*sic*) measure . . . if the protected property is used to support the military effort', provided, of course, that it satisfies the test of a military objective.[134] The suggestion is made by the ICRC that 'in case of a contradiction between [Protocol I] and a rule of the [Cultural] Convention, the latter is applicable'.[135] Does this mean that the protection of Protocol I goes no further than the Cultural Convention? That would be a surprising result, given the clear language of the former. Here the ICRC seem contradictory in stating that the obligation under Protocol I is 'stricter than that imposed by the . . . Hague Convention since it does not provide for any derogation even where military necessity imperatively requires such a waiver'.[136] Even allowing for the fairly elastic interpretation of international agreements, the following statement of the ICRC seems strange at first sight: 'when parties to the

---

[127] Art. 1.
[128] Art. 53.
[129] I. Detter de Lupis, *The Law of War*, Cambridge University Press, 1987, p. 250.
[130] See also M. Bothe, K. J. Partsch and W. Solf, *New Rules for the Victims of Armed Conflicts*, Martinus Nijhoff, 1982, p. 332.
[131] *Ibid.*, p. 329. See the Trial of the Major War Criminals, vol. XXII, p. 497.
[132] Arts. 52, para. 1, and 53, sub-para. (c).
[133] Art. 53.
[134] Bothe *et al.*, *New Rules*, pp. 332–3.
[135] ICRC *Commentary*, para. 2046.
[136] *Ibid.*, para. 2072.

Protocol are also parties to the [Cultural] Convention . . . , these derogations continue to apply . . . If one of them is a party to the Protocol and not to the [Cultural] Convention, no derogation is possible.' Can it be that the obligations of a party to Protocol I vary according to whether or not it is also a party to the Cultural Convention? This may be explained by the contractual nature of international agreements and the provisions of Art. 30 of the Vienna Convention on the Law of Treaties.[137] The United Kingdom would be well advised either to ratify the Cultural Convention before ratifying Protocol I or to make an appropriate reservation on ratifying Protocol I.

Another important difference between Protocol I and the Cultural Convention is the omission in the former of the loss of protection where cultural property is used by the enemy for military purposes, the classic example being the cathedral tower being used as an observation post. The United Kingdom made a statement on signature of Protocol I that if cultural objects are 'unlawfully used for military purposes they will thereby lose protection from attacks directed against such unlawful military uses'. Similar statements were made on ratification by Italy and the Netherlands.[138] It seems that the ICRC is of the opinion that the United Kingdom approach is admissible,[139] although there is nothing in the text of Protocol I that would appear to support it, so it must be based on the context of the negotiations. On the other hand, Germany seems prepared to accept the restrictions appearing on the face of Protocol I, since no statement on this point was made on ratification, yet the German manual[140] states that 'cultural property which the enemy uses for military purposes shall also be spared so far as possible'. It may be that the German forces are expected to be fighting on their own territory, so the German perspective may be different from that of the United Kingdom, whose forces have historically fought on the territory of other states.

Finally, Solf considered that the property qualifying for protection under Protocol I is substantially the same as that qualifying for special protection under the Cultural Convention[141] and that the words 'acts of hostility' rather than 'attacks' would include the demolition of a cultural object,[142] for example, by defenders wanting to clear a field of fire.

The cultural bridge referred to earlier in this chapter poses something of a conundrum for the defenders who cannot attack it until the enemy uses it. So how do they deny the enemy passage across the river? One answer might be to lay charges and put up warning signs, but to blow up the bridge only if the enemy actually starts to cross it.

---

[137] See paras. 2 and 4 of that article.
[138] Roberts and Guelff, *Documents*, pp. 465–6.
[139] ICRC *Commentary*, paras. 2072, 2079.
[140] Germany, *Der Schutz*, para. 906.
[141] Bothe *et al.*, *New Rules*, p. 333.
[142] *Ibid.*

The Gulf War of 1990–91

Iraq contains some of the earliest monuments of civilization, including Ur of the Chaldees, Uruk and Nippur. The mounds which remain of ancient cities are features in the desert that might, if they were not cultural sites, be regarded as military objectives in giving forces a vantage point. There was evidence to suggest that Iraq had adopted a policy of placing military objectives close to archaeological sites to protect the former from attack.[143] One account refers to the allied bombing of Iraqi military aircraft shelters at Tallil air base in southern Iraq and in camouflaged positions on roads near the base. They were all destroyed by precision attacks although they were in sight of the ziggurat of Ur, an important cultural monument.[144] But it was clear that the allies had target lists[145] and that although Iraqi aircraft, command posts and troops had been placed near civilian areas, including schools and religious sites, the allies would avoid bombing anything of religious significance. A photograph in *The Independent*[146] above an article by Geoffrey Best shows damage to a structure close to a mosque which is intact.

Although the allied target lists for the bombing campaign were restricted to military objectives and, therefore, excluded cultural property, it is alleged that the lists did include two items of a cultural nature, though probably not amounting to cultural property in the sense of the common heritage of mankind, one being a statue of Saddam Hussein in Baghdad and the other an Iraqi war memorial, and that both were removed from the list by the US Secretary of Defence.[147] The writer has not been able to verify this allegation from officially published sources, but if it is taken as a hypothetical question the removal of such items from the target list would seem correct.

The US Department of Defense report to Congress[148] contains information about the steps taken by the allies to protect cultural property. Lists were drawn up of historical, archaeological and religious installations in Iraq and Kuwait that were not to be targeted. Analysts were also asked to look at a six-mile radius around listed targets for schools, hospitals and mosques which would necessitate special care in planning. The weapon systems, munitions, time of attack and direction of attack, desired impact point and level of effort were carefully planned.[149]

[143] DOD Report, p. 615. See also G. Hill, Conflict threatens ancient sites, *The Times*, 28 February 1991.
[144] B. Brown and D. Shukman, *All Necessary Means*, BBC Books, 1991, at p. 53.
[145] DOD Report, p. 100. See also M. Evans, Freedom of the sky, *The Times*, 5 February 1991; Brown and Shukman, *All Necessary Means*, p. 16.
[146] 4 February 1991.
[147] T. Matthews *et al.*, The Secret History of the War, *Newsweek*, 18 March 1991, p. 20.
[148] DOD Report, p. 100.
[149] See also On International Policies and Procedures regarding the Protection of Nature and Cultural Resources during Times of War, 19 January 1993, published as an appendix to the *Review* of Boylan, p. 201.

Conclusions

The rules for the protection of cultural property are quite complicated and seem, at first sight, to be redundant because civilian property is immune from direct attack in any event. Nor is cultural property any less likely than other civilian property to be damaged as a side effect of attacks on military objectives in the vicinity. If movable, it may, of course, be attractive to the cultured looter, but looting is prohibited anyway.

What seems more important is a ban on the use of cultural property for military purposes so that there is no need to attack it, and this is provided by Protocol I, though there may be *rare* cases where it is essential to use such property for military purposes. The protection of the Cultural Convention can be waived relatively easily. The definition of cultural property defies analysis and there is, perhaps, a case for harmonizing the various treaty provisions dealing with cultural property, since different treaties provide different protection for different property.

The advantage of the special rules on cultural property is in making attacking commanders more aware of the existence of such property, particularly if it is marked, or contained in a published list which is available to him. Much more responsibility is, however, placed on the authorities of the defending state to compile and publish lists, to register property under special protection, to mark property, to establish refuges and arrange the transfer of cultural property in good time to those refuges, to have a policy of non-defended localities or demilitarized zones. This is a substantial undertaking which requires a lot of peacetime planning and preparation and the allocation of personnel and money. Like civil defence, however, it is unlikely to be allocated sufficient priority in the competition for resources.

The tendency of states not to appoint protecting powers undermines the efficacy of the Cultural Convention, and the Director-General of UNESCO may have to fill the vacuum by persuading the parties to the conflict to accept his proposals for commissioners-general and generally by becoming active in trying to protect cultural property in wartime.

Should a state not party to the Cultural Convention be contemplating ratification of Protocol I and wish to take advantage of the derogations permitted by the Convention, it may wish to ratify the convention first or enter an appropriate reservation on ratification of the protocol. A statement on ratification of Protocol I to the effect that cultural property loses its protection if it is used for military purposes would, in any event, be advisable.

6

Environmental protection

Introduction

Although the law of war has been mainly concerned with the protection of human life,[1] various principles of customary law can work towards the protection of the environment.[2] First, the principle that military operations are to be directed against the enemy armed forces[3] and military objectives. Secondly, that any damage or destruction caused in war must be dictated by military necessity[4] and not by some other motive, for example revenge or lust for destruction. There must be some reasonable connection between the destruction of property and the overcoming of the enemy forces.[5] Thirdly, the damage or destruction must be proportionate to the military gain sought.[6]

[1] It has been described as 'anthropocentric in scope and focus' by the Office of the Judge Advocate General, Canadian Forces, in a Note on the Current Law of Armed Conflict relevant to the Environment in Conventional Conflicts, Ottawa Conference of Experts, July 1991. P. Painchaud, in Environmental Weapons and the Gulf War, Ottawa Conference of Experts, makes the point that in the case of various attacks on dams, dykes and irrigation systems in the Sino-Japanese War, the Second World War and the Korean War the military planners did not consider the environmental consequences.

[2] The environment referred to in this chapter is the natural environment, not the man-shaped environment referred to by A. Roberts, Failures in protecting the environment, in P. J. Rowe, *The Gulf War 1990–91 in International and English Law*, Routledge, 1993, p. 121, though it includes areas cultivated by humans.

[3] The preamble to the St Petersburg Declaration of 1868.

[4] Hague Regulations 1907, Art. 23(g). This also applies, by virtue of Art. 53 of the Civilian Convention, to destruction caused by an occupying power; and if that destruction is not militarily necessary and is extensive, those responsible commit a grave breach of the Convention, see Art. 147. The occupying power is only the administrator and usufructuary of property in occupied territory, Hague Regulations, Art. 55.

[5] The Hostages trial, VIII WCR 66.

[6] According to Bothe, increased awareness in the world of environmental problems must have an impact on the proportionality rule, M. Bothe, The Protection of the Environment in Time of Armed Conflict, Ottawa Conference of Experts, July 1991. Bothe also mentions that the 'dictates of public conscience' in the Martens preamble to Hague Convention No. IV of 1907 will include environmental concerns. Roberts, Environment, p. 116, also mentions the principle of humanity as being relevant.

Devastation as a method of warfare

Early writers thought it permissible for a belligerent to attain the object of war by laying waste to a country and destroying food and provender to prevent the enemy from subsisting there. But it was thought wrong to carry out devastation if it was motivated by hate and passion.[7] Those writers seem to have accepted devastation by way of legitimate reprisals; to create a barrier in one's own[8] or allied territory[9] against invasion; or to harass an invading force.[10] Even the devastation of enemy-held territory was regarded as legitimate[11] if it was done to deny the area to enemy forces.[12] It followed, therefore, that General Rendulic, who laid waste to large areas of northern Norway to impede an expected Soviet army advance, was acquitted by a US war crimes tribunal.[13]

Protection of the environment

Despite the practice of states over the centuries of inflicting damage on the environment in war,[14] including the many historical examples of a 'scorched earth' policy as mentioned above, early law of war treaties were concerned more with the protection of human beings than with the protection of objects or of the environment.[15] Even though the artillery barrages of the First World War and the bombing of the Second World War caused severe environmental damage, it was not until defoliants,[16] daisy-cutter bombs and Rome ploughs were used, and until consideration was given to the possibility of causing precipitation to

[7] As in the French devastation of the Palatinate in 1674 and 1689.

[8] Compare the actions of Peter the Great in Russian territory in 1709. This right in national territory is still recognized by Protocol I, Art. 54, para. 5.

[9] As in the devastation in front of the lines of Torres Vedras in Portugal by Wellington.

[10] As in the burning of Moscow in 1812.

[11] As in the case of the Shenandoah valley during the American Civil War.

[12] For a more detailed study of early writers and military practice, see G. Best, *Humanity in Warfare*, Methuen, 1983, pp. 65–6, 206–7. See also L. Doswald-Beck, The value of the 1977 protocols, in M. A. Meyer, *Armed Conflict and the New Law*, British Institute of International and Comparative Law, 1989, p. 160.

[13] The Hostages trial, VIII WCR 34, 69. It is questionable whether, had Protocol I applied, a tribunal would have come to the same conclusion.

[14] McCoubrey speaks of the ancient Roman practice of putting salt on the fields of the enemy to render them infertile, H. McCoubrey, *International Humanitarian Law*, Dartmouth, 1990, p. 162. M. Saalfeld, Umweltschutz in bewaffneten Konflikten, *Humanitäres Völkerrecht Informationsschriften*, 1992, No. 1, p. 15, refers to various mentions in the Bible of such practices, e.g. 'and that the whole land thereof is brimstone, and salt, and burning, that it is not sown, nor beareth, nor any grass groweth therein' (Deut. 29:23), but also points to historical examples of orders of military leaders prohibiting the destruction of crops, e.g. the biblical injunction in sieges not to cut down fruit trees for use for military purposes 'for the tree of the field is man's life' (Deut. 20:19).

[15] See Saalfeld, Umweltschutz, for a review of the limited environmental protection provisions in customary and early treaty law.

[16] Aldrich points out that so far as he was aware defoliants were deliberately used in South Vietnam and Laos only where the consent of the governments had been obtained—G. H. Aldrich, Prospects for US ratification of Protocol I, *American Journal of International Law*, 1991, p. 14.

flood enemy supply routes in Vietnam, that attention was paid to techniques in war that were specifically aimed at the environment.[17] World-wide concern for the environment was expressed in the World Charter for Nature,[18] which recognizes that 'nature shall be secured against degradation caused by warfare or other hostile activities'. The relevant provisions are:

5. Nature shall be secured against degradation caused by warfare or other hostile activities . . .
20. Military activities damaging nature shall be avoided.

It is arguable that both these provisions are covered by those of Protocol I, Art. 57 (precautions in attack), which protects civilian objects from attack and from incidental damage, and Arts. 35 and 55 (protection of the environment). Although it is not a binding treaty obligation, one would expect states that had voted in favour of this resolution to issue internal instructions, perhaps in military manuals, or laws to ensure compliance.[19] But, as McCoubrey argues,[20] it is not a simple matter and there are delicate judgements to be made. The need to protect the lives of combatants needs to be balanced against the protection of the environment; any health hazards to the civilian population caused by the use of chemical herbicides will have to be taken into account;[21] and the extent of the damage to the environment and its capacity to regenerate will need to be considered.

Current law

Property protection

There are various rules which provide, in effect, that property is not to be damaged unless military necessity so requires.[22] They can indirectly help to protect the environment.

[17] See P. J. Rowe, *Defence: the Legal Implications*, Brassey, 1987, at pp. 116–17; F. Kalshoven, *Constraints on the Waging of War*, International Committee of the Red Cross, 1987, p. 81; McCoubrey, *Humanitarian Law*, p. 163, refers to the possibility of 'cloud-seeding' being considered during the Vietnam war.
[18] UN General Assembly Resn. (1982) 22 *International Legal Materials* 455.
[19] N. A. Robinson, Draft Articles with Commentary on a Convention securing Nature from Warfare or other Hostile Activities, paper for the Ottawa Conference of Experts, July 1991, speculates that, because this resolution was a 'soft law' instrument, Iraq, which had voted in favour, felt free to breach the principle. Szasz defines 'soft law' as norms which are not, strictly speaking, binding on states but which may nevertheless influence their actions: P. C. Szasz, Study of Proposals for Improvements to Existing Legal Instruments relating to the Environment and Armed Conflicts, Ottawa Conference of Experts, July 1991. L. C. Green, The Environment and the Law of Conventional Warfare, Ottawa Conference of Experts, is of the opinion that the International Law Commission's Art. 19 (on criminal liability for breach of environmental obligations) in its draft Declaration on State Responsibility lacks any legal significance. Roberts, Environment, p. 111, refers to other treaties and bilateral agreements that have an impact on environmental issues in wartime.
[20] McCoubrey, *Humanitarian Law*, pp. 162–3.
[21] I. Detter de Lupis, *The Law of War*, Cambridge University Press, 1987, p. 227.
[22] Hague Regulations, Reg. 23(g). This is reinforced by the provisions of Regs. 22 (means of

Environmental protection

There are three treaty provisions dealing directly with the protection of the environment during armed conflicts. First, the Convention on the Prohibition of Military and any other Hostile Use of Environmental Modification Techniques, 1977 (ENMOD Convention); secondly, Art. 35.3 of Protocol I; and thirdly, Art. 55 of Protocol I. There is also a prohibition, in Protocol III to the Weapons Convention,[23] on incendiary attacks on forests or other kinds of plant cover, unless they are being used to 'cover, conceal or camouflage combatants or other military objectives, or are themselves military objectives'.[24]

The United Kingdom is a party to the ENMOD Convention, which was negotiated under the auspices of the UN Conference of the Committee on Disarmament and entered into force on 5 October 1978. The United Kingdom is not yet a party to Protocol I[25] or the Weapons Convention. It is of interest to analyse the texts of these three treaty provisions, which bear some resemblance to each other.

ENMOD Convention

Art. I.1 is an undertaking by states party:

not to engage in military or any other hostile use of environmental modification techniques having widespread, long-lasting or severe effects as a means of destruction, damage or injury to any other State Party.

Westing refers to this as a ban on actions carried out with the deliberate intent to manipulate the environment for hostile purposes but suggests that it ought to include reasonable expectation, since such deliberate intent is difficult to establish in the absence of an admission by the perpetrator.[26]

It is worth mentioning here that non-hostile uses of environmental modification techniques are not caught by the convention.[27]

Art. II defines such techniques as those 'for changing—through the deliberate manipulation of natural processes—the dynamics, composition or structure of the Earth, including its biota, lithosphere, hydrosphere and atmosphere, or of outer space'.

injuring the enemy are not unlimited) and 25 (no attacks on undefended places) as well as the Martens clause in the preamble. The same principles apply in occupied territory under Reg. 55 of the Hague Regulations and Art. 53 of the Civilian Convention. By virtue of Art. 147 of the Civilian Convention, extensive and wanton destruction of property can amount to a grave breach and a war crime.

[23] Art. 2, para. 4.
[24] For an area of land as military objective, see chapter 2.
[25] But has announced its intention to ratify, see the written answer by Douglas Hogg in Hansard (Commons) of 22 October 1993.
[26] A. H. Westing, The Environmental Modification Conference of 1991, *Humanitäres Völkerrecht Informationsschriften*, 1992, No. 2, p. 71.
[27] J. Goldblat, Legal protection of the environment against the effects of military activities, *Bulletin of Peace Proposals*, vol. 22, No. 4 (1991), p. 5; Robinson, Draft Articles.

In submitting the text of the treaty[28] to the UN General Assembly, the UN Conference of the Committee on Disarmament also submitted a set of under-standings. The first relates to the meaning of the terms 'widespread, long-lasting or severe' and defined them as follows:

1. Widespread: encompassing an area on the scale of several hundred square kilometres.

2. Long-lasting: lasting for a period of months, or approximately a season.

3. Severe: involving serious or significant disruption or harm to human life, natural and economic resources or other assets.

The understanding was expressly said to be exclusively for the ENMOD Convention and was without prejudice to the interpretation of similar terms in any other international agreement.

Another understanding included a list of examples of phenomena that could be caused by environmental modification techniques:

earthquakes, tsunamis,[29] an upset in the ecological balance of a region; changes in weather patterns (clouds, precipitation, cyclones of various types, and tornadic storms); changes in climate patterns; changes in ocean currents; changes in the state of the ozone layer; and changes in the state of the ionosphere.

McCoubrey refers to the problems for allied air operations of ash and gritty particles released by the natural eruption of Mount Vesuvius in 1944 and specu-lates as to the military effects that could be caused by bombing volcanoes.[30]

Some commentators seem to think that the convention has a wider scope than seems apparent on a reading of Arts. I and II. One speaks of deliberate[31] destruction of a forest to deprive the enemy of shelter[32] as being caught by the convention. It is difficult to follow the logic of this argument, since the conven-tion deals only with 'deliberate human manipulation of the natural processes, as distinct from conventional acts of warfare which might result in adverse effects on the environment',[33] except in cases of such extensive destruction of, for example, the tropical rain forest as to cause a climatic change and to lead to the inference that that change was intended. Westing[34] is nearer the mark when he

---

[28] 1108 UNTS 151–78. See also A. Roberts and R. Guelff, *Documents on the Laws of War*, 2nd ed., Clarendon Press, 1989, p. 377.

[29] The Japanese word for tidal waves—see Detter de Lupis, *Law of War*, at p. 229.

[30] H. McCoubrey and N. D. White, *International Law and Armed Conflict*, Dartmouth, 1992, p. 263.

[31] Rather than incidental, say, to a severe bombardment.

[32] Szasz, Study of Proposals. This may be a reference to the statement made in 1976 by the US negotiator that such use is prohibited only if it upsets the ecological balance of a region, see J. Goldblat, The ENMOD Convention: a critical review, *Humanitäres Völkerrecht Informationsschriften*, 1993, No. 2, p. 82. In fact, Szasz expresses doubt later in his paper about whether Iraq's deliberate spillage of oil and setting on fire of oil wells, if not done for the purpose of deliberately damaging the environment, would have been a violation of the convention if carried out by a party to it.

[33] Goldblat, ENMOD Convention, p. 81.

[34] A. H. Westing, The environmental modification conference of 1991, *Humanitäres Völkerrecht Informationsschriften*, 1992, p. 71.

says that an environmentally devastating attack with nuclear weapons would not readily fall within the purview of the ENMOD Convention, since the ensuing environmental modification might well be presented as unintended collateral effects. This is the nub of the problem. It will be difficult to prove that nuclear weapons were used for the purpose of environmental modification rather than for the simple destruction of the targets at which they were aimed.

The environmental protection of the ENMOD Convention applies to all states party, and not just the states in conflict. It extends to the environment at large.[35] Although Art. I.1 specifically refers to destruction, damage or injury to any other state party, it can still be caused by manipulation of the environment at large.

Szasz raises but leaves open the question of whether the essential terms of the ENMOD Convention have already become part of customary international law.[36]

As Goldblat has pointed out, one of the greatest difficulties with a convention which does not impose an absolute ban is verification—establishing that the environmental changes were due to human activity and that they were brought about by deliberate, hostile intent.[37] The procedures laid down in the convention for a consultative committee of experts and for referring complaints to the UN Security Council[38] are intended to alleviate this problem.

A review conference took place in 1992 to assess the convention in the light of the Gulf War of 1990–91 and was attended by forty states party, but little of substance emerged save for the understanding that under certain conditions the use of herbicides could be equated with environmental modification techniques prohibited under Art. II of the Convention.[39]

Protocol I

Although it comes into operation only during armed conflicts, occupation and liberation struggles involving states party, within those situations Art. 35.3 of Protocol I seems also to protect the environment at large and not merely the territories of the parties to the conflict.

Art. 35, para. 3, of Protocol I, which is in the part dealing with methods and means of warfare, prohibits the employment of 'methods and means of warfare which are intended, or may be expected, to cause widespread, long-term and severe damage to the natural environment'.

Art. 55 of Protocol I,[40] which is in the part dealing with the protection of the

---

[35] Szasz, Study of Proposals.
[36] *Ibid.*
[37] Goldblat, ENMOD Convention, p. 83.
[38] Art. V.
[39] A. Bouvier, Protection of the natural environment in time of armed conflict, 1991, *International Review of the Red Cross*, p. 563.
[40] Not of the 'Geneva convention' as suggested by A. Taylor, M.P., Hansard (Commons), 15 March 1991, col. 1381.

civilian population against the effects of hostilities,[41] requires care to be taken in warfare 'to protect the natural environment against widespread, long-term and severe damage'. It repeats the prohibition on methods and means in Art. 35 para. 3 but with the additional qualification 'and thereby to prejudice the health or survival of the population'.[42] It also prohibits *attacks* [43] against the environment by way of reprisals.

It is important to emphasize the point made by Bothe,[44] that Arts. 35 and 55 only come into play once the military planner has surmounted two hurdles: first, that the object to be attacked is a military objective and, secondly, that the rule of proportionality will not be violated. After that he must have regard to the specific rules on environmental protection. It is likely, though, that if the environmental damage is going to be widespread, long-term and severe, the military planner may well fall at the second hurdle in any event.[45]

Kalshoven has criticized the vague formulation of Protocol I and suggested that express prohibitions would have been more useful.[46] This is a dilemma always faced by those negotiating law of war treaties. If the treaty imposes a specific ban, states will find other ways of achieving the same result. If the language is more general, so as to catch all foreseeable means, states will argue about its scope of application and the intentions of the negotiators.

Representatives of the ICRC have suggested that these articles prohibit not only attacks on the environment as such but also making use of the environment as a tool of warfare.[47] Although one normally looks to the ENMOD Convention when thinking about the manipulation of the environment for hostile purposes, the ICRC may be right about the effect of Protocol I. However, before Protocol I applied it would have to be established that there was a risk of environmental damage by such manipulation.

It is not specifically a grave breach of the protocol to violate Arts. 35 and 55.

---

[41] And, therefore, applies only in the limited circumstances laid down in Art. 49.3, i.e. affecting the civilian population on land.

[42] Kalshoven considers that, as only long-term damage is envisaged, 'health' and 'survival' have to be interpreted in the sense of future health or survival—Kalshoven, Reaffirmation and development of international humanitarian law, *Netherlands Yearbook of International Law*, 1978, p. 130. M. Bothe, K. J. Partsch and W. Solf, *New Rules for the Victims of Armed Conflicts*, Martinus Nijhoff, 1982, p. 346, point out that the committee report states that 'population' is not preceded by the usual qualification 'civilian' because it is the whole population that is protected, irrespective of combatant status, and 'health' was included because, even if the population survived, it might suffer from, e.g., congenital defects.

[43] 'Attack' means an act of violence against the adversary, see chapter 1, and is a narrower concept than methods and means of warfare.

[44] Bothe, Protection.

[45] Fleck seems to be of the view that legal protection of the environment is based on proportionality rather than on an absolute ecological standard—D. Fleck, Environment: legal and policy perspectives, in H. Fox and M. A. Meyer (eds.), *Effecting Compliance*, British Institute of International and Comparative Law, 1993, p. 147.

[46] Kalshoven, *Constraints*, p. 81.

[47] A. Bouvier and H. P. Gasser, Protection of the Natural Environment in Time of Armed Conflict, Ottawa Conference of Experts, July 1991.

But an indiscriminate attack launched in the knowledge that it would cause excessive damage to the environment would be a grave breach.[48]

The treatment of the same subject in two different articles and in slightly different terms seems to have been the result of an attempt to accommodate different approaches to the problem suggested by delegates to the CDDH.[49] It was decided to leave the matter in two separate articles because Art. 55 deals with the protection of the civilian population while Art. 35 deals with the prohibition of unnecessary injury and has a wider scope, including transnational damage. The United Kingdom protested that there was no need for environmental provisions in Art. 35, since they were to be found, in the context of civilian protection, in Art. 55 and that the ultimate purpose of protecting the environment was to protect the civilians living in it. The logic of this dissenting view seems very compelling.[50] Both provisions contain the words 'which are intended or may be expected'. They seem to introduce an objective element into the test of whether the articles have been breached. Strangely, it does not even seem to be necessary to prove that actual damage has been caused, although, if it has, that would be evidence from which intent or expectation could be inferred. On the wording of the articles it is not clear whether 'or may be expected' means may be expected by the attacker or may be expected by an objective onlooker.[51]

Another difference between the scope of Art. 35 and that of Art. 55 is that the former relates to all methods or means of warfare, whether on land, at sea or in the air, whereas Art. 55 is in the part dealing with the protection of the civilian population, civilians and civilian objects on land against the effects of hostilities.[52] Art. 55 extends to a state's territorial waters, but only Art. 35 applies to damage on the high seas.[53]

Protocol I has been criticized on the grounds that it antedates the modern environmental law of peace in which the environment is protected even in the absence of proved specific damage (the principle of precaution which is absent

[48] Art. 85, para. 3(b).

[49] Bothe *et al.*, *New Rules*, p. 345.

[50] See ICRC *Commentary*, paras. 1449, 1459.

[51] Kalshoven, Reaffirmation, p. 130, refers to the concept of 'objective expectation'. Bothe *et al.*, *New Rules*, p. 347, refer to 'objectively foreseeable collateral effects'.

[52] Art. 49, para. 2. Kalshoven, *Constraints*, p. 96, points out that Art. 55 is intended to prevent consequential prejudice to the health or survival of the population.

[53] M. Bothe, at a meeting of the Committee for the Protection of Human Life in Armed Conflict at the twelfth Congress of the International Society for Military Law and the Law of War, Brussels, May 1991. However, Rauch considers that the provisions of Section I, Part IV, of Protocol I cover the collateral effects on land of operations against enemy warships and merchant ships—E. Rauch, *The Protocols Additional to the Geneva Conventions... and the Convention on the Law of the Sea: Repercussions in the Law of Naval Warfare*, Institute of International Law, Kiel, Duncker & Humblot, 1984, pp. 60, 141. S. Witteler, Der Krieg im Golf und seine Auswirkungen auf die natürliche Umwelt, *Humanitäres Völkerrecht Informationsschriften*, January–July 1991, p. 53, comments that Art. 35, being wider in scope, allows a more broadly based assessment of environmental damage to be made, such as the entire Iraqi oil-letting episode during the Gulf War of 1990–91.

from the protocol).[54] However, it must be said that the use of the words 'or may be expected' does incorporate a precautionary element, though less far-reaching than the Montreal Protocol.[55]

It has been pointed out that it is strange that the protection of the natural environment in Arts. 35 and 55 of Protocol I is absolute, not being subject to any considerations of military necessity or proportionality, and is therefore more rigid than the protection of human life. Of course, it is only methods or means of warfare that cause, or may be expected to cause, widespread, long-term and severe damage to the natural environment that are forbidden.[56] This takes account of national defence interests, for it allows less severe environmental damage to be caused if it is militarily necessary. Reference has been made to military plans to burn oil installations in a harbour, since that would deny the use of both the harbour and the oil to a potential enemy and, although there would be environmental damage, it would not be on an international scale.[57] It is noteworthy that the word 'attack' is not to be found in Arts. 35 and 55, only the words 'use' or 'employ'. The word 'use' has in the past been found in treaties which impose a complete ban. The view has been expressed that perhaps the natural environment is more important than human life because human life depends on the environment for its very existence.[58] On the other hand, as Kalshoven has stated, the Protocol I provisions are really aimed at unconventional methods of warfare such as herbicides specifically designed to damage the environment and, therefore, will affect only high-level planners and decision-makers rather than those at lower levels carrying out attacks with conventional weaponry.[59]

Relationship between the ENMOD Convention and Protocol I

Bothe puts the differences between the two instruments most succinctly by saying that, in the case of the convention, the environment is the weapon and, in the case of Protocol I, the environment is the victim.[60] Rowe gives the classic example of a technique caught by the ENMOD Convention as an attempt to modify the weather so as to cause a drought.[61] However, causing a drought by

---

[54] M. Bothe, The protection of the environment in time of armed conflict, *GYIL* 34 (1991), p. 54, at p. 57.

[55] Protocol on Substances that Deplete the Ozone Layer, Montreal, 1987.

[56] This is a reference to the natural environment as a whole and not to a local site of nature. In the words of Witteler, Der Krieg im Golf, p. 51, *die natürliche Umwelt in Sinne eines grösseren ökologischen Gesamtsystems.*

[57] S. B. Magnusson, *Brussels Congress,* 1991.

[58] A. P. V. Rogers, Military necessity and the rule of proportionality, *Military Law and Law of War Review,* vol. 1/2, 1980, Addendum.

[59] Kalshoven, Reaffirmation, p. 130. He adds that even in the case of the higher-level planners, the 'widespread, long-term and severe' principles apply. See also, Bothe *et al.*, *New Rules,* p. 348.

[60] Bothe, *Brussels Congress,* 1991. See also the ICRC *Commentary* at para. 1450.

[61] Rowe, *Defence*, p. 117.

destroying reservoirs would not be a breach of the convention. Furthermore, the convention applies to damage to another state while Protocol I applies to any environmental damage,[62] so would apply to damage in a state's own territory, on the high seas or, for example, in Antarctica.

The ENMOD Convention seems to be of an absolute nature. If the environmental consequences occur, the convention applies even if those consequences were neither intended nor foreseen.[63] On the other hand, in the case of Protocol I, the consequences must have been intended or foreseen, but the damage need not necessarily have occurred. Even if it does occur, liability does not arise if it could not have been foreseen.[64] Finally, the ENMOD Convention applies to any hostile uses of environmental modification techniques, whereas Protocol I applies only in declared wars, armed conflicts and hostile occupations of enemy territory.[65]

It is unfortunate that similar terminology is used in both the ENMOD Convention and Protocol I. The former speaks of 'widespread, long *lasting or* severe' damage while the latter refers to 'widespread, long-*term and* severe' damage. But the terms are interpreted differently in the two instruments. It is immediately apparent that the terms are disjunctive in the ENMOD Convention and conjunctive in Protocol I; in the former case the convention applies if any of the criteria are satisfied, while in the latter they must all be satisfied. The understanding relating to the ENMOD Convention is set out above but there is no equivalent understanding with regard to Protocol I. Witteler[66] comments that the threshold cannot be so low as to prevent normal military activity nor so high as not to prevent the most conspicuous cases of environmental damage but that it is impossible to lay down any fixed standards such as the area affected, or the proportion of territory or of an environmentally sensitive area affected.

According to those who negotiated Protocol I, 'long-term' was understood to relate to a period of decades and was not intended to include damage on the scale of the battlefield damage suffered in France in the First World War or to battlefield damage incidental to conventional warfare.[67] Only the expression 'long-term' was explained in the report of the negotiating committee.[68] One can only assume that it was considered that the other terms did not need explanation. An examination of the various commentaries on Protocol I leads one to infer that 'severe' means prejudicing the continued survival of the civilian population or involving the risk of major health problems and that 'widespread' means more

---

[62] ICRC *Commentary*, para. 1452.
[63] Szasz, Study of Proposals.
[64] *Ibid.*
[65] *Ibid.*, see Art. 1(3) of the Protocol.
[66] Witteler, Der Kreig im Golf, p. 51.
[67] See para. 27 of the Report of Committee III, *Official Records of the Diplomatic Conference on the Reaffirmation and Development of International Humanitarian Law applicable in Armed Conflict*, Geneva (1974–77), Berne 1978, vol. XV, p. 269.
[68] Bothe *et al.*, *New Rules*, p. 346.

than the standard of several hundred square kilometres considered in connection with the ENMOD Convention. Antoine's suggestion that widespread means *less* than the standard laid down by the ENMOD understanding seems inconsistent with the generally accepted interpretations of 'long-term' and 'severe'; perhaps he means *less stringent*.[69] Witteler[70] makes much of the differences in the size of states, saying that damage which would obliterate Luxembourg would hardly be noticed in Russia, but it seems to the writer that this is only a factor to be taken into account, since severe environmental damage is of concern to the whole of mankind. Witteler also makes the interesting point that, since Art. 55 of Protocol I is not concerned with individual attacks,[71] the cumulative effect on the environment of individual attacks may amount to a breach of the article.[72]

A comparison of the ENMOD Convention with the environmental articles of Protocol I highlights the point made by Painchaud that a distinction is necessary between the deliberate manipulation of the environment for military purposes and the environmental consequences of military operations. He points out that the destruction of a chemicals factory can have two objects: to weaken the industrial potential of the enemy or to create pollution which will curtail the enemy's freedom of movement. It is difficult to follow his argument that the second tactic is an attempt to manipulate the environment. It is certainly not manipulation in the sense of the ENMOD Convention.[73] He goes on to suggest that environmental weapons should be placed in two categories: first degree weapons, which use the environment as an immediate instrument, and second degree weapons, which make use of an intermediate instrument to act on the environment. To these might be added third degree weapons—those which, though not intended to do so, have environmental consequences.

Other provisions of Protocol I

Indispensable objects. It is prohibited to attack agricultural areas, crops, drinking water or irrigation installations for the purpose of denying them for their sustenance value to the adverse party unless they are used solely as sustenance for the enemy armed forces or in direct support of military action.[74] An example of crops being used in direct support of military action is where, for example, a wheat field is used as cover by advancing infantry.

It has been suggested that the right to carry out a scorched earth policy on national territory under national control as a defence against invasion is still

---

[69] See P. Antoine, International humanitarian law and the protection of the environment in time of armed conflict, *International Review of the Red Cross*, 1992, p. 526.

[70] Witteler, Der Krieg im Golf, p. 51.

[71] He presumably means parts of an attack.

[72] Witteler, Der Krieg im Golf, p. 52.

[73] Painchaud, Environmental Weapons.

[74] Protocol I, Art. 54.

preserved.[75] Kalshoven refers to a Netherlands law of 1896 which allows the authorities to inundate parts of Netherlands territory to impede an invasion. Although this would damage crops, it would not be done to deny them for their sustenance value and so there would be no breach of Protocol I.[76]

Dangerous forces. One commentator observes that exceptions to the provisions of Art. 56 of Protocol I may be made in several important instances on grounds of military necessity and that the required justification is bound to be subjective, leaving the military commander much room for discretion.[77] Goldblat says that the commander is required to balance such unquantifiable notions as human suffering and the demands of war and that responsibility is passed to commanders to decide, in the heat of battle, what is lawful.

Of course, the scope of Art. 56 is limited to dams, dykes and nuclear electricity generating stations and there is no international legal instrument protecting facilities containing other dangerous materials such as chemical works[78] or oil installations.[79] Furthermore, the article is concerned with loss of human life, so that the environment is only indirectly protected and it would be possible to conceive of a situation in sparsely populated territory where loss of water through the destruction of a dam could have severe ecological consequences. Regret has been expressed that environmental concerns have not been reflected in the 'grave breach' provisions of Protocol I.[80] But, of course, deliberately indiscriminate attacks and attacks on works containing dangerous forces in the knowledge that there will be excessive collateral damage are grave breaches of Protocol I[81] and may encompass environmental damage.

Particular weapons[82]

Conventional weapons. The environmental provisions examined above were not intended to cover damage ordinarily caused by conventional means and methods of warfare.[83]

[75] Canada, Note on the Current Law of armed Conflict relevant to the Environment in Conventional Conflicts, paper by the Office of the Judge Advocate General for the Ottawa Conference of Experts, July 1991, referring to Protocol I, Art. 54, para. 5.

[76] Kalshoven, *Constraints*, p. 96.

[77] Goldblat, Legal Protection, p. 3.

[78] Szasz, Study of Proposals; or factories containing toxic substances—Goldblat, in an intervention at the Ottawa Conference of Experts, July 1991.

[79] Kalshoven, in an intervention at the Ottawa Conference of Experts, July 1991, said that a proposal at the Diplomatic Conference to include oil installations in Art. 56 was defeated.

[80] Bothe, Ottawa Conference, 1991; Bothe, *GYIL*, p. 58.

[81] Art. 85.3(b), (c).

[82] Bouvier and Gasser, Natural Environment, point out that Art. 36 of Protocol I, which requires parties introducing new weapons to ensure their compatibility with the requirements of international law, also requires those parties to ensure compatibility with the environmental standards laid down by Protocol I.

[83] ICRC *Commentary*, para. 1454; Bothe *et al.*, *New Rules*, p. 348; Doswald-Beck, The value of the 1977 protocols, p. 162.

Mines and other remnants of war. According to the ICRC,[84] unexploded mines are a serious and constant threat to the environment. Other commentators have referred to the UN General Assembly resolution on the remnants of war[85] and stress that such remnants may constitute significant environmental degradation.[86] This argument is not always valid. Unexploded munitions cannot damage the environment unless they contain toxic chemicals or heavy metals.[87] They may make areas inaccessible or unusable, but that may even encourage the growth of the natural vegetation. Clearance of mines now tends to be addressed in cease-fire arrangements.[88] The Mines Protocol to the Weapons Convention contributes to environmental protection by prohibiting the indiscriminate use of mines, restricting the use of remotely delivered mines and requiring the recording of certain minefields.[89]

Nuclear weapons. The use of nuclear weapons may have environmental consequences.[90] However, negotiations at the CDDH were based on an ICRC draft which specifically stated that it was not intended to deal with the problem of nuclear weapons.[91] It was only on this basis that the nuclear powers were prepared to enter into negotiations. The United Kingdom and the United States made declaratory statements on signature that the rules established by Protocol I are not intended to have any effect on and do not regulate or prohibit the use of nuclear weapons. Similar statements were made on ratification by Italy, the Netherlands and Germany. The effect is that environmental damage caused by nuclear weapons is not covered by Protocol I at all.[92] States are still being

[84] ICRC *Commentary*, para. 1443. The ICRC takes the view that problems arising from the material remnants of war are also covered by Arts. 35 and 55; *Commentary*, para. 1455. This concern is reflected in Goldblat, Legal protection, who talks about incidental damage being caused to cropland by mines and refers to the damage to the environment caused by the remnants of war, particularly the chemical component of some munitions.

[85] A/RES/37/215 of 20 December 1982.

[86] Szasz, Study of Proposals, who expresses the view that the resolution remains at best hortatory and cannot even be categorized as *de lege ferenda*.

[87] See A. R. G. Price, *Possible Environmental Threats from the Current War in the Gulf*, Greenpeace, 2 February 1991, p. 14.

[88] UN Security Council Resn. 686 of 2 March 1991 called upon Iraq to provide information and assistance in identifying Iraqi mines, booby-traps and other explosives and chemical and biological weapons in Kuwait and the parts of Iraq temporarily occupied by allied forces.

[89] For a more detailed treatment of the subject, see A. P. V. Rogers, A commentary on the Protocol on Prohibitions or Restrictions on the Use of Mines, etc., *Military Law and Law of War Review*, 1987; Mines, booby-traps and other devices, 1990, *International Review of the Red Cross*; The Mines Protocol: Negotiating History, ICRC Report on a Symposium on Anti-personnel Mines, Montreux, 21–23 April 1993.

[90] See, e.g., Rowe, *Defence*, p. 117; Rauch, *The Protocols*, p. 143.

[91] The ICRC, in the introduction to its June 1973 version of the Draft Additional Protocols to the Geneva Conventions of August 12, 1949, stated: 'Problems relating to atomic, bacteriological and chemical warfare are subjects of international agreements or negotiations by governments, and in submitting these draft Additional Protocols the ICRC does not intend to broach those problems. It should be borne in mind that the Red Cross as a whole, at several International Red Cross Conferences, has clearly made known its condemnation of weapons of mass destruction and has urged governments to reach agreements for banning their use.'

[92] Kalshoven, *Constraints*, p. 104, said that the drafting history of Protocol I shows that any new

encouraged by the international community to reach agreement 'on the elimination and complete destruction of such weapons.'[93]

Incendiary weapons. It is prohibited to make forests or other kinds of plant cover the object of attack by incendiary weapons unless they are used to cover, conceal or camouflage combatants or other military objectives or are themselves military objectives.[94]

Chemical and bacteriological weapons, which are weapons that could have environmental effects, are, subject to the 'no first use' reservations with regard to chemical weapons, prohibited.[95] The precise definition of a chemical weapon is somewhat obscure. Rowe has suggested that chemical herbicides can be brought within the regime of the 1925 Geneva Gas Protocol, particularly in the light of the interpretation given it by the UN General Assembly in 1969.[96] The operative part of the resolution declares as contrary to international law, in particular the Gas Protocol, the use in international armed conflicts of 'any chemical agents of warfare—chemical substances, whether gaseous, liquid or solid—which might be employed because of their direct toxic effects on man, animals or plants'. It will be noted that the United Kingdom abstained in the voting, so, as a 'soft law' instrument, its relevance to the UK is limited. In any event, General Assembly resolutions are not law, nor is the Assembly a court or legal body having power to interpret the law. A UN resolution could, depending on the voting pattern, be *some* evidence of the views of the international community. The Chemical Weapons Convention of 1993 now contains, for the first time, a definition of chemical weapons. It does not come into force until the sixty-fifth instrument of ratification and then, at the earliest, on 13 January 1995.

Szasz is doubtful whether chemical and bacteriological weapons should be included in any study of the environmental effects of war, since chemical weapons have only short-term effects in a given area and that only in the event of bacteriological weapons creating a persistent epidemic could their effect be categorized as environmental.[97] Such might be the case if, for example, land

rules embodied in the protocol were not written with a view to the potential use of nuclear weapons and that Arts. 35, para. 3, and 55 are obvious examples of new rules. Those who argue that Protocol I applies to nuclear weapons, e.g. Rauch, *The Protocols*, p. 71, and Witteler, Der Krieg im Golf, p. 50, seem to ignore the essentially contractual nature of the basis of the relationship between states party.

[93] Principle 26 of the Declaration of the UN Stockholm Conference of 1972. Green, The Environment, points out that the conference did not deal with harm to the environment caused by conventional weapons or by the remnants of war and that the Declaration is not a legally binding document.

[94] Art. 4, para. 4, of Protocol III to the UN Conventional Weapons Convention of 1981. Kalshoven, Reaffirmation, p. 157, says that the exceptions deprive the paragraph of virtually all practical significance.

[95] Geneva Gas Protocol of 1925 and Bacteriological Weapons Convention of 1972. According to Goldblat, Legal protection, p. 5, the Gas Protocol also protects plants. In so far as the Gas Protocol bans any use of chemical and bacteriological weapons, this must be true.

[96] Rowe, *Defence*, p. 117. The resolution is No. 2603 A(XXIV) of 16 December 1969.

[97] Szasz, Study of Proposals.

that had been used for biological experiments were declared unfit for human habitation or agriculture for a lengthy period.

Fuel-air explosive. Apparently, this was used in the Gulf War of 1990–91 for the clearance of minefields,[98] which is perfectly legitimate.

Effect on neutral states

Article 1 of the Hague Neutrality Convention of 1907 provides that the territory of neutral powers is inviolable. Bothe considers that this is sufficiently wide to cover environmental damage, points out that during the Second World War compensation was paid to Switzerland for collateral damage on Swiss territory from attacks on targets in neighbouring Germany and concludes that the normal peacetime rules relating to trans-frontier pollution apply.[99]

The Gulf War of 1990–91

Oil pollution

Environmental concerns certainly affected allied military planning. It is reported that the allies decided not to attack four Iraqi super-tankers inside the Gulf which were contravening UN Security Council Resolution 665 because of the environmental consequences of so doing.[100] This was being more environmentally conscious than the law requires, since there is nothing in international law to prevent a party to an armed conflict attacking and sinking enemy super-tankers or nuclear submarines.[101]

It is reported that in January 1991 Iraq opened the oil valves of the Sea Island Terminal in Kuwait and the Mina Al-Bakr terminal in Iraq, causing massive oil spills into the Persian Gulf,[102] and perhaps even more on land in Kuwait, and

---

[98] Hansard (Commons), 2 May 1991 at col. 484 and, 17 June 1991, at col. 16.

[99] Bothe, Ottawa Conference, 1991. See also Bothe, *GYIL*, pp. 59–60; and Bouvier, Natural environment, p. 568. Some authors, e.g. G. Plant, Environmental damage and the law of war, in H. Fox and M. A. Meyer (eds.), *Effecting Compliance*, British Institute of International and Comparative Law, 1993, p. 163, refer in this connection to principle 21 of the 1972 Stockholm Declaration (confirmed in UN General Assembly Resn. 2996) that each state has a responsibility to ensure that activities under its jurisdiction or control do not cause damage to the environment of other states or areas beyond national jurisdiction. But this is only a 'soft law' instrument. Green, Ottawa Conference, 1991, said it could be ignored and Kalshoven, Reaffirmation, said it had been incorporated, so far as possible, in Protocol I, Arts. 35 and 55.

[100] G. van Hegelsom, *Brussels Congress,* 1991.

[101] H. P. Gasser, Some legal issues concerning ratification of the 1977 Geneva protocols, in M. A. Meyer (ed.), *Armed Conflict and the New Law*, British Institute of International and Comparative Law, 1989, pp. 91–2. For the contrary view, see Rauch, *The Protocols*, pp. 143–51, who also deals with offshore oil installations at pp. 151–3.

[102] Estimates seem to vary. The DOD Report (United States, *Conduct of the Persian Gulf War*, Department of Defense final report to Congress, April 1992), p. 624, mentions 7 million to 9 million

that in February 1991 Iraq sabotaged hundreds[103] of Kuwaiti oil wells, setting over 500 on fire, causing huge daily emissions of sulphur dioxide, nitrous oxide and carbon dioxide.[104] So much smoke resulted that Kuwait City was in darkness for two days out of every three. The oil fires deposited soot on five-eighths of Kuwait. It was estimated that the environmental damage to Kuwait would take ten to twenty years to repair. The smoke plume extended over Iran, Afghanistan, Pakistan and India, black rain fell 600 miles away in Turkey and blackened snow fell in the Himalayas.[105] The large amounts of sulphur caused rain to be highly acidic and the smoke reduced daytime temperatures but also reduced night-time cooling. It was estimated that the main fall-out effects would be within 2,000 km.[106] UNESCO described the oil fires as the largest environmental catastrophe since Chernobyl.[107] While predictions of a 'nuclear winter' appear to have been exaggerated, there seems little doubt that the atmosphere in the region was dangerously polluted, involving damage to agriculture and risks to the health of the local population, particularly in increased lung cancer.[108] It seems that if the ENMOD Convention applied it would cover the damage done to the atmosphere.[109] Although the oil spillage was the world's largest, a combination of the Gulf's high salinity and the hot sun in the region caused the bulk of the oil to evaporate,[110] so the actual damage may not have been so severe or long-term as may first have been feared.[111] However, Iraq is not a party to the convention, though as a signatory it is obliged to refrain from acts which would defeat the object and purpose of the convention.[112] It is doubtful whether the breach by one

barrels; the Greenpeace report mentions 11 million barrels on pp. 1 and 11 and 6 million to 8 million barrels on p. 3 (Price, *Environmental Threats*); and J. Guthrie, Ottawa Conference of Experts, July 1991, spoke of 5 million to 6 million barrels, of which Saudi Arabia recovered about 1 million and 70 per cent of which evaporated.

[103] The DOD Report, p. 624, mentions 590 damaged or destroyed well heads, of which 508 were set on fire and eighty-two damaged to allow oil to flow freely.

[104] One estimate was of 40,000, 3,000 and 500,000 tonnes respectively each day—Robinson, Draft Articles. The Parliamentary Under Secretary of State for the Environment, T. Baldry, M.P., mentioned a Kuwaiti estimate of a rate of burn of 5 million to 6 million barrels a day, which, he said, would be 'more severe and widespread' than had previously been feared, Hansard (Commons), 15 March 1991, col. 1387.

[105] Robinson, Draft Articles, who gives a very graphic account of the pollution effects; and Guthrie, Ottawa Conference, July 1991.

[106] Study by the Parliamentary Office of Science and Technology, quoted in Hansard (Commons), 15 March 1991, col. 1388.

[107] Paper entitled 'Basis and Objectives of the Meeting of Experts on the Use of the Environment as a Tool of Conventional Warfare', presented by B. Mawhinney, Ottawa Conference of Experts, July 1991.

[108] Painchaud, Environmental Weapons. As to the potential environmental problems in the Gulf, see Price, Environmental threats. E. Nicholson, M.P., stated that 'the incomplete combustion of oil-producing carcinogens may cause cancer', Hansard (Commons), 15 March 1991, col. 1346.

[109] Goldblat, Legal protection, p. 4.

[110] *The Times*, 8 May 1991; Guthrie, Ottawa Conference, July 1991.

[111] The ENMOD Convention did not apply in the Gulf War. If it had, one would still have had to look at the damage actually done.

[112] Vienna Convention on the Law of Treaties, Art. 18.

party of one provision of many in a convention could be said to defeat its object and purpose, and it is arguable, in any event, whether the techniques adopted were those envisaged by the convention.[113]

There was speculation that Iraq had done all this to impede naval and military operations by the allied forces. However, some commentators consider that Iraq's action in respect of the Kuwaiti oil wells was an act of revenge rather than an act dictated by military necessity,[114] done systematically rather than inadvertently, and was wholly out of proportion to any military gain.[115] Others suggested that it was intended to contaminate Saudi Arabian desalination plants,[116] or to deny the allies the fruits of victory.[117]

The Iraqi actions seem to have violated Art. 23(g) of the Hague Regulations, which prohibits the destruction of enemy property unless imperatively demanded by the necessities of war. A similar provision, applicable in occupied territory, appears in Art. 53 of the Civilian Convention, and the damage in Kuwait would certainly appear to fall into the category of 'extensive' so as to amount to a grave breach of that convention.[118]

It has been suggested[119] that, even in the case of a charge based on Art. 23(g) of the Hague Regulations or Art. 53 of the Civilian Convention, a plea of military necessity might have been based on the need to prevent or hamper an allied advance into Kuwait, as in the case of General Rendulic. However, had it been desired to produce smoke as an obscurant, that could have been done without completely destroying oil wells.[120] Alternatively, Iraq could have argued that the oil wells were legitimate military objectives because it was essential to deny their use to enemy mechanized forces.[121] Any tribunal would, therefore, have to look at the reasons for the destruction of the oil wells and the oil

---

[113] Goldblat, in an intervention at the Ottawa Conference of Experts, 1991, said that setting oil on fire was analogous to releasing volcanic energy through an explosion. However, that still does not amount to manipulation of natural processes as envisaged by Art. II of the ENMOD Convention.

[114] G. Plant, Elements of a New Convention on the Protection of the Environment in time of Armed Conflict, Ottawa Conference of Experts, July 1991; Painchaud, Environmental Weapons. Goldblat, Legal protection, points out that, even if Protocol I had applied in the Gulf War, it would not have helped Iraq, since Arts. 35 and 55 allow no exception on grounds of military necessity, such as to repel a marine invasion. Kalshoven, in an intervention at the Ottawa Conference of Experts, July 1991, described Iraq's actions as wanton destruction of property. His views seemed to be shared by many delegates except, perhaps, Green, who pointed out the defences available to Iraq, and Sur, who emphasized that the conference was not a court and had no access to the evidence.

[115] Robinson, Draft Articles, who described what happened as the largest single human-induced air and oil pollution event.

[116] J. Arnold, M.P., Hansard (Commons), 15 March 1991, col. 1365.

[117] Roberts, Environment, p. 147.

[118] Art. 147.

[119] Goldblat, Legal protection, p. 4.

[120] For example, by opening the valves and setting light to them—W. H. Parks, in an intervention at the Ottawa Conference of Experts, 1991.

[121] Green, Environment. As O. Bring pointed out in an intervention at the Ottawa Conference, 1991, however, Iraq would have had to show that it was militarily necessary to attack the oil installations.

spillages to ascertain whether it was done to deny use of installations or areas to the enemy or to blind 'spy' satellites or whether it was simply an act of wanton destruction or of revenge against Kuwait and the allies.[122] In examining Iraq's motives the tribunal would, no doubt, take account of the fact that before hostilities started Saddam Hussain was threatening to cause environmental damage.[123] That would indicate environmental terrorism rather than a resort to military necessity. A tribunal would also have to consider the question of proportionality. That would include an examination of the methods used to determine whether the military aim could have been achieved in less devastating ways.

Also to be considered is the principle that a state is under a duty to pay compensation for damage caused by violations of the law of armed conflict.[124] This principle was applied in the case of Iraq following the Gulf conflict by Security Council Resolution 687,[125] which confirms Iraq's liability to pay compensation for damage caused as a result of the invasion and occupation of Kuwait, including environmental damage and the depletion of natural resources. 'Environmental damage' would include the costs of cleaning up the damage and 'depletion of natural resources' would include compensation for oil spilt or burnt off. The Security Council purported to be acting under chapter VII of the UN Charter (action with respect to threats to the peace, breaches of the peace, and acts of aggression), so they were acting under the *jus ad bellum* rather than under the Hague principles. At all events, Resolution 687 was accepted by Iraq as a condition of the cease-fire.[126]

The allied response to Iraq's actions was prompt. On 24 January 1991 Iraq started releasing oil into the Gulf. The US Department of Defense immediately established an oil spill task force and on 27 January US air strikes against oil manifolds upstream of the al-Ahmadi terminal stopped the flow of oil into the Gulf. On the same day, US teams of experts were sent to Saudi Arabia to provide technical assistance and booms were supplied.[127] The UK also provided anti-pollution equipment which was flown to the Gulf on 28–30 January.[128] These actions helped local efforts to limit the damage and went beyond the

---

[122] F. J. Hampson, Liability for war crimes, in Rowe (ed.), *Gulf War*, p. 254. The DOD Report, p. 626, confirms that oil spillages and smoke did not hamper allied operations at all.

[123] See, e.g., *The Independent*, 24 September 1990.

[124] Hague Convention IV of 1907 concerning the laws and customs of war on land, Art. 3. The convention is considered to reflect customary international law. Szasz, Study of Proposals, refers in this connection to the work of the International Law Commission in codifying the responsibility of states for acts prohibited by international law, including a provision on responsibility for massive pollution of the atmosphere or the sea. However, damage caused in the course of military activities is excluded from the commission's considerations.

[125] S/RES/687(1991) of 3 April 1991, para. 16. See also H. Fox, Reparations and state responsibility, in Rowe (ed.), *Gulf War*, p. 261.

[126] Fox, Reparations, p. 264.

[127] *The Conduct of the Persian Gulf Campaign*, US Department of Defense Interim Report to Congress, July 1991 (DOD Interim Report).

[128] Hansard (Commons), 15 March 1991, col. 1334.

requirements of Protocol I, to which the United States and United Kingdom
were not even parties. In fact there is no obligation of the law of armed conflict
to limit environmental damage caused by the enemy's actions.[129] Roberts is
nevertheless critical of what he perceives as the allied lack of effective response
to Iraq's environmental threats.[130] Apart from clearer statements that such acts
are unlawful, which Roberts acknowledges may have achieved nothing, it is
difficult to see what else might have been done, short of reprisal action which
might have made things even worse.

It is of interest to speculate whether, had Iraq been a party to Protocol I[131] as
well as Kuwait, the environmental damage would have fallen within the 'widespread, long-term and severe' criteria of Arts. 35 and 55. It seems likely that the
widespread and severe tests would have been satisfied, but what of the long
term?[132] That test does not seem to be satisfied.[133] The report, prepared before
the event, by the Meteorological Office estimated that the only possible long-
term effect would be the impact of carbon dioxide on global warming and that
that would be almost negligible;[134] the effect on the Asian monsoon would
be within normal annual fluctuations.[135] McCoubrey, however, refers to the
increased incidence of respiratory disease due to ozone-laden smog caused by
the oil fires.[136]

Allied planners, on the other hand, were very concerned to reduce the environmental impact of their attacks. For example, they attacked oil refineries producing petrol that had immediate military use but avoided attacks on Iraq's
long-term oil production capacity.[137]

Roberts tends to damn with faint praise the allied efforts to reduce environmental damage,[138] saying that allied actions were 'less wanton and gratuitous

[129] Except, possibly, Art. 58(c) of Protocol I, which refers to precautions to protect civilians from
the dangers resulting from military operations; see chapter 4.

[130] Roberts, Environment, p. 148.

[131] The ENMOD Convention did not apply, as Iraq was not a party. Even if it had, it is extremely
doubtful whether Iraq's actions would have violated the convention, as it was not a deliberate
manipulation of the natural processes. For the opposing arguments, see Roberts, Environment,
p. 138, and Plant, Environmental damage, at p. 168.

[132] Rauch, *The Protocols*, p. 147, studies the *Amoco Cadiz* disaster, which caused an oil slick 100
km long and 10 km wide, deposited 64,000 metric tons of oil ashore and polluted 200–300 km of
coastline. He also examines the case of the leaking oil well in the Nowruz field off the coast of Iran
in 1983, when an estimated 5,000 barrels of oil a day leaked into the Persian Gulf. He concludes
that the damage in both cases was 'widespread' within the meaning of Protocol I, reaches no
conclusion as to the 'long-term and severe' criteria, but considers that the element of objective
expectation suffices to render such methods and means of warfare unlawful.

[133] See Plant, Environmental damage, p. 169. Even Witteler, Der Krieg im Golf, p. 52, who argues
for a more restrictive interpretation of these terms, considers that there would not have been a breach
of Art. 55. Saalfeld, Umweltschutz, p. 31, comes to the same conclusion and complains that the
provisions of Protocol I do not do enough to protect the environment.

[134] Quoted by T. Dalyell, M.P., Hansard (Commons), 15 March 1991, col. 1337.

[135] Quoted by R. Hughes, M.P., Hansard (Commons), 15 March 1991, col. 1374.

[136] McCoubrey and White, *International Law*, p. 236.

[137] DOD Report, p. 97.

[138] Roberts, Environment, p. 141.

than the Iraqi oil crimes in Kuwait, and that some, but only some, significant efforts were made to avoid or reduce certain kinds of environmental damage'. He is obviously referring to all kinds of damage caused by the allied bombing, not just damage to the natural environment, but it is not clear what evidence he relies on for his stance. Plant disagrees with Roberts in characterizing the damage to the Iraqi civil and industrial infrastructure as an 'environmental' question.[139]

Roberts's statement is surprising, given the lengths that the allies went to in identifying targets and selecting appropriate methods and means of attack. In the words of Aldrich,[140] 'there had probably never previously been in the Twentieth Century a conflict in which attacks were made with the accuracy of those by the Coalition forces.'

Nuclear facilities

In attacking Iraqi chemical and nuclear facilities, precautions were taken to prevent the escape of dangerous forces.[141] It is of interest to note that the US Air Force attacks on the Iraqi nuclear power stations did not create a risk of radioactive contamination.[142]

Goldblat[143] criticizes the bombing on the grounds that no military necessity could be shown. He says that Iraq's reactors were not large enough to produce the quantities of plutonium needed for nuclear weapons and they were not used in 'regular, significant and direct support of military operations'.[144] But there were intelligence reports that Iraq was developing nuclear weapons[145] and evidence has since emerged, through the visits of UN inspectors, that Iraq was doing so.[146] That would certainly have justified the attacks. Attacks on power stations[147] are justified if the power stations are military objectives. The only difference in the case of nuclear power stations is the risk of radioactive contamination. If a power station can be attacked in such a way that there is no such risk, the attack is lawful. Even if there is an escape of radioactive material, it

[139] Plant, Environmental damage, p. 161.
[140] In a letter dated 6 April 1993 to the writer.
[141] Mr Lennox-Boyd in a written parliamentary answer, Hansard (Commons), 26 June 1991, col. 487.
[142] Painchaud, Environmental Weapons, quoting *Le Devoir*, 1991. See also the evidence of the UK Secretary of State in *Preliminary Lessons of Operation Granby*, House of Commons Defence Committee, Tenth Report, HMSO, 1991, p. 11.
[143] Goldblat, Legal protection, p. 2.
[144] These words are taken from Geneva Protocol I of 1977, Art. 56, which did not apply in the Gulf conflict.
[145] DOD Report, p. 97.
[146] See, e.g., Douglas Hurd, the Foreign Secretary, in *The Times*, 2 August 1991.
[147] According to Gasser, the installations attacked in Iraq were research installations, not power stations—H. P. Gasser, Humanitäres Völkerrecht in Aktion, *Humanitäres Völkerrecht Informationsschriften*, January–July 1991, p. 32.

would then be a question of proportionality:[148] how severe the pollution caused
and its effects on the civilian population and the environment.

Diverting rivers

The *Manual of Military Law* makes the bold statement, without quoting any
authority, that there is no rule 'to prevent measures being taken to dry up springs
and to divert rivers and aqueducts'.[149]

Following the invasion of Kuwait by Iraqi forces in August 1990, it was at
first estimated that an attack to free Kuwait would cost in excess of 100,000
casualties. Newspaper reports indicated that some experts had suggested an
alternative[150]—turning off Iraq's water supply—since, with the completion of
the Ataturk dam in Turkey in January 1991, 328 of the 400 cubic metres of
water discharged every second by the rivers Tigris and Euphrates could have
been siphoned off before it reached Iraq.[151] The question arises whether this
would have been lawful.

Applying the manual, the answer would be in the affirmative. But would the
answer still be the same today? Had the ENMOD Convention, to which the
United States and United Kingdom are parties, applied, it might have been
violated, bearing in mind Iraq's dependence on the two rivers for its water
supply, though there would be an argument about whether the threshold of
Art. II of the convention had been crossed.[152] But the convention did not apply,
because Iraq was not a party.[153] Had Protocol I applied to the Gulf War, it is
questionable whether there would have been a violation of Arts. 35 and 55,
given the regenerative capacity of the desert, but there might well have been a
breach of Art. 54, since it could hardly be argued that the action had not been
intended to starve the civilian population.

Painchaud[154] speculates about the reasons why the allies did not make use of
this method of warfare: did they fear chemical or bacteriological retaliation, did
they hold back for legal reasons, was Turkey opposed,[155] were the allies afraid
of public opinion? He thinks the answer was a combination of these factors. It
could have been kept in reserve for possible reprisal purposes had Iraq used

[148] This is recognized in Protocol I, Art. 56, para. 1, which speaks of 'consequent *severe* losses
among the civilian population'.

[149] Page 42.

[150] *Evening Standard*, 15 November 1990.

[151] Painchaud, Environmental Weapons, considers that if Iraq's water supply had been cut off in
this way, Iraq would have been able to sustain its population and armed forces for only a few days.

[152] South Korea, on accession to the convention, made a statement that it included 'any technique
for deliberately changing the natural state of rivers', see Roberts and Guelff, *Documents*, p. 385.

[153] DOD Report, p. 606.

[154] Painchaud, Environmental Weapons.

[155] Pazarci, in an intervention at the Ottawa Conference, 1991, said that Turkey would not use its
waterways as a weapon of war.

chemical or bacteriological warfare, but it was confirmed in Parliament that the allies never envisaged the use of environmental techniques.[156]

Conclusions

The following conclusions may be reached about the law as it currently stands.

1. Natural processes must not be deliberately manipulated for hostile purposes if that would have widespread, long-lasting or severe effects.

2. The environment as such may not be attacked.

3. In the conduct of military operations, care must be taken to spare the environment.

4. Damage which is not militarily necessary may not be inflicted.

5. When attacking a military objective, methods or means should be chosen which, commensurate with military success, cause the least environmental damage.

6. Any environmental damage caused must be proportionate to the military objective to be attained.

7. It is prohibited to employ methods or means of warfare which are intended, or may be expected, to cause widespread, long-term and severe damage to the environment and thereby prejudice the health or survival of the population.

In addition, there are other rules that protect the environment, for example the protection of forests from incendiary attack, the rules on dangerous forces and the protection of objects that are indispensable to the survival of the civilian population.[157]

The threshold for the applicability of the environmental provisions in warfare is very high. It is unlikely that military commanders would be involved in environmental manipulation. As for Protocol I, even the severe pollution caused in the Gulf War of 1990–91 does not seem to have fallen within the widespread, long-term and severe criterion.

The future

There is no doubt that there is greater interest now than in recent memory in environmental protection and that political leaders ignore that interest at their peril.[158] Modern developments have had both negative and positive effects.

---

[156] Lennox-Boyd, Hansard (Commons), 26 June 1991, col. 487. It was agreed between the allies in advance that water supplies would not be attacked, see Defence Committee Report, p. 10.

[157] A complete list appears in the ICRC Report, *Protection of the Environment in Time of Armed Conflict* (Report for the Forty-eighth Session of the UN General Assembly), ICRC, 1993.

[158] As Painchaud, Environmental Weapons, puts it, 'the use of environmental weapons is proving to be more and more costly from a political point of view'.

Precision weapons can be used to strike targets with reduced risk of environmental damage but, on the other hand, the increase in the number of nuclear power stations, chemical facilities and dams has increased the risk of attacks that might have environmental consequences. Some commentators consider that customary law now requires the avoidance of unnecessary damage to the environment.[159] While that formulation may be disputed, it is clear that, under the customary law rule of proportionality, military commanders must take into account the consequences for the civilian population when planning attacks and that would include the effect on the population of environmental damage.[160]

There have been calls for what might be described as a fifth Geneva Convention, or Ecocide Convention,[161] to protect the environment, with some peacetime principles,[162] such as the precautionary principle,[163] responsibility for damage caused to the environment outside the limits of national jurisdiction, impact assessments,[164] and the duty to warn of trans-boundary escapes, being applied in wartime and a 'protecting power' for the environment modelled on the ICRC[165] and protective emblems being established.[166] Some consider that breaches of Arts. 35 and 55 of Protocol I should be grave breaches.[167] One useful suggestion is that environmentally sensitive areas should be declared non-defended localities.[168] This might work in respect of small areas or those containing no objects of military significance. In the case, for example, of areas containing offshore oil installations, however, the coastal state might be reluctant to declare them undefended. Falk complains that existing law is deficient in being based on customary principles, sweeping generalizations and vaguely defined terms, with

[159] B. Mawhinney's conclusions at the Ottawa Conference, 1991.

[160] Parks, in an intervention at the Ottawa Conference, 1991, said that in planning the ground and air campaign to liberate Kuwait, great care was taken to protect the environment and that any attack on the environment is a two-edged sword. See also, Bothe, *GYIL*, p. 58.

[161] R. Falk, The environmental law of war: an introduction, in G. Plant (ed.), *Environmental Protection and the Law of War*, Belhaven, 1992, at p. 94.

[162] The writer shares the opinion of Green, The Environment, that the law of war is *lex specialis* and, to the extent to which it conflicts with the *lex generalis*, it prevails. Others like Kiss expressed the view at the Ottawa Conference, 1991, that the peacetime rules for the protection of the environment, like those for the protection of human rights (subject to derogations), are not suspended in wartime.

[163] See Bothe, *GYIL*; ICRC Report to UN General Assembly, p. 21.

[164] See the authorities quoted by Szasz, Study of Proposals. In the case of the European Union the requirement for impact assessments is laid down in Council Directive 85/337, see P. Sands and D. Alexander, Assessing the impact, *New Law Journal*, 1 November 1991, p. 1487.

[165] Bothe, *GYIL*, p. 62, considers that the ICRC could take the lead by clearing the way for organizations expert in dealing with pollution problems to combat the environmental hazards occurring as a consequence of military activity.

[166] G. Plant, Elements. S. Hughes, M.P., made a similar point in Parliament, Hansard (Commons), 15 March 1991, col. 1357. Szasz, Study of Proposals, considers that such a body could have norm-making, monitoring and dispute-resolving functions.

[167] ICRC Report to UN General Assembly, p. 21.

[168] Goldblat, Legal protection, p. 6; Bouvier, Protection, p. 577; Antoine, Environment, p. 532. See Protocol I, Arts. 59 and 60. The differences between the two articles are briefly explained in chapter 4.

too much subjectivity and loopholes and a lack of means of implementation.[169] There have also been calls for objective criteria for assessing what amounts to 'widespread, long-term and severe damage' and a suggestion that the ICRC might evaluate the matter.[170] There is growing concern in the world that states should be made responsible for removing the remnants of war and clearing up environmental damage caused by war. It is for consideration whether, when troops are lent to another country to assist in its defence, responsibility for dealing with the remnants of war and environmental damage should be dealt with in the treaty or memorandum of understanding governing the deployment of troops. Fleck calls for an updating of standards for the legal protection of the environment in line with the dictates of public conscience, and an examination of the rules on criminal responsibility, internal armed conflicts and neutrality.[171] Plant demands a lowering of the threshold of environmental harm in Protocol I, an extension of Art. 56 of Protocol I to severe damage to the natural environment, an extension of the Weapons Convention to fuel–air explosives, the special protection of environmentally sensitive areas and the institution of a Green Cross type of organization.[172]

Green[173] doubts the utility of negotiating yet another treaty and suggests that the International Law Commission might be charged by the UN Security Council with drafting principles of customary law for the protection of the environment which could be made binding by a resolution of the Council.

Anyway, as noted above, there is already a respectable body of treaty law which, whether directly or indirectly, protects the environment. It may be that energies would be better directed towards encouraging states to adhere to those instruments,[174] and reflecting them, and any 'soft law' instruments to which they had subscribed, in national law and military manuals,[175] than in negotiating new, and in some cases somewhat fanciful, texts.

---

[169]Falk, Environmental law of war, p. 93. His criticisms are shared by Roberts, Environment, p. 125.

[170]M. Saalfeld and H. P. Gasser, *Brussels Congress,* 1991; Bothe, *GYIL*, p. 58. Indeed, the ICRC studied these matters at meetings of experts in 1992 and 1993, see ICRC Report to UN General Assembly.

[171]Fleck, Environment, pp. 148–9.

[172]Plant, Environmental damage, pp. 172–4.

[173]Green, The Environment.

[174]This was the feeling of many delegates to the Ottawa Conference, 1991, and at the London Conference on a 'Fifth Geneva Convention on the Protection of the Environment in Time of Armed Conflict', June 1991 (see the rapporteur's executive summary), was the thrust of the resolution of the Sixth Committee of the UN General Assembly (A/C.6/47/L.2/Rev.1), and seems to be the view of Roberts, Environment, p. 152; Fleck, Environment, p. 152; A. Bouvier, Recent studies on the environment in time of armed conflict, 1992, *International Review of the Red Cross*, p. 577; the ICRC, Report to UN General Assembly, p. 24; and McCoubrey, see McCoubrey and White, *International Law*, p. 237.

[175]Fleck refers to the steps taken in this regard in the German manual, *Humanitäres Völkerrecht in bewaffneten Konflikten. Handbuch*, Bundesministerium der Verteidigung, 1992: Fleck, Environment, p. 154.

7

Criminal responsibility

For the purposes of this chapter a commander may be defined as a soldier having either direct authority over a body of troops or authority over a geographical area in which troops are stationed.[1] Depending on the circumstances, a commander may be a corporal commanding a section or a general commanding an army group.

The war crimes trials

Commanders

Criminal responsibility
Liability is clear if the commander commits a war crime himself or orders the commission of a war crime, but very often his responsibility will be less sharply defined because he will be remote from the scene of the crime or from those who have committed it.

The commander has always been held responsible for the outcome of the orders he gives[2] but the concept of a superior's responsibility for the acts of his subordinates where those acts do not flow from that superior's orders is a comparatively recent development of the law of war.[3] It started with the trial of General Yamashita after the Second World War and has found confirmation in Protocol I,[4] which provides that a superior is responsible for the offences of his subordinates if he knew, or ought to have known, of them and failed to take steps to prevent them. The criminal responsibility of commanders may be summarized as follows.

[1] See Queen's Regulations for the Army, HMSO, 1975, para. 2.001.
[2] T. Meron, Henry the Fifth and the law of war, *American Journal of International Law*, 1992, pp. 16–21.
[3] Cassese comes to the same conclusion, see A. Cassese, *Violence and Law in the Modern Age*, Polity, 1988, p. 84.
[4] Art. 86, para. 2.

Commanders are responsible for the orders they give and so if the orders are unlawful they are as responsible in law as those who carry out the orders.[5]

Criminal responsibility does not automatically attach to the commander for all acts of his subordinates. The court in the Von Leeb case said that: 'a high commander cannot keep completely informed of the details of military operations of subordinates and most assuredly not of every administrative measure. He has the right to assume that details entrusted to responsible subordinates will be legally executed.'[6] There must be an unlawful act by the commander or a failure to supervise his subordinates constituting a dereliction of duty on his part.

A commander may be required to pass on for execution by his subordinates an order from a superior commander. Sometimes this order may be issued without consultation with the intermediate commander; sometimes it is passed on by the intermediate commander's staff as a matter of routine without the personal knowledge or involvement of the intermediate commander. The court in the Von Leeb case also dealt with this situation and said that, within certain limitations, a commander is entitled to assume that orders issued by his superiors and the state which he serves are issued in conformity with international law. 'He cannot be held criminally responsible for a mere error of judgment as to disputable legal questions.' To be held criminally responsible, the intermediate commander 'must have passed the order to the chain of command and the order must be one that is criminal upon its face, or one which he is shown to have known was criminal'.[7]

Commanders have a duty to prevent crimes being committed by their subordinates. That may engage the criminal responsibility of the commander if he fails to carry out that duty or has condoned offences. General Yamashita, the Japanese military commander of the Philippines during the Second World War, was found guilty by a US military commission of unlawfully disregarding and failing to discharge his duty as commander to control the operations of members of his command, permitting them to commit brutal atrocities and other high crimes, thereby violating the law of war.[8] On his petition to the US Supreme Court, that court held that he had an affirmative duty to take such measures as were in his power and appropriate in the circumstances to protect prisoners of war and the civilian population.[9] While not disagreeing with this principle, Walzer[10] is critical of the findings in the Yamashita case because the circumstances were such that he was unable to exercise effective control over the troops under his command. This notion formed the basis of the scathing dissenting

---

[5] The Dostler trial, I WCR 22. General Dostler was found guilty of having ordered the illegal shooting of fifteen prisoners of war.

[6] High Command trial, XII WCR 76.

[7] *Ibid.*, p. 74.

[8] Yamashita trial, IV WCR 3.

[9] *Ibid.*, pp. 43–4.

[10] M. Walzer, *Just and Unjust Wars*, Pelican, 1980, pp. 319–22.

judgement of Mr Justice Murphy.[11] The latter, rightly in the opinion of the writer, criticized the legal basis cited by the Supreme Court[12] for holding a commander responsible for controlling his subordinates, but it is submitted that there should be no difficulty in accepting the general principle that an officer, by the nature of his appointment, carries some responsibility for the acts of his subordinates and it is right that a military tribunal should assess the level of that responsibility in the particular circumstances of the case. The following questions arise about the commander's duty:

1. Is the commander liable for not taking steps in advance to prevent the commission of offences?

2. To what extent is knowledge of the commission of offences required as the basis of liability for not intervening to stop offences?

3. What is the extent of the duty to enquire whether offences are being committed?

4. Is there a difference between the duty as a commander and liability for war crimes committed by others?

Duty to take steps

Responsibility may arise if war crimes were committed as a result of the commander's failure to discharge his duties either deliberately or by culpably or wilfully disregarding them, not caring whether this resulted in the commission of war crimes or not,[13] for example if the commander had reasonable grounds for suspecting that men under his command were going to commit war crimes and failed to do anything about it.[14]

Knowledge

Proof of knowledge, actual or inferred, is necessary.[15] Although General Sawada was away on duty when prisoners of war were denied that status, he did subsequently ratify the death sentences that had been imposed upon them.[16] On the other hand, General Hisakasu's responsibility did not arise because he was away on duty until after the execution of the victim.[17]

Knowledge can be inferred from the surrounding circumstances, for example the widespread nature, severity or notoriety of offences,[18] the prevailing state of discipline, and the participation in offences of officers in the command chain between the commander and troops committing offences.[19] The repeated occur-

---

[11] IV WCR 51.
[12] *Ibid.*, p. 43.
[13] The Baba Masao trial, abstracted in XV WCR 69.
[14] The trial of Schonfeld and others, abstracted at XV WCR 69.
[15] The Seeger trial, IV WCR 88.
[16] V WCR 4.
[17] V WCR 79.
[18] The Yamashita trial, IV WCR 1.
[19] The Rauer trial, IV WCR 85.

rence of offences by troops under one command may amount to *prima facie* evidence of the responsibility of the commander for those offences.[20] The commander will be liable for offences committed during his temporary absence from duty if they arise out of a general prescribed policy he has formulated.[21] But knowledge will not be inferred if the offences are not of sufficient magnitude or duration to constitute notice to the accused.[22] Milch was acquitted for lack of proof that he had guilty knowledge[23] but this may have been due to the fact that he was charged with being 'a principal in, accessory to, ordered, abetted, took a consenting party in and was connected with' plans for certain offences.

The leading case on the question of knowledge is the Yamashita trial.[24] There was no doubt that widespread atrocities had been committed in the area of his command, but Yamashita claimed that he was unaware of them, since communications were bad and he was totally preoccupied in dealing with the conduct of the military campaign. The case is unsatisfactory in that, while there was *some* evidence that the accused knew of some war crimes, the prosecution case seems to have been based on imputed knowledge. In its judgement the commission did not specifically state the basis of its finding. That it was based on imputed knowledge may be inferred from the following passage:

It is absurd, however, to consider a commander a murderer or a rapist because one of his soldiers commits a murder or rape. Nevertheless, where murder and rape and vicious, revengeful actions are widespread offences, and there is no effective attempt by a commander to discover and control the criminal acts, such a commander may be held responsible, even criminally liable, for the lawless acts of his troops, depending upon their nature and the circumstances surrounding them.[25]

Later on the commission concluded:

that during the period in question you failed to provide effective control of your troops as was required by the circumstances.[26]

One is driven to the conclusion that the commission found as a matter of fact that, despite his protestations to the contrary, Yamashita did know of the atrocities.

Want of knowledge of the contents of a report drawn up for a commander is not a defence, since failure to acquaint himself with the contents of reports drawn up for his special benefit is a dereliction of duty.[27] Again, much depends on the circumstances of the case. If the commander is busy conducting a military

[20] IV WCR 85.
[21] The Hostages trial, abstracted at XV WCR 76.
[22] The Pohl trial, VII WCR 63–4.
[23] IV WCR 88.
[24] IV WCR 1.
[25] IV WCR 35.
[26] *Ibid.*
[27] The Hostages trial, VIII WCR 71, quoted with approval in the High Command trial, XII WCR 112.

operation, he may simply not have the time to read all reports, even those drawn up for him personally. He may have to put some on one side until time becomes available. But, if he does so, that will require him at least to enquire as to the subject matter of those reports so that he can decide on their priority. If he is told that a report deals with, say, the massacre of civilians by troops under his command, he is put under a duty to do something about it. He cannot simply turn a blind eye. He must give appropriate orders to his staff.

Duty to enquire

A duty to enquire arises when a commander is put on notice or ought, in the circumstances, to have been put on notice.[28] Tschentscher was acquitted because the activities of his subordinates were not of sufficient magnitude or duration to constitute notice.[29] Commanders also have a duty to establish proper procedures to ensure that war crimes are not committed and to ensure that those procedures work efficiently. Otherwise they are liable only if they know crimes are being committed and fail to take steps to prevent them, or are at fault in having failed to acquire such knowledge.[30]

Practical examples of the commander's duties relating to the handling of prisoners of war would include ensuring that proper procedures were instituted and instructions issued, personnel and material made available, occurrences reported, enquiries conducted and periodic inspections carried out. During the Gulf War of 1990–91 the United Kingdom established a special prisoner-of-war guard force consisting of three infantry battalions advised by a military lawyer. The responsibility for prisoners of war does not end when they are transferred to another country under Art. 12 of the Prisoner of War Convention, so the United Kingdom set up a prisoner-of-war monitoring team, which included a military lawyer, to monitor the treatment of prisoners of war handed over to the allies.[31]

After the Second World War, Major Rauer was charged in respect of three separate killings by troops under his command of a total of twelve allied airmen. He was acquitted of the first set of killings but convicted of the other two, presumably on the basis that, although he had not given the orders for the killings, he had created a climate in which it was known by his subordinates that they would not be punished for killing prisoners of war. He took no steps to investigate the killings and accepted at face value assurances that prisoners of war had been killed while attempting to escape. The court may have thought that he had been put on notice after the first set of killings.[32]

---

[28] The Yamashita trial, IV WCR 94–5; the Doctors' trial, VII WCR 63; the Pohl trial, VII WCR 63.
[29] The Pohl trial, VII WCR 63.
[30] The Tokyo trial, abstracted at XV WCR 73.
[31] N. Pearce, *The Shield and the Sabre*, HMSO, 1992.
[32] The Rauer trial, IV WCR 113.

A commander may also be liable for war crimes committed in an area under his control by persons not under his command.[33] Thus commanders of occupied territory were held responsible for crimes committed by the *Einsatzgruppen* of the Security Police and SD of which they had knowledge and neglected to suppress[34] and for crimes committed in occupied territory without their consent or approval by SS units under the direct command of Heinrich Himmler.[35] At first sight this decision seems somewhat harsh but it seems to be based on the proposition that the commander derives his authority over occupied territory under international law and this does not take into account national regulations or chains of command. He has certain responsibilities which he cannot set aside or ignore by reason of the activities of his own state within his area. He is the instrument by which the occupation exists.[36] Cassese[37] draws some interesting parallels between the war crimes trials and the massacres in the Sebra and Shatila camps in 1982.[38] He considers that since Israeli troops wielded effective power over the Phalangist troops, once they knew the slaughter had started they were under a duty to stop it and, afterwards, to seek out and punish those responsible. In the von Manstein case[39] the accused was acquitted of having 'ordered, authorized and permitted' mass murders of civilians by paramilitary and police detachments operating in his area of command, but he was found guilty of violating Arts. 43 and 46 of the Hague Regulations by failing in his duty as a military commander to ensure public order and safety and to respect family honour and individual rights. According to the *Manual of Military Law*[40] this finding turned on the precise degree of subordination of the task force police units to the accused in his capacity as commander-in-chief, and his actual knowledge of their role and activities.

Duty/liability
Greenwood puts this duty thus:

A commander has a duty to ensure that forces under his command behave in accordance with the laws of armed conflict and may be convicted of a war crime if he fails to restrain them from unlawful behaviour.[41]

Hampson has summarized the position of the commander as follows:

It could be argued that a commander should only be responsible where the facts were of sufficient notoriety or involved breaches on such a scale that alleged ignorance of the

---

[33] High Command trial, XII WCR 74 *et seq.*
[34] *Ibid.*
[35] The Hostages trial, VIII WCR 69–70.
[36] High Command trial, XII WCR 77.
[37] Cassese, *Violence and Law*, p. 84.
[38] See the Kahan Report, 22 *International Legal Materials* (1983), p. 473.
[39] *Annual Digest*, 1949, Case No. 192.
[40] Page 178.
[41] C. J. Greenwood, *Command and the Laws of Armed Conflict*, Strategic and Combat Studies Institute, Army Staff College, Camberley, 1993, p. 35.

violations must, in effect, have been wilful. At the other end of the spectrum, a commander could be held responsible for failing to institute effective mechanisms to prevent
violations and to ensure that any possible breach was reported to him.[42]

There is a very fine distinction between complicity in war crimes committed by
others on the one hand and an omission to act, which may itself amount to a war
crime, on the other. In the Milch trial, one of the questions considered by the
tribunal was 'did he fail to act, thereby becoming *particeps criminis* and accessory to' the offences.[43] It seems that Hampson's above statement covers both
aspects. The first sentence deals with complicity in the breaches complained
of. The second sentence deals with complicity not in war crimes committed by
others but in breach of duty by the commander. As Hampson[44] indicates, the
duty of the commander in this respect may be inferred from the requirement
of the Geneva Conventions for states to take measures necessary for the suppression of all acts contrary to the provisions of the conventions.

In borderline cases it may be best to charge the commander in respect of
dereliction of duty rather than as a party to war crimes committed by others.

It is suggested that the commander also has a duty to bring to trial those under
his command who have committed grave breaches of the Geneva Conventions
or other serious war crimes.[45] This duty can be inferred from the duty placed on
states by the Geneva Conventions 'to search for persons alleged to have committed grave breaches and to bring them to justice.'[46]

Evidence
The evidential provisions at the war crimes trials were relaxed, especially with
regard to the admission of hearsay evidence. Rowe refers to the difficulties in
a wartime situation of obtaining sufficient admissible evidence to secure a conviction but points out that the exclusion of evidence that may be unreliable
ensures that the accused receives a fair trial.[47] For example, at the war crimes
trials, membership of a group was *prima facie* evidence of responsibility for
the activities of that group.[48] It is questionable whether such provisions would

[42]F. J. Hampson, Liability for war crimes, in P. J. Rowe (ed.), *The Gulf War 1990–91 in International and English Law*, Routledge, 1993, p. 245.
[43]IV WCR 90.
[44]Hampson, Liability, p. 245
[45]Alleged killings of prisoners of war by British troops during the Falklands war of 1982 were
referred to the Crown Prosecution Service, which instructed the Metropolitan Police Commissioner
to investigate, see, e.g., *The Times*, 20 August 1992 and 9 November 1993, but the Director of Public
Prosecutions decided not to mount a prosecution.
[46]Greenwood, *Command*, p. 34. See, e.g., Art. 146 of the Civilian Convention. The duty is now
confirmed in Protocol I, Art. 87, para. 3.
[47]P. J. Rowe, in his memorandum to the Foreign Affairs Select Committee, Third Report from the
Foreign Affairs Committee, *The Expanding Role of the UN and its Implications for UK Policy*,
Appendix to the Minutes of Evidence, 1993, p. 313.
[48]See Art. 8(ii) of the British royal warrant of 14 June 1945 with regulations for the trial of war
criminals, published in the *Manual of Military Law*, p. 347.

be acceptable today. Protocol I[49] provides that no one shall be convicted of an offence except on the basis of individual penal responsibility. The War Crimes Act of 1991 contains no provision for the relaxation of the law of evidence in trials to which the Act relates.

Staff officers

For the purposes of this chapter a staff officer may be defined as an officer on the staff of a commander who assists the commander in carrying out his duties.[50]

A staff officer is not guilty of a war crime by virtue only of his knowledge of illegal acts or of the outcome of his commander's orders which he approved from the point of view of form and issued on his commander's behalf.[51] Unlike a commander, a staff officer cannot normally be found guilty of a war crime for failure to act, because he has no command responsibility.[52] There is an implication in the war crimes reports[53] that a staff officer is not liable for failing to pass to his commander information about war crimes on the grounds that a staff officer's duty to pass information to his superiors stems from national regulations rather than international law.

There must, therefore, be some personal involvement on the staff officer's part, such as when he issues orders on his own behalf,[54] drafts them himself[55] or influences policy,[56] or events[57]—for example, where he presents a policy paper which is adopted by the commander, or, it is suggested, where he deliberately conceals offences committed by others by failing to bring them to his commander's notice. It will be for a tribunal to decide, depending on the facts of the case, whether a staff officer is liable as an accessory.

The responsibility of staff officers was considered more recently by the Ministry of Defence in its examination of material in its possession relating to Kurt Waldheim when he was a junior staff officer at headquarters Army Group E in the Balkans during the Second World War. While it seems in one or two cases that he was aware of the existence of captured commandos and of their intended fate, known as special treatment,[58] there was no evidence of any complicity on his part in the matter sufficient to form the basis of war crimes responsibility.[59]

---

[49] Art. 75, para 4(b).
[50] For more information about the British army staff structure, see Queen's Regulations for the Army, chapter 4.
[51] The Hostages trial, VIII WCR 34–92.
[52] The High Command trial, XII WCR at p. 81.
[53] XV WCR 77–8.
[54] XII WCR 81–2 and the Woehler trial, XII WCR 113–18.
[55] The High Command trial, XII WCR at p. 118.
[56] Tokyo trial abstracted in XV WCR 78.
[57] The Isayama trial, V WCR 60.
[58] *Sonderbehandlung.*
[59] United Kingdom, *Review of the results of investigations . . . and the involvement . . . of Lieutenant Waldheim*, HMSO, 1989.

Protocol I

Basic principle

Protocol I reinforces the grave breach provisions of the Geneva Conventions by introducing grave breach provisions of its own.[60] One example is wilfully, in violation of Art. 51 para. 2 of Protocol I,[61] making individual civilians or the civilian population the object of attack and thereby causing death or serious injury to body or health. Clearly, this applies to those who carry out the attack, but what of their military superiors? On the basis of general legal principles, the criminal responsibility of the commander who orders such an attack or otherwise takes an active part in encouraging or acquiescing in it is implied.

The commander as a party to war crimes committed by his subordinates (Protocol I, Art. 86, para. 2)

Protocol I deals specifically with the problem addressed in the Yamashita case of the commander who has knowledge, express or implied, of breaches of the law of war and does nothing. He becomes liable for a breach[62] committed by a subordinate if he knew, or had information which should have enabled him to conclude in the circumstances at the time, that his subordinate was committing or was going to commit such a breach and did not take all feasible measures within his power to prevent or repress[63] the breach.[64]

Partsch is critical of this provision because it is unbalanced: it deals with the responsibility of the commander, but the corresponding responsibility of the subordinate who receives an unlawful order is not dealt with.[65] He also criticizes the failure to set out clearly the three conditions for the commander's responsibility laid down in the Yamashita case: that he knew of the breach, that he had the power to prevent it, that he did nothing to do so.[66] He accepts that the second

---

[60] Art. 85.

[61] Which provides that the civilian population as such, as well as individual civilians, shall not be the object of attack. Acts or threats of violence the primary purpose of which is to spread terror among the civilian population are also prohibited.

[62] This provision is not limited to grave breaches, ICRC *Commentary*, p. 1012.

[63] According to Partsch, 'repress' means action under penal law; 'suppress' means other action, e.g. disciplinary measures—M. Bothe, K. J. Partsch and W. Solf, *New Rules for the Victims of Armed Conflicts*, Martinus Nijhoff, 1982, p. 524.

[64] Art. 86, para. 2.

[65] Bothe *et al.*, *New Rules*, p. 524.

[66] Rowe considers that where a commander 'fails to take steps that he might take to prevent an offence taking place (without ordering that the offences be committed), he may also be liable' and refers to Smith and Hogan, *Criminal Law*, 7th ed., 1992, p. 132, where the authors state: 'where [the defendant] has a right to control the actions of another and he deliberately refrains from exercising it, his inactivity may be a positive encouragement to the other to perform an illegal act, and therefore an aiding and abetting [of the offence committed]', see P. J. Rowe, Response from the United Kingdom Group of the International Society for Military Law and the Law of War to the criminology questionnaire, 1994 (to be published in the *Military Law and Law of War Review*).

condition is included in the words 'all feasible measures in his power' but considers that the first condition has been extended by inclusion of the words 'had information which should have enabled him to conclude in the circumstances at the time'. However, this may have been an attempt at the CDDH to articulate the thought processes of the tribunal in the Yamashita case, which was faced with a denial of knowledge yet had evidence which led it to believe that he must have known.

Problems of interpretation arise when the English and French texts of this passage are compared:

1.   Had information which should have enabled them to conclude in the circumstances at the time.

2.   *Possédaient des informations leur permettant de conclure, dans les circonstances du moment.*

At first sight the use of the words 'should have' in the English text seems to introduce an element which is not present in the French version and various authorities suggest that the French text should prevail.[67] But both texts seem to lead to the same result, since in either case the tribunal will have to decide whether the information was such that knowledge can be inferred.

De Preux[68] lists some of the factors that a tribunal might take into account in deciding whether constructive knowledge of the superior could be established: the tactical situation, the level of training and instruction of subordinate officers and their troops (particularly on the Geneva Conventions and Protocols and the handling of prisoners of war) and their character traits, the means of attack allocated or available in an area densely populated by civilians or lack of medical services. He adds that a commander cannot absolve himself from responsibility by invoking temporary absence as an excuse or by pleading ignorance of reports addressed to him. Here one has to be careful because no one is to be convicted of a war crime except on the basis of individual penal responsibility.[69] A tribunal has to look at all the circumstances before it can find constructive knowledge. A temporary absence is one of the factors that it would take into account. The fact that a report is addressed to a commander does not mean that he sees it or is even aware of its existence. It is frequently the case in practice that a report addressed to the commander is first seen by the chief of staff, who decides whether the commander needs to be made aware of it or not. The chief of staff may well pass it to another staff officer for action. Again, the tribunal would have to look at the circumstances before coming to any conclusion. It might be more inclined to find against a commander if it concluded that he was deliberately turning a blind eye to reports or information about war crimes committed by those under his command, especially where the offences were widespread and a matter of public notoriety.

[67] Bothe *et al.*, *New Rules*, p. 525; ICRC *Commentary*, p. 1013.
[68] ICRC *Commentary*, pp. 1013–14.
[69] Protocol I, Art. 75, para. 4(b).

De Preux[70] also refers to the difficulty of establishing *mens rea* in cases of failure to act, particularly in cases of negligence, points out that the Geneva Conventions do not contain any provision qualifying negligent conduct as criminal, recalls that one delegation at the CDDH thought that the words 'should have' implied responsibility incurred by negligence and concludes that negligence is not necessarily criminal: 'it must be so serious that it is tantamount to malicious intent'. In English criminal law the level of negligence required to constitute an offence depends on the nature of the offence. A relatively small amount of negligence will suffice for driving without *due* care and attention; yet gross negligence is required for manslaughter.[71] In military law, negligence has to be blameworthy and deserving of punishment.[72]

The writer does not share the view of de Preux[73] that the concept of the superior 'should be seen in terms of a hierarchy encompassing the concept of control'. If so, there would be no need for 'persons under his control' to be specifically included in the text of Art. 87, para. 3, of Protocol I. Since the two texts are different, and deal with different situations, they must have been intended to impose different liabilities.

It is debatable whether Art. 86, para. 2, of Protocol I has affected the liability of staff officers in respect of failure to act. It is of interest that the term 'commander' is not used in this provision, but the word 'superiors'. It is certainly arguable that 'superiors' encompasses staff officers at a superior headquarters. They would indeed be well placed to do something about suppressing breaches by issuing appropriate orders or instructions, if it lay within their competence to do so, or passing the matter to another staff division or to the commander with appropriate recommendations if it did not.

Duty of commanders to deal with breaches (Protocol I, Art. 87, para. 3)

Apart from being liable to be considered a party to war crimes committed by his subordinates, a commander is in any event under a general duty to maintain discipline, and that includes a duty to take action in respect of war crimes committed, or about to be committed, by his subordinates or by other persons under his control.[74] Protocol I is curiously drafted in that when dealing with the suppression of breaches it does not place any direct responsibility on commanders.[75] It places the responsibility on the high contracting parties and the parties to the conflict to ensure that commanders:[76]

---

[70]ICRC *Commentary*, pp. 1011–12.
[71]*R.* v. *Prentice and others*, [1993] 4 All ER 935.
[72]*Manual of Military Law*, Part I, HMSO, 1972 (reprinted 1992), pp. 311, 350.
[73]ICRC *Commentary*, p. 1013.
[74]The Yamashita trial, IV WCR 1.
[75]Unlike, e.g., Art. 57, para. 2a, which states that 'those who plan or decide upon an attack shall . . . ', or Art. 85, dealing with grave breaches, which, again, is based on personal liability.
[76]Art. 87. This provision of Protocol I depends for its effectiveness on the introduction by the

1. Prevent and, where necessary, suppress and report to the competent authorities breaches of the Geneva Conventions and Protocol I. This applies in relation to members of the armed forces under their command and also other persons under the control of commanders. (Art. 87, para. 1.)

2. Make members of the armed forces under their command aware of their obligations under the conventions and protocol. This applies commensurate with the commander's level of responsibility. (Art. 87, para. 2.)

3. If aware that persons are going to commit or have committed breaches of the conventions or Protocol I, initiate such steps as are necessary to prevent those breaches and, where appropriate, initiate penal or disciplinary action against the violators. This applies in relation to subordinates or other persons under the control of the commander. (Art. 87, para. 3.)

If the offence were not a grave breach but some other serious war crime, the issue would arise as to the appropriate charge. An example might be a soldier who altered his ammunition to produce a dum-dum round. The answer would depend on the legal system being applied. Under British military law a soldier can be charged under the appropriate section of the Army Act 1955, for example s. 30 (looting), s. 34 (disobeying a lawful command), s. 36 (disobeying standing orders), s. 44 (damaging public property), s. 63 (offences against the civilian population), s. 64 (scandalous conduct), s. 66 (disgraceful conduct) and s. 69 (prejudicial conduct). Under the Royal Warrant of 14 June 1945, authorized officers may convene military courts to try persons who are within the limits of their command for war crimes.[77]

It is submitted that even if the state, or party to the conflict, to which the commander belongs fails to issue the appropriate instructions, the tests enunciated in the war crimes trials would still apply to him.

Members of the armed forces under command include not only those who are regularly under command but also those who are placed under command temporarily[78] and, within a sector of occupied territory for which a commander is responsible, the term 'persons under control' includes the population of that sector and even troops operating in that sector which are not directly subordinate to him.[79]

The law of war is becoming very complicated. One cannot really expect every soldier and officer to know every article and every nuance of the Geneva Conventions and Protocols, let alone the other conventions and writings. It suffices

---

parties of implementing legislation or regulations. The German manual places a positive obligation on the disciplinary superior to act when he learns of a breach of international humanitarian law, see Germany, *Humanitäres Völkerrecht in bewaffneten Konflikten—Handbuch*, Bundesministerium der Verteidigung, 1992, para. 1213.

[77] For a more extensive discussion of the royal warrant, see A. P. V. Rogers, War crimes trials under the royal warrant, 39 (1990), *International and Comparative Law Quarterly* 780.

[78] ICRC *Commentary*, p. 1019.

[79] *Ibid.*, p. 1020; the List trial, VIII WCR 69–71. See also the discussion earlier in this chapter under the heading 'Knowledge'.

if they understand the general principles of the law of war and then receive
training or instructions specifically related to their mission. Legal advisers should
be on hand[80] to advise commanders about appropriate levels of instruction. The
important thing is that commanders are alert to the implications of the law of
war and take them into consideration, seeking expert advice where necessary,
when issuing orders or instructions and take steps to prevent or report breaches
of which they become aware, including instituting formal disciplinary action
when necessary.

Partsch is critical of the drafting of Art. 87 para. 3 of Protocol I, saying that
it does not conform to Art. 86 para. 2.[81] However, the use of the word 'aware'
may have been an attempt by the draftsmen to cover both actual and constructive knowledge, so that one could argue that both paragraphs are consistent.

The level at which a commander's responsibility arises will depend on the
circumstances. A corporal commanding a section would be responsible for
ensuring that the soldiers under his command acted in accordance with the law
of war by issuing appropriate orders and instructions and reporting offenders to
officers having disciplinary powers. Although he could not be expected to carry
out formal law of war training, he might, depending on the circumstances, be
under a duty to remind his soldiers about the aspects of their law of war training that were relevant to the tactical situation in which they found themselves.
Although Partsch suggests[82] that Art. 87 para. 2 of Protocol I goes no further
than Art. 83 of the Protocol,[83] it does make it clear that the responsibility for
instructing others in the law of war is not limited to those who are involved in
running formal courses.

International Law Commission

The International Law Commission has been considering a draft code of crimes
against the peace and security of mankind for some years. In 1991[84] it prepared
a draft article, Article 3, on responsibility which reads, in part:

An individual who aids, abets or provides the means for the commission of a crime
against the peace and security of mankind or conspires in or directly incites the commission of such a crime is responsible therefor and is liable for punishment.

This formulation may, in suitable cases, engage the liability of staff officers as
persons who 'provide the means'.

---

[80]Protocol I, Art. 82.
[81]Bothe *et al.*, *New Rules*, p. 529. Art. 86, para. 2, deals with the legal responsibility of the
commander if he fails to act to deal with breaches.
[82]Bothe *et al.*, *New Rules*, p. 529.
[83]Which deals with dissemination.
[84]UN Doc. A/46/405.

The commission had previously adopted an article, Article 12, on the responsibility of the superior, which is almost identical to the wording of Protocol I.[85]

Military discipline and superior orders[86]

Military effectiveness depends on the prompt and unquestioning obedience of
orders to such an extent that soldiers are prepared to put their lives at risk in
executing those orders. During military operations decisions, actions and instructions often have to be instantaneous and do not allow time for discussion or
attention by committees. It is vital to the cohesion and control of a military force
in dangerous and intolerable circumstances that commanders should be able to
give orders and expect their subordinates to carry them out.[87] In return for this
unswerving obedience the soldier needs the protection of the law so that he does
not afterwards risk his neck for having obeyed an order which later turns out to
be unlawful.

Until the 1920s obedience to orders was usually regarded as a complete
defence to a charge.[88] If anybody had to accept responsibility for the outcome
of orders it must be he who gave them.

But the decisions of the German supreme court in the hospital ship cases[89]
indicated otherwise: that the defence of superior orders would provide no justification where the act was manifestly and indisputably contrary to international
law.

The Nuremberg trial and the war crimes trials virtually put an end to the
superior orders defence because all too often it was claimed that the accused was
only obeying orders. Taken to its logical extreme in a hierarchical society, that
would mean that officers at every level of command could plead superior orders
and only the head of state would be criminally responsible. The passing of
responsibility had to stop. So in anticipation of such defences the rule, at least
as it was understood by the victorious allies, was that accused could not escape
punishment for complying with an order that was manifestly illegal and committing acts which both violated the unchallenged rules of warfare and outraged the
general sentiment of humanity.[90]

[85] 'The fact that a crime against the peace and security of mankind was committed by a subordinate
does not relieve his superiors of criminal responsibility, if they knew or had information enabling
them to conclude, in the circumstances at the time, that the subordinate was committing or was going
to commit such a crime and if they did not take all feasible measures within their power to prevent
or repress the crime.'
[86] This part of this book deals only with superior orders under *international* law. For a more
detailed discussion of this problem, see A. P. V. Rogers, The defence of superior orders in international law, 1991 *Military Law Journal*, p. 17.
[87] G. J. Cartledge, *The Soldier's Dilemma: When to Use Force in Australia*, Australian Government Publishing Service, 1992, pp. 174–5.
[88] *Manual of Military Law*, 7th ed., HMSO, 1929, p. 83.
[89] *Annual Digest* 1923–24, Case Nos. 231, 235.
[90] Amendment 34 to the *Manual of Military Law*, 7th ed., HMSO, 1944.

Art. 8 of the Nuremberg Charter seemed even stricter, providing only that superior orders might be considered in mitigation of punishment. However, in its judgement the International Military Tribunal (IMT) said that the true test was not the existence of the order but whether a moral choice was, in fact, possible.[91] The International Law Commission also referred to moral choice when codifying the Nuremberg principles.[92] Perhaps the crimes dealt with by the International Military Tribunal were so obviously illegal that the finer points of the defence did not fall to be considered.

National war crimes tribunals, on the other hand, seem to have allowed a little more latitude.[93] The US tribunal in the *Einsatzgruppen* case indicated that the defence of duress might be available in suitable cases[94] and also raised manifest illegality in the following passage: 'If the nature of the ordered act is manifestly beyond the scope of the superior's authority, the subordinate may not plead ignorance to (sic) the criminality of the order.'[95] In the High Command trial the court held that, as orders relating to prisoner-of-war labour were not criminal on their face, it was a matter which a field commander had the right to assume was properly determined by higher authority.[96] On the other hand, a plea by von Falkenhorst that he had passed on Hitler's commando order as a reprisal and had no means of verifying the facts set out in the order was not accepted by a British military court, presumably on the basis that von Falkenhorst could have verified the facts in his command area.[97] Anyway, the Geneva Conventions of 1929 prohibited reprisals against prisoners of war.

The question of manifest illegality is well dealt with in the following passage:

The true test in practice is whether an order, illegal under international law, on which an accused has acted was or must be presumed to have been known to him to be so illegal or was so obviously illegal . . . or should have been recognized by him as being so illegal.[98]

To the writer this seems a clear reference to establishing *mens rea*.

What is the current legal thinking on the position under international law of those who carry out orders that are illegal? On the whole, modern theorists have rejected superior orders as a complete defence but are divided into two camps:

[91] Trial of the Major War Criminals before the International Military Tribunal, Nuremberg, 1948, vol. XXII, p. 497. For more about the Nuremberg trials, see R. K. Woetzel, *The Nuremberg Trials in International Law*, Stevens, 1962.

[92] D. Schindler and J. Toman, *The Laws of Armed Conflicts*, 3rd ed., Martinus Nijhoff, 1988, p. 923.

[93] A useful discussion of the defence of superior orders in these cases is at XV WCR, pp. 157–60.

[94] As did the other tribunal referred to in XV WCR 170 *et seq*.

[95] *US v. Ohlendorf*, No. 9, Trials of War Criminals before the Nuremberg Military Tribunals under Control Council Law No. 10, vol. IV, pp. 470–1.

[96] XII WCR 88–9.

[97] XI WCR 18, at p. 26. See also M. H. F. Clarke, The Status of Guerillas and Irregular Forces, unpublished, 1976.

[98] XV WCR 158.

those, epitomized by Dinstein, who consider that superior orders are no defence at all and those, represented by Green, who say that superior orders ought to be a defence if the orders are not manifestly illegal.[99]

Those who negotiated Protocol I, however, were not able to agree on any text dealing with the defence of superior orders.[100] During the negotiations a text was put forward by the ICRC which provided that superior orders were no defence to an accused if 'in the circumstances at the time, he should have reasonably known that he was committing a grave breach . . . and that he had the possibility of refusing to obey the order'. Several delegations opposed this text on the basis that it created special rules for grave breaches while war crimes remained regulated by customary law, and the text did not receive approval by the necessary two-thirds majority, so was not adopted, leaving the matter to be governed by customary law.[101]

The writer finds the logic of the Dinstein school of thought more compelling, especially in that the key to the problem is the question of *mens rea*, and after a study of the authorities has come to the following conclusions.[102]

The position under international law may be summarized as follows. Soldiers[103] have a duty to obey lawful orders and a duty not to comply with unlawful orders. The fact that a soldier acted on the basis of orders from a superior will not relieve him of personal responsibility if, as a result, he commits a war crime. When he is tried for a war crime, the orders he received may be relevant in establishing *mens rea* or to defences such as mistake of fact or duress. In any event, superior orders will normally be taken into account in mitigation of punishment. Although there is some weight of academic authority in favour of allowing a limited exception to the principle that ignorance of the law is no excuse[104] in cases where a soldier has acted in good faith on the basis of superior orders in circumstances where the law is not clear or controversial, the point is not settled and it is difficult to conceive of circumstances where such a defence

[99] Y. Dinstein, *The Defence of Obedience to Superior Orders in International Law*, Leyden, 1965, and L. C. Green, *Superior Orders in National and International Law*, Sijthoff, 1976. In his article Superior orders and the Geneva conventions and protocols, in H. Fox and M. A. Meyer (eds.), *Effecting Compliance*, British Institute of International and Comparative Law, 1993, Green refers to 'obvious' illegality. McCoubrey seems to be a follower of the Green school. Referring to the International Military Tribunal and war crimes tribunal judgements, he states the position thus: 'superior orders may protect a subordinate from criminal responsibility but only if he or she neither knew nor ought to have known, upon the basis of normal professional competence, them to have been unlawful'—H. McCoubrey and N. D. White, *International Law and Armed Conflict*, Dartmouth, 1992, p. 341.

[100] Kalshoven, *Constraints on the Waging of War*, International Committee of the Red Cross, 1987, p. 134.

[101] Green, Superior orders and the Geneva conventions and protocols, pp. 196–7.

[102] Rogers, Superior orders, p. 24.

[103] Whatever their rank.

[104] H. McCoubrey, *The Idea of War Crimes and Crimes against the Peace since 1945*, University of Nottingham Research Papers in Law, June 1992, No. 2, p. 25, says that the root of the *ignorantia juris* principle lies in knowledge and application not of one but two, municipal and public international, legal systems.

might be raised.[105] It is to be hoped that in such cases the accused will not be prosecuted or, if prosecuted, given the benefit of any doubt by the court.

Of course, the court in any trial would determine the law. If a superior has made a mistake of law, that will not affect his liability and therefore the liability of the soldier. The soldier's act is illegal, so there is no defence. If prosecuted, the soldier could be given the benefit of the doubt only by the court's exercising its inherent right not to convict if it thought that to do so would not be in the interests of justice.

It is argued by the authors of the US Army pamphlet on international law[106] that there should be an exception to the *ignorantia juris* principle in international law because international law 'does not in some cases possess either the exactness or the degree of publicity which pertains to municipal law'. However, in the case there quoted of Flick[107] the plea of ignorance of local law was allowed only in mitigation of punishment and the scuttled U-boats[108] case also referred to seemed to turn on issues of fact (knowledge of the surrender) rather than on the question of knowledge of the law (the terms of the act of surrender).

Many military men—understandably, given the importance of orders in the military context—cling tenaciously to the manifest illegality test. They will find academic support too. McCoubrey states that 'It would thus be strongly arguable that the defence of superior orders, with the strict "ought to know" qualification, survived 1945 and remains a feature of modern law.'[109] Cartledge[110] considers that both *mens rea* and manifest illegality are important. He refers to various national manuals and court rulings to the effect that the prosecution must show that the accused either knew that the order was unlawful or could reasonably be expected to have known it. He says that there is a parallel with some military offences such as insubordination which require the prosecution to prove that the accused knew or ought to have known that the complainant was his superior officer.

But perhaps *mens rea* and manifest illegality are the same thing or, at least, lead to the same result. This can only be demonstrated by examples.

Example 1. The accused is ordered to and does bomb a military aircraft factory which later turns out to be a musical instruments factory.

Here there is no war crime: there is neither *mens rea* nor manifest illegality.

Example 2. The accused is ordered to and does shoot and kill a man passing by who is dressed in civilian clothes. He is an enemy guerilla commander.

---

[105] Because it is only the most serious and obvious war crimes that are likely to be tried.

[106] United States, *International Law,* vol. II, Department of the Army, Pamphlet 27-161-2, 1962, p. 246. McCoubrey makes the same point: 'potentially a conflict between two systems of law is involved, the detailed resolution of which lies beyond the reasonably expected competence of the average soldier or indeed junior officer'—McCoubrey and White, *International Law and Armed Conflict,* p. 342.

[107] IX WCR 1.

[108] I WCR 55.

[109] McCoubrey, *War Crimes,* p. 25.

[110] Cartledge, *The Soldier's Dilemma,* pp. 176–84.

Here there is no war crime because the person attacked is a legitimate target. The questions of *mens rea* and manifest illegality do not arise.

Example 3. Against a background of enemy guerilla operations the accused is ordered to shoot and kill a man passing by who is dressed in civilian clothes on the grounds that he is an enemy guerilla commander. In that belief the soldier complies with the order. It turns out that the man is an innocent civilian.

Although at first sight a man appearing to be a civilian ought not to be attacked, the soldier would say that he had no *mens rea* for a war crime because he had no reason to believe the facts to be other than as stated in the order. He would, no doubt, also claim that the order, in its context, was not manifestly unlawful.

Example 4. A soldier is ordered to and does use riot control gas to clear an enemy trench. He is prosecuted for violating the Geneva Gas Protocol of 1925[111] and claims that the protocol does not include riot control agents, but the tribunal finds against him on this point of law.

In this case the fact that he was ordered to use gas is irrelevant to the issue of criminal responsibility, so questions of *mens rea* and manifest illegality do not arise. Ignorance of the law is no excuse. However, it is to be hoped that the tribunal would make allowance for the fact that the law on this point is the subject of controversy and either acquit or impose only a nominal punishment.

Example 5. A long-range patrol ambushes a group of enemy soldiers and in the exchange of fire kills all its members except one who is wounded. A soldier is ordered to kill the wounded man because the patrol cannot take him with them and if he is left behind he may endanger the patrol by reporting its existence.

The order is illegal, so the soldier carrying it out would be liable to prosecution for a grave breach of Protocol I.[112] Here, it is submitted, neither the *mens rea* nor the manifest illegality test is going to help the defence.

Example 6. Prior to an infantry assault, the artillery commander is ordered by the divisional commander to, and does, destroy a village which is an enemy guerilla stronghold. The village is devastated as a result and most civilians living there are killed or injured, but none of the guerillas, since they are in protected positions.

It might be alleged that this attack was indiscriminate and that those involved were criminally liable. The test suggested by Fenrick[113] is that:

in all but the most blatant cases of indiscriminate attacks, subordinates would be entitled to assume that their superiors had carried out the attack precautions specified in Art. 57 of Protocol I and, as a result, they could not be held personally liable for any violation which occurred as a result of superior orders.

[111] Of course, the situation would be different if the states party to the conflict were parties to the Chemical Weapons Convention of 1993, which prohibits the use of riot control agents as a method of warfare.

[112] Protocol I, Arts. 41 and 85, para. 3(e).

[113] W. J. Fenrick, The rule of proportionality and Protocol I in conventional warfare, *Military Law Review*, 1982, p. 115.

Both the artillery commander and the commanding officer of the artillery regiment involved in the bombardment would have been involved in the planning of the attack, so could not rely on superior orders, but what of battery and troop commanders? They would probably realize that they were firing at areas in a village but might say that on the basis of the orders they had received and the information in their possession they had no reason to believe that the targets that had been identified for them were not military targets and carried out the orders they had received, so it would be a question of *mens rea* rather than manifest illegality. In this context, issues such as recklessness might be considered by the tribunal.

It is difficult to think of an example of a case where applying the *mens rea* and manifest illegality tests would lead to different results except, possibly, those where the law is unclear or controversial.

The International Law Commission, in its draft code of crimes against the peace and security of mankind, which include 'exceptionally serious war crimes', makes no reference to manifest illegality in its draft article on superior orders, prepared in 1991,[114] which reads as follows:

The fact that an individual charged with a crime against the peace and security of mankind acted pursuant to an order of a Government or a superior does not relieve him of criminal responsibility if, in the circumstances at the time, it was possible for him not to comply with that order.

This seems close to the formula adopted by the Commission when codifying the Nuremberg principles, does not include the manifest illegality test and is consistent with the line adopted in this chapter.[115]

[114]UN Doc. A/46/405.
[115]H. S. Levie, The rise and fall of an internationally codified denial of the defence of superior orders, *Military Law and Law of War Review*, 1991, p. 183, at p. 204, makes the interesting point that because of the failure of any international body to draft a provision on superior orders, that defence will be available to somebody charged with a violation of the law of war. Green, Superior orders and the Geneva conventions and protocols, in Fox and Meyer, *Effecting Compliance*, comments that, if adopted, the International Law Commission draft provides a limited defence of superior orders in the case of exceptionally serious war crimes but that in the case of grave breaches and other war crimes the matter is governed by customary law.

8

The military lawyer's perspective

The military lawyer's involvement in law on the battlefield may take one or more of several forms: as a negotiator in international conferences, as a writer of military manuals or as an instructor on the law of war, as a legal adviser to a commander or his staff or as a prosecutor in war crimes proceedings. In all these areas he can make a useful contribution to the understanding and implementation of the law.

Negotiator

At an international conference where treaty texts are being negotiated, the military lawyer may be part of a national delegation. Apart from providing the delegation with technical advice on the law of the war, he ought to be able to bring realism into the debate to ensure that participants are aware of the practical effect of the proposals that are being made; he should also be able to act as a link between the advocates of humanity and the advocates of military necessity in finding common ground, compromise and solutions. He should see that the rules that are being negotiated are capable of being understood, accepted by those to whom they apply and implemented in practice. This will involve endeavouring to make sure that the language is unambiguous and consistent. Here the search for compromise is a severe obstacle to clarity. Treaty texts sometimes contain emotive and politicized language,[1] or loose drafting,[2] or provisions which may be misunderstood if they are not considered in the context of other

---

[1] E.g. Art. 1, para. 4, of Protocol I, which speaks of armed conflicts in which peoples are fighting against colonial domination and alien occupation and against racist regimes.

[2] Such as Art. 51, para. 4(c), of Protocol I, which refers to attacks the effects of which cannot be limited as required by the protocol, so importing elements of proportionality into a rule dealing with distinguishing between the armed forces and civilians. It would have been clearer and more logical for there to have been a separate article dealing with proportionality.

provisions,[3] or provisions which are inconsistent with those of previous treaties,[4] or which lead to uncertainty,[5] or whose meaning is downright obscure.[6]

The military lawyer should, at least, be aware of lack of consistency or looseness of drafting and bring it to the attention of the conference so that corrections can be made.

Sometimes these difficulties are caused by a combination of factors. The need to find consensus sometimes leaves room for different interpretations. Pressure of time, late-night sittings, eagerness to clinch a deal after long and hard-fought negotiations also play their part.

An example is Art. 5 of the Mines Protocol to the Weapons Convention. This provides that remotely delivered mines may be used only within an area that is a military objective or which contains military objectives and then only if either they are fitted with neutralizing mechanisms or 'their location can be accurately recorded in accordance with Article 7(1)(a)'. On looking at Art. 7(1)(a) one finds that it provides that the parties to the conflict shall record the location of all pre-planned minefields laid by them.

The meaning of Art. 5 is, therefore, opaque. It might be interpreted as meaning that remotely delivered mines without neutralizing mechanisms can be used only for laying pre-planned minefields or, perhaps, that they can be used without recording in all cases when such use was not pre-planned.

With such widely divergent interpretations possible, the reference to Art. 7(1)(a), therefore, makes no sense at all. It is necessary to examine the negotiating history to find out what the parties to the negotiations intended.[7] The reference to Art. 7(1)(a) was a clumsy attempt by the delegates (including the writer!) suffering from the effects of a late-night sitting towards the end of a busy conference to ensure that remotely delivered mines not fitted with neutralizing mechanisms were to be used only if their location could be accurately recorded. Art. 7(1)(a) was the only provision for the *mandatory* recording of mines, paragraph 2 being merely exhortatory.

[3] E.g., when considering the status of British military advisers to the Kuwaiti armed forces captured by Iraq during the invasion of Kuwait in 1990, it was not enough to consider the Prisoner of War Convention. In fact, their status as *civilian* protected persons was confirmed by the Civilian Convention. See, further, F. J. Hampson, Liability for war crimes, in P. J. Rowe (ed.), *The Gulf War 1990–91 in International and English Law*, Routledge, 1993, p. 246.

[4] Because law of war treaties are self-standing and do not repeal and replace previous treaties dealing with the same subject matter, their relationship with each other may be difficult, if not impossible, to ascertain, as in the case of the cultural property texts referred to in chapter 5 above. The problem is exacerbated by the use of similar language in different treaties to mean different things, as in the ENMOD Convention and the ecological provisions of Protocol I.

[5] E.g. the failure to mention in Art. 53 of Protocol I that if cultural property is used for military purposes it loses its protection or the rather loose language of the Cultural Convention, which refers to property of great importance, property of very great importance and property of relative importance, see chapter 5 above.

[6] E.g. the term 'pre-planned' in the Mines Protocol to the Weapons Convention.

[7] This is set out in full in A. P. V. Rogers, The Mines Protocol: negotiating history, in ICRC, *Symposium on Anti-personnel Mines, Report*, International Committee of the Red Cross, 1993.

As agreement on this text had been achieved only at a very late stage after prolonged and intense arguments, nobody wanted to reopen the issue, even when its obscurity became evident.

The military lawyer will also be looking for realistic proposals. During the CDDH a proposal that stretcher bearers should carry a Red Cross flag was objected to by the medical colonel in the Soviet delegation on the grounds that stretcher bearers need both hands to carry the stretcher and do not have a spare hand for flag carrying! One provision that is regarded by some as unrealistic is the requirement of Protocol I to give effective advance warning of attacks which may affect the civilian population, unless circumstances do not permit. The writer finds the provision realistic enough. If to do so would endanger the attacker, circumstances probably would not permit the giving of a warning. On the other hand, there is no reason why minefields designed to channel the enemy in a certain direction should not be clearly marked. That would achieve the military aim and at the same time protect the civilian population. It may be possible when one's own territory is under attack to pass warnings through loyal civil channels without endangering the military operation. So much depends on the prevailing circumstances, but it is right that commanders should be obliged to consider the possibility of warnings.

Manual writer

It goes without saying that the manual writer must be a master of the subject matter who can express himself clearly and unequivocally. Where the law is unclear or controversial he should say so but still provide guidance to readers. In the opinion of the writer, therefore, it would be better to treat civilians working in military objectives as civilians exempt from direct attack but vulnerable to the incidental dangers of an attack on that objective than to describe them as having quasi-combatant status. To do that would only confuse the uninitiated. Even where the treaty texts are straightforward, as in the Geneva Conventions of 1949, practical guidance and practical examples should be provided. Where the treaty texts are complicated, such as the rules on indiscriminate attacks in Protocol I, the texts will need careful explanation.

The writer will also have to consider carefully at whom the manual is aimed.

Obviously, military lawyers prefer to work from the treaty texts, but need explanatory footnotes, or a commentary, and cross-references.[8] The latter are especially important. For example, the definition of 'military objective' cannot be looked at in isolation; attention must also be drawn to specific rules on objects such as dams, dykes and nuclear electricity generating stations. Generally speaking, though, military lawyers do not need a legal treatise because in

[8] Such as from Art. 78 of Protocol I to Art. 49 of the Civilian Convention.

practice time will not be available for studying problems in depth. They need to be in a position to give prompt and accurate legal advice. They do not need a learned discussion of whether or not an enemy combatant is to be classed as a military objective; they just need to know that it is permissible to attack enemy combatants. Where the law is controversial, as in the case of economic targets, the manual writer will have to make a decision on the guidance to be given. It may require political clearance. Military lawyers also may need practical examples like specimen rules of engagement.

Specialists, such as those handling prisoners of war, may need a special manual giving practical guidance on how to implement the Prisoner of War Convention, for example, the layout of a prisoner-of-war camp, orders for sentries, censorship, matters of diet or recreational facilities.

Commanders and staff officers require manuals which are written in clear, straightforward and non-legal language, perhaps expressed in the form of a series of rules or propositions. Some rules or propositions will need explanatory examples. The definition of 'military objective' in Protocol I, for instance, will be of limited use to the commander without an explanation of what it means, particularly concepts such as 'in the circumstances ruling at the time', and without concrete examples, particularly in the case of items of a civilian nature such as lines of communication. The circumstances in which an area of land may be a military objective must also be explained. The same is true of the rule of proportionality. Historical examples can help to clarify the meaning and application of the rule. In other cases, manuals may go beyond the treaty texts by laying down practical guidelines or instructions. It would be dangerous to set out the law on reprisals without saying at what level, according to national rules, reprisal action should be sanctioned. Otherwise the doctrine might be seized upon as an excuse for the commission of war crimes. In the case of cultural property, manuals can specify the level at which a decision to waive protection should be taken. The obligation to take precautions in attack can be summarized on the lines suggested in chapter 3 and checklists can be developed in the light of experience.

Junior officers probably need a pamphlet explaining the basic principles of the law of war.[9] Soldiers and junior noncommissioned officers do not need a manual at all, a brief summary being all that is required.[10] Rules of engagement cards may well suffice. Different cards can be produced for different situations. While parties to the Geneva Conventions and Protocols have a duty to disseminate them, it is left to the parties to decide how best to do so.[11]

The structure of a manual can be based on the subject matter, such as the conduct of combat, occupation, relations between belligerents and so on[12] or on

---

[9] E.g. the British Army pamphlet *The Law of Armed Conflict* (Army Code 71130).

[10] As in the British forces card JSP 381, Aide Memoire on the Law of Armed Conflict.

[11] See, e.g., Protocol I, Art. 83, and ICRC *Commentary*, para. 3382.

[12] As in the German manual, *Humanitäres Völkerrecht in bewaffneten Konflikten—Handbuch*, Bundesministerium der Verteidigung, 1992.

the tactical situation such as exercise of command, conduct in action or problems arising in support areas.[13] Again, the structure will depend on the readership: military lawyers may prefer the subject-matter approach while infantry officers may prefer the tactical approach. Certainly, it would be of advantage to include a 'teeth arm' officer in the editorial team.

Instructor

Protocol I recognizes the importance of legal advisers in providing advice on the instruction to be given to the armed forces on the law of war.[14]

Many of the considerations affecting manual writers apply to instructors too: clarity, firm guidance, tailoring the presentation or course to the audience, special presentations for specialist subjects, practical guidance. Obviously those with first-hand experience of the conduct of combat or operational deployments and the legal problems arising will speak with greater authority. Syndicate work is essential to reinforce points made in formal presentations and should preferably involve the discussion of problems among groups drawn from different disciplines. Best is the inclusion of realistic law of war problems in exercise scenarios. Here the military lawyer can be of great assistance to exercise planners but also to exercise controllers to ensure that legal problems are included in the exercise plans and recognized as such, and that action is taken accordingly.

Adviser

Protocol I specifically lays down a requirement for legal advisers to be available to advise commanders about the Geneva Conventions and Protocols.[15]

Like the manual writer, the adviser must be an expert in the subject. The experience of the writer is that the adviser will not have the time to acquire the necessary knowledge once the armed conflict, or the state of tension leading up to an armed conflict, has started. Advice is always needed very quickly, often in a matter of hours or at the very most overnight. This does not leave time for learning or research or more than the barest consultation. It means that the adviser must have attended courses and studied the treaty texts, commentaries, law books and military manuals beforehand so that answers to questions can be given almost instinctively. His burden will be eased if checklists have been prepared in peacetime, for example a list of legal points to be considered when examining target lists or plans of attack or draft rules of engagement

---

[13]As in F. de Mulinen, *Handbook on the Law of War for the Armed Forces*, ICRC, 1987.
[14]Art. 82.
[15]Art. 82.

or a model memorandum of understanding between allies. He should be aware of the traps inherent in obscure wording of treaty texts and how they should be interpreted. His advice must be practical. The commander or staff or Ministry of Defence officials involved do not, unless they specifically ask for it, want a legal essay with considerations, conditions and reservations. The adviser should have considered all that before preparing his advice. Those who have consulted him will want to know what action they can take within the law and, if various courses are open, the advantages and disadvantages of each, with recommendations.

It is not enough for the legal adviser to know about the law of war in the abstract. He must also know which countries have ratified or acceded to which conventions and with what reservations or statements. He needs to be aware of the legal background to the conflict, whether or not an armed conflict exists, whether it is an international or non-international armed conflict and between which states or factions, what UN Security Council resolutions have been passed and their content, what bilateral or multilateral agreements have been entered into and their effect. Here he may be lacking information, because these things will have been dealt with at a higher level, but he must have the information. Without it his advice may be useless.

The legal adviser must also be pro-active. Legal problems may not be recognized by commanders and their staff. As noted in chapter 7, commanders must be alert to law of war issues and take them into account in operational planning. Here the legal adviser can perform a useful function by briefing commanders about likely pitfalls and in advising them on procedures to be adopted to ensure compliance with the law. He may also be able to make suggestions for reducing the incidental effects of military operations by, say, creating demilitarized zones, or by drawing attention to the world-wide concern for the protection of the environment. For this purpose the legal adviser must be informed about what is going on, anticipate problems and provide advice in advance. This means that the lawyer must attend briefings so he is aware of the military situation and that he must be accessible to all divisions of the staff of a headquarters, preferably reporting direct to the chief of staff, and not be tucked away in the personnel division or the civil affairs division.

Nevertheless, in the context of multinational deployments under UN auspices or under the auspices of a regional defence organization like NATO, the civil affairs division of a headquarters is becoming increasingly important and busy and may well need dedicated legal staff to negotiate host-country support agreements and agreements between the contributing nations and resolve legal problems arising from their implementation. Such lawyers can also play a useful part in law on the battlefield in ensuring that the necessary steps are taken to introduce or plan for the precautions against the effects of attacks dealt with in chapter 4, or for the protection of cultural property dealt with in chapter 5, identifying legal problems and ensuring that solutions are found.

Finally, the military lawyer has a very important role to play in public relations and media briefings. Allegations and counter-allegations about violations of the law of war, about massacres and atrocities are rife during armed conflict. It is very important that those responsible for making public statements are well informed about the law of war and are quick to correct misapprehensions and false allegations. Likewise, if the enemy are violating the law of war by, for example, placing military objectives close to cultural objects, or by using hostages as 'human shields', such violations need to be brought to the attention of the world community. The military lawyer can help in identifying these breaches and explaining the legal background.

When during the Gulf War of 1990–91 bombs fell on the market town of Fallujah the RAF spokesman, Group Captain Henderson, was quick to explain that this was due to the malfunctioning of a bomb which was aimed at a bridge, a legitimate target because it was on a main supply line.[16] This was exactly the right thing to do to forestall allegations that the Royal Air Force was deliberately bombing civilians. The military lawyer can help to ensure that press lines are legally accurate. He can also draw attention to statements in the media which are legally incorrect and need correction.

Prosecutor

The prosecutor will have to decide, first, whether the alleged offence should be made the subject of a prosecution at all. If it was a grave breach of the Geneva Conventions, there is a duty to do so under international law.[17] If it was another breach of the law of war, it is suggested that the prosecutor has discretion but should advise prosecution in the case of serious war crimes not amounting to grave breaches, such as direct attacks on civilians or the civilian population.[18] In the case of minor violations it would suffice if corrective action were recommended.

In deciding, secondly, whether an individual is responsible for an alleged war crime arising out of conduct in action and, if so, whether he should be prosecuted, the military lawyer will need to consider the situation as it appeared to the accused at the time in the light of the information available to him then. That will involve consideration of the tactical situation, the time available for a decision, the heat of the moment, and so on. Where it is a question of assessing proportionality, it will involve examining very many factors: the method and timing of attack, the weapons available and used and their effect, the orders given by higher authority, the intelligence available about the target and its surroundings, the military gain expected from the attack, the likely civilian casualties and

---

[16] *The Times*, 19 February 1991.
[17] See, e.g., Art. 129 of the Prisoner of War Convention or Arts. 85 and 86 of Protocol I.
[18] See the classification by Hampson, War crimes, p. 256.

damage, and the context of the operation as whole. In the case of a commander, the prosecutor will have to consider whether he committed the offence himself as principal or accessory, or whether he should be charged in respect of his failure to act to suppress or repress offences committed by others.

It is suggested that in the rare case when the law is controversial or obscure, and the accused acted in good faith, the prosecutor will advise no prosecution.

Final remarks

Although some ambiguities remain, and although the law has become complicated, especially with regard to the protection of cultural property, Protocol I provides a useful code of conduct in combat which achieves a reasonable balance between military and humanitarian considerations. Any perceived imbalance between the rights and duties of defenders and attackers can be redressed by applying the rule of proportionality. Of course, Protocol I cannot stand by itself as a document issued to military personnel. It has to be incorporated into military manuals with explanatory commentaries, cross-references and practical guidance, but it does form the foundation of those manuals on the subject of law on the conduct of combat, or law on the battlefield, which previously had been somewhat neglected. Had Protocol I applied to the allied forces in the Gulf War of 1990–91, it is suggested, they would have had no difficulty in complying with its provisions.

Works cited

Adler, G. J., Targets in war, legal considerations, *Houston Law Review*, 1980.

Aldrich, G. H., New life for the laws of war, *American Journal of International Law*, 1981.

Aldrich, G. H., Prospects for US ratification of Protocol I, *American Journal of International Law*, 1991.

Alexandrow, E., *International Legal Protection of Cultural Property*, Sofia, Sofia Press, 1979.

Algase, R. C., Islamic law in warfare, *Military Law and Law of War Review*, 1977.

Allen, C., *Thunder and Lightning*, London, Her Majesty's Stationery Office, 1991.

Antoine, P., International humanitarian law and the protection of the environment in time of armed conflict, *International Review of the Red Cross*, 1992.

Arbuckle, T., Rhodesian bush war strategies and tactics, *Royal United Services Institute Journal*, 1979.

Baker, J. R., and Crocker, H. G., *The Laws of Land Warfare*, Washington, US Department of State, 1919.

Barclay, T., *The Law and Usage of War*, London, Constable, 1914.

Barras, R., and Erman, S., Forces armés et développement du droit de la guerre, *Military Law and Law of War Review*, 1982.

Beeston, R., Civilian casualties take on a key role, *The Times*, 11 February 1991.

Berber, F. J., *Völkerrechtliche Verträge*, 3rd ed., Nördlingen, Beck, 1983.

Best, G., *Humanity in Warfare*, London, Methuen, 1983.

Best, G., *Law and War since 1945*, Oxford, Clarendon Press, 1994.

Best, G., World War Two and the law of war, *Review of International Studies*, 1981.

Binney, M., Dubrovnik's scars laid bare, *The Times*, 8 February 1992.

Blix, H., Area bombardment: rules and reasons, *British Yearbook of International Law*, 1978.

Bothe, M., The protection of the environment in time of armed conflict, *German Yearbook of International Law*, 1991.

Bothe, M., The Protection of the Environment in Time of Armed Conflict, paper for the Ottawa Conference of Experts, July 1991.

Bothe, M., Partsch, K. J., and Solf, W., *New Rules for the Victims of Armed Conflicts*, The Hague, Martinus Nijhoff, 1982.

Bouvier, A., Protection of the natural environment in time of armed conflict, *International Review of the Red Cross*, 1991.

Bouvier, A., Recent studies on the environment in time of armed conflict, *International Review of the Red Cross*, 1992.

Bouvier, A., and Gasser, H. P., Protection of the Natural Environment in Time of Armed Conflict, paper for the Ottawa Conference of Experts, July 1991.

Boylan, P. J., *Review of the Convention for the Protection of Cultural Property in the event of Armed Conflict*, Paris, UNESCO, 1993.

Brown, B., and Shukman, D., *All Necessary Means*, London, BBC Books, 1991.

Bruderlein, C., Custom in international humanitarian law, *International Review of the Red Cross*, 1991.

Campbell, J., Rings of disaster, *Evening Standard*, 3 July 1991.

Canada, Note on the Current Law of Armed Conflict relevant to the Environment in Conventional Conflicts, paper by the Office of the Judge Advocate General for the Ottawa Conference of Experts, July 1991.

Carcione, M. M., Protection de biens culturels en cas de conflit armé, paper for the sixteenth Round Table of the International Institute for Humanitarian Law, 1991.

Carnahan, B. M., Additional Protocol I: a military view, *Akron Law Review*, 1986.

Carnahan, B. M., Protecting civilians under the draft Geneva protocol, 18 *Air Force Law Review*, 1976.

Cartledge, G. J., *The Soldier's Dilemma: When to Use Force in Australia*, Canberra, Australian Government Publishing Service, 1992.

Cassese, A., *Violence and Law in the Modern Age*, Cambridge, Polity Press, 1988.

Cauderay, G. C., Visibility of the distinctive emblem on medical establishments, units and transports, *International Review of the Red Cross*, 1990.

Clarke, M. H. F., The status of guerillas and irregular forces, unpublished, 1976.

Clarke, M. H. F., Glynn, T., and Rogers, A. P. V., Combatant and prisoner of war status, in M. A. Meyer (ed.), *Armed Conflict and the New Law*, London, British Institute of International and Comparative Law, 1989.

Craig, D., Should Australia ratify the 1944 protocol additional to the 1949 Geneva conventions? *Defence Force Journal*, 1989.

De Mulinen, F., *Handbook on the Law of War for the Armed Forces*, Geneva, International Committee of the Red Cross, 1987.

De Smet, A., General report on civilian support to the armed forces, *Military Law and Law of War Review* [to be published].

Detter de Lupis, I., *The Law of War*, Cambridge, Cambridge University Press, 1987.

De Vattel, E., *Le Droit des gens*, 1758.

De Visscher, C., Les lois de la guerre et la théorie de la nécessité, *Revue Général de Droit International Public*, 1917.

Dinstein, Y., Siege warfare and the starvation of civilians, in A. J. M. Delisson and G. J. Tania (eds.), *Humanitarian Law of Armed Conflict, Challenges Ahead*, The Hague, Martinus Nijhoff, 1991.

Dinstein, Y., *The Defence of Obedience to Superior Orders in International Law*, Leyden, Sijthoff, 1965.

Dowty, A., Sanctioning Iraq: the limits of the new world order, *Washington Quarterly*, 1994.

Draper, G. I. A. D., Humanitarianism in the modern law of armed conflict, in M. A. Meyer (ed.), *Armed Conflict and the New Law*, London, British Institute of International and Comparative Law, 1989.

Draper, G. I. A. D., The new law of armed conflict, *Royal United Services Institute Journal*, 1979.

Doswald-Beck, L., The value of the 1977 protocols, in M. A. Meyer, *Armed Conflict and the New Law*, London, British Institute of International and Comparative Law, 1989.

Evans, M., Freedom of the sky, *The Times*, 5 February 1991.

Falk, R., The environmental law of war: an introduction, in G. Plant (ed.), *Environmental Protection and the Law of War*, London, Belhaven, 1992.

Fauchille, P., Le bombardement aérien, *Revue Général de Droit International Public*, 1917.

Fenrick, W. J., The rule of proportionality and Protocol I in conventional warfare, *Military Law Review*, 1982.

Fleck, D., Die rechtlichen Garantien des Verbots von unmittelbaren Kampfhandlungen gegen Zivilpersonen, *Military Law and Law of War Review*, 1966.

Fleck, D., Environment: legal and policy perspectives, in H. Fox and M. A. Meyer (eds.), *Effecting Compliance*, London, British Institute of International and Comparative Law, 1993.

Fox, H., Reparations and state responsibility, in P. J. Rowe (ed.), *The Gulf War 1990– 91 in International and English Law*, London, Routledge, 1993.

Garner, J. W., *International Law and the World War*, vol. 1, London, Longman, 1920.

Gasser, H. P., Humanitäres Völkerrecht in Aktion, *Humanitäres Völkerrecht Informationsschriften*, Bonn, German Red Cross, and Bochum, Ruhr University, 1991.

Gasser, H. P., Some legal issues concerning ratification of the 1977 Geneva protocols, in M. A. Meyer (ed.), *Armed Conflict and the New Law*, London, British Institute of International and Comparative Law, 1989.

Gehring, R. W., Loss of civilian protection, *Military Law and Law of War Review*, 1980.

Germany, *Der Schutz von Kulturgut bei bewaffneten Konflikten*, Bonn, Federal Ministry of Defence publication Zdv 15/9, 1964.

Germany, *Humanitäres Völkerrecht in bewaffneten Konflikten—Handbuch*, Bonn, Bundesministerium der Verteidigung, 1992.

Germany, Report concerning the execution of the [Cultural Convention] by the Federal Republic of Germany, *Military Law and Law of War Review*, 1978.

Goldblat, J., Legal protection of the environment against the effects of military activities, *Bulletin of Peace Proposals*, 1991.

Goldblat, J., The ENMOD Convention: a critical review, *Humanitäres Völkerrecht Informationsschriften*, 1993.

Goldman, R. K., The legal regime governing the conduct of operation Desert Storm, *University of Toledo Law Review*, 1992.

Gonsalves, E. L., Armed forces and the development of the law of war, *Military Law and Law of War Review*, 1982.

Green, J. H., The destruction of the abbey of Monte Cassino, *British Army Review*, 1988.

Green, L. C., Superior orders and the Geneva conventions and protocols, in H. Fox and M. A. Meyer (eds.), *Effecting Compliance*, London, British Institute of International and Comparative Law, 1993.

Green, L. C., *Superior Orders in National and International Law*, Leyden, Sijthoff, 1976.

Green, L. C., *The Contemporary Law of Armed Conflict*, Manchester, Manchester University Press, 1993.

Green, L. C., The Environment and the Law of Conventional Warfare, paper for the Ottawa Conference of Experts, July 1991.

Green, L. C., The new law of armed conflict, *Canadian Yearbook of International Law*, 1977.

Greenspan, M., *The Modern Law of Land Warfare*, Berkeley, University of California Press, 1959.

Greenwood, C. J., *Command and the Laws of Armed Conflict*, Camberley, Strategic and Combat Studies Institute, Army Staff College, 1993.

Greenwood, C. J., Customary international law and the first Geneva protocol of 1977 in the Gulf conflict, in P. J. Rowe (ed.), *The Gulf War 1990–91 in International and English Law*, London, Routledge, 1993.

Greenwood, C. J., Reprisals and reciprocity in the new law of armed conflict, in M. A. Meyer (ed.), *Armed Conflict and the New Law*, British Institute of International and Comparative Law, 1989.

Grotius, H., *De Jure Belli ac Pacis*, 1642.

Hall, W. E., *A Treatise on International Law*, 8th ed. by A. Pearce Higgins, Oxford, Clarendon Press, 1924.

Hampson, F. J., Belligerent reprisals and the 1977 protocols, *International and Comparative Law Quarterly*, 1988.

Hampson, F. J., Liability for war crimes, in P. J. Rowe (ed.), *The Gulf War 1990–91 in International and English Law*, London, Routledge, 1993.

Hampson, F. J., Means and methods of warfare in the conflict in the Gulf, in P. J. Rowe (ed.), *The Gulf War 1990–91 in International and English Law*, London, Routledge, 1993.

Hanke, H. M., The 1923 Hague Rules of Air Warfare, *International Review of the Red Cross*, 1993.

Hill, G., Conflict threatens ancient sites, *The Times*, 28 February 1991.

Hine, P., Despatch by the joint commander of Operation Granby, 2nd supplement to the *London Gazette*, 28 June 1991.

Holland, T. E., *The Laws of War on Land*, Oxford, Clarendon Press, 1908.

Howard, M., On balance, Bush must go to war, *The Times*, 5 November 1990.

ICRC, *Protection of the Civilian Population against the Dangers of Hostilities*, Report No. 3 to the Conference of Government Experts, Geneva, International Committee of the Red Cross, 1971.

ICRC, *Protection of the Environment in Time of Armed Conflict*, Report for the Forty-eighth Session of the United Nations General Assembly, Geneva, International Committee of the Red Cross, 1993.

Infeld, D. L., Precision guided missiles demonstrated their pinpoint accuracy in Desert Storm; but is a country obligated to use precision technology to minimize collateral civilian injury and damage? *George Washington Journal of International Law and Economics*, 1992.

Jochnick C., and Normand, R., The legitimation of violence: a critical history of the laws of war, *Harvard International Law Journal*, 1994.

Johnson, D. H. N., The legality of modern forms of aerial warfare, *Royal Aeronautical Society Journal*, 1968.

Kadelbach, S., Zwingende Normen des humanitären Völkerrechts, *Humanitäres Völkerrecht Informationsschriften*, 1992.

Kalshoven, F., *Constraints on the Waging of War*, Geneva, International Committee of the Red Cross, 1987.

Kalshoven, F., The reaffirmation and development of international humanitarian law, *Netherlands Yearbook of International Law*, 1978.

Karsten, P., *Law, Soldiers and Combat*, Westport, Greenwood, 1978.

Keaney, T. A., and Cohen, E. A., *Gulf War Air Power Survey, Summary Report*, Washington, Government Printing Office, 1993.

Keenan, T. P. Jr., Die Operation Wüstensturm aus der Sicht des aktiven Rechstberaters, *Humanitäres Völkerrecht Informationsschriften*, 1991.

Krüger-Sprengel, F., Le concept de proportionalité dans le droit de la guerre, *Military Law and Law of War Review*, 1980.

Kuehl, D. T., Air power *v.* electricity: electric power as a target for strategic air operations, *Journal of Strategic Studies* [to be published, 1995].

Lauterpacht, H., The problem of the revision of the law of war, *British Yearbook of International Law*, 1952.

Levie, H. S., The rise and fall of an internationally codified denial of the defence of superior orders, *Military Law and Law of War Review*, 1991.

Luttwak, E., Supplies, not troops, should be the main target of jets in Kuwait, *The Times*, 16 February 1991.

McCoubrey, H., *International Humanitarian Law*, Aldershot, Dartmouth, 1990.

McCoubrey, H., *The Idea of War Crimes and Crimes against the Peace since 1945*, University of Nottingham Research Papers in Law, 1992.

McCoubrey, H., The nature of the modern doctrine of military necessity, *Military Law and Law of War Review, 1991.*

McCoubrey, H., and White, N. D., *International Law and Armed Conflict*, Aldershot, Dartmouth, 1992.

Masters, J., *The Road past Mandalay*, London, Michael Joseph, 1961.

Matthews, T., *et al.*, The secret history of the war, *Newsweek*, 18 March 1991.

Mawhinney, B., Basis and Objectives of the Meeting of Experts on the Use of the Environment as a Tool of Conventional Warfare, paper for the Ottawa Conference of Experts, July 1991.

Meek, A. D., Operation Centre, *British Army Review*, 1994.

Meron, T., Henry the Fifth and the law of war, *American Journal of International Law*, 1992.

Meyrowitz, H., Buts de guerre et objectifs militaires, *Military Law and Law of War Review*, 1983.

Middle East Watch, *Needless Deaths in the Gulf War*, New York: Human Rights Watch, 1991.

Moderhack, R., *Braunschweig, das Bild der Stadt in 900 Jahren*, vol. 1, Brunswick, Städtisches Museum Braunschweig, 1985.

Morgan, J. H., *The German War Book*, London, John Murray, 1915.

Obradovic, K., La protection de la population civile dans les conflits armés internationaux, in A. Cassese, *The New Humanitarian Law of Armed Conflict*, Naples, Editoriale Scientifica, 1979.

Oppenheim, L., *International Law*, vol. 2, 7th ed. by H. Lauterpacht, London, Longman, 1952.

Painchaud, P., Environmental Weapons and the Gulf War, paper for the Ottawa Conference of Experts, July 1991.

Parks, W. H., Air war and the law of war, 32 *Air Force Law Review*, 1990.

Pearce, N., *The Shield and the Sabre*, London, Her Majesty's Stationery Office, 1992.

Phillips, G. R., Rules of engagement: a primer, *Army Lawyer*, 1993.

Pictet, J., *Commentary* on the IV Convention relating to the Protection of Civilian Persons in Time of War, Geneva, International Committee of the Red Cross, 1958.

Plant, G., Elements of a new Convention for the Protection of the Environment in Time of Armed Conflict, paper for the Ottawa Conference of Experts, July 1991.

Plant, G., Environmental damage and the law of war, in H. Fox and M. A. Meyer (eds.), *Effecting Compliance*, London, British Institute of International and Comparative Law, 1993.

Price, A. R. G., Possible environmental threats from the current war in the Gulf, *Greenpeace*, 2 February 1991.

Rauch, E., Attack restraints, target limitations, *Military Law and Law of War Review*, 1979.

Rauch, E., Conduct of combat and risks run by the civilian population, *Military Law and Law of War Review*, 1982.

Rauch, E., Le concept de nécessité militaire dans le droit de la guerre, *Military Law and Law of War Review*, 1980.

Rauch, E., *The Protocol Additional to the Geneva Conventions for the Victims of Armed Conflicts and the United Nations Convention on the Law of the Sea: Repercussions on the Law of Naval Warfare*, Berlin, Duncker & Humblot, 1984.

Risley, J. S., *The Law of War*, London, Innes & Co., 1897.

Roberts, A., Civil defence and international law, in M. A. Meyer (ed.), *Armed Conflict and the New Law*, London, British Institute of International and Comparative Law, 1989.

Roberts, A., Failures in protecting the environment, in P. J. Rowe, *The Gulf War 1990–91 in International and English Law*, London, Routledge, 1993.

Roberts, A., The laws of war and the Gulf conflict, *Oxford International Review*, 1990/91.

Roberts, A., and Guelff, R., *Documents on the Laws of War*, 2nd ed., Oxford, Clarendon Press, 1989.

Robinson, N. A., Draft Articles with Commentary on a Convention securing Nature from Warfare or other Hostile Activities, paper for the Ottawa Conference of Experts, July 1991.

Rogers, A. P. V., A commentary on the Protocol on Prohibitions or Restrictions on the Use of Mines, *Military Law and Law of War Review*, 1987.

Rogers, A. P. V., Conduct of combat and risks run by the civilian population, *Military Law and Law of War Review*, 1982.

Rogers, A. P. V., Military necessity and the rule of proportionality, *Military Law and Law of War Review Addendum*, 1980.

Rogers, A. P. V., Mines, booby-traps and other devices, *International Review of the Red Cross*, 1990.

Rogers, A. P. V., The defence of superior orders in international law, *Military Law Journal*, 1991.

Rogers, A. P. V., The Mines Protocol: negotiating history, in ICRC, *Symposium on Antipersonnel Mines, Report*, Geneva, International Committee of the Red Cross, 1993.

Rogers, A. P. V., War crimes trials under the royal warrant, *International and Comparative Law Quarterly*, 1990.

Rosenblad, E., Area bombing and international law, *Military Law and Law of War Review*, 1976.

Rousseau, C., *Le Droit des conflits armés*, Paris, Pedone, 1983.

Rowe, P. J., Memorandum to the Foreign Affairs Select Committee, in *The Expanding Role of the UN and its Implications for UK Policy*, London, Third Report from the Foreign Affairs Select Committee, 1993.

Rowe, P. J., *Defence: the Legal Implications*, London, Brassey, 1987.

Rowe, P. J., Response from the United Kingdom Group of the International Society for Military Law and the Law of War to the criminology questionnaire, to be published in the *Military Law and Law of War Review*, 1994.

Saalfeld, M., Umweltschutz in bewaffneten Konflikten, *Humanitäres Völkerrecht Informationsschriften*, 1992.

Sandoz, Y., Swinarski, C., and Zimmerman, B., with Pictet, J., *Commentary on the Additional Protocols of 8 June 1977 to the Geneva Conventions of 12 August 1949*, Geneva, Martinus Nijhoff, 1987.

Sands, P., and Alexander, D., Assessing the impact, *New Law Journal*, 1 November 1991.

Schachter, O., United Nations law in the Gulf conflict, *American Journal of International Law,* 1991.

Schindler, D., and Toman, J., *The Laws of Armed Conflicts*, 3rd ed., Dordrecht, Martinus Nijhoff, 1988.

Schwarzenberger, G., *International Law*, vol. II, London, Stevens, 1968.

Schwarzenberger, G., The revision of the law of war, *British Yearbook of International Law*, 1952.

Shotwell, C. B., Food and the use of force, *Military Law and Law of War Review*, 1991.

Skarstedt, C. I., Armed forces and the development of the law of war, *Military Law and Law of War Review*, 1982.

Smith, J. C., and Hogan, B., *Criminal Law*, 7th ed., London, Butterworth, 1992.

Spaight, J. M., *Air Power and War Rights*, London, Longman, 1924.

Spaight, J. M., *Air Power and War Rights*, London, Longman, 1947.

Spaight, J. M., Non-combatants and air attack, 9 *Air Law Review*, 1938.

Spaight, J. M., *War Rights on Land*, London, Macmillan, 1911.

Spieker, H., Martens'sche Klausel, *Humanitäres Völkerrecht Informationsschriften*, 1988.

Stone, J., *Legal Controls of International Armed Conflict*, London, Stevens, 1954.

Switzerland, *Botschaft über die Zusatzprotokolle zu den Genfer Abkommen*, Berne, Swiss Federal Council, 1981.

Switzerland, *Gesetze und Gebräuche des Krieges*, Berne, Swiss Army Regulation 51.7/II d, 1987.

Szasz, P. C., Study of Proposals for Improvements to existing Legal Instruments relating to the Environment and Armed Conflicts, paper for the Ottawa Conference of Experts, July 1991.

Toman, J., *La Protection des biens culturels en cas de conflit armé*, Paris, UNESCO, 1994.

United Kingdom, *Queen's Regulations for the Army*, London, Her Majesty's Stationery Office, 1975.

United Kingdom, *Manual of Military Law*, 7th ed., London, Her Majesty's Stationery Office, 1929.

United Kingdom, *Manual of Military Law*, Part I, London, Her Majesty's Stationery Office, 1972 (reprinted 1992).

United Kingdom, *Manual of Military Law*, Part III, London, Her Majesty's Stationery Office, 1958.

United Kingdom, *Preliminary Lessons of Operation Granby*, House of Commons Defence Committee Tenth Report, Her Majesty's Stationery Office, 1991.

United Kingdom, *Review of the Results of Investigations ... and the Involvement ... of Lieutenant Waldheim*, report by the Ministry of Defence, London, Her Majesty's Stationery Office, 1989.

United Kingdom, *The Law of Armed Conflict*, British Army Pamphlet, Army Code 71130, 1981.

United States, *Commander's Handbook on the Law of Armed Conflict*, Washington, Department of the Air Force, Pamphlet 110-34, 1980.

United States, *Conduct of the Persian Gulf Campaign*, Washington, Department of Defense interim report to Congress, July 1991.

United States, *Conduct of the Persian Gulf War*, Washington, Department of Defense final report to Congress, April 1992. Appendix O to the report, entitled The Role of the Law of War, is published in 31 I.L.M. 612, 1992.

United States, *International Law*, vol. II, Washington, Department of the Army, Pamphlet 26-161-2, 1962.

United States, *International Law—The Conduct of Armed Conflict and Air Operations*, Washington, Department of the Air Force, Pamphlet 110-31, 1976.

United States, *Law of Land Warfare*, Washington, Department of the Army, Manual 27-10, 1956.

Van Dongen, Y., *The Protection of the Civilian Population in Time of Armed Conflicts*, Groningen, Groningen University, 1991.

Walzer, M., *Just and Unjust Wars*, Harmondsworth, Pelican, 1980.

Waters, G., *Gulf Lesson One: the Value of Air Power*, Canberra, Air Power Studies Centre, 1992.

Westing, A. H., The environmental modification conference of 1991, *Humanitäres Völkerrecht Informationsschriften*, 1992.

Westlake, J., *International Law*, Part II (War), Cambridge, Cambridge University Press, 1913.

Wheaton, H., *International Law*, 7th English ed. by A. B. Keith, London, Stevens, 1944.

Witteler, S., Der Krieg im Golf und seine Auswirkungen auf die natürliche Umwelt, *Humanitäres Völkerrecht Informationsschriften*, 1991.

Woetzel, R. K., *The Nuremberg Trials in International Law*, London, Stevens, 1962.

Wortley, B. A., Observations on the revision of the 1949 Geneva 'Red Cross Conventions', *British Yearbook of International Law*, 1983.

Würkner-Theis, G., *Fernverlegte Minen und humanitäres Völkerrecht*, Frankfurt am Main, Peter Lang, 1990.

Index